A
BOOK
IS A PRESENT
YOU CAN OPEN
AGAIN
AND
AGAIN
This Book Belongs To
RITA CRAYTHORNE
B258 © Mary Engelbreit

THE FORCES OF DESTINY

Reincarnation, Karma and Astrology

For
Jamie, Alexander and Dominic

THE FORCES OF DESTINY

Reincarnation, Karma and Astrology

Penny Thornton

WEIDENFELD AND NICOLSON
LONDON

Published in Great Britain by
George Weidenfeld & Nicolson Limited
91 Clapham High Street
London SW4 7TA

ISBN 0 297 810162

Typeset at The Spartan Press Ltd,
Lymington, Hants
Printed in Great Britain by
Butler & Tanner Ltd, Frome and London

Contents

Acknowledgements

I owe a great debt of gratitude to the many people who have, in their individual ways, helped the creation of this book. Maurice Bailey, Eon Begg, Sarah Bradpiece, Meg Bond, Antoinette Carr, Roger Coghill, Barbara Downing, Kathy Eldon, Madaleine Etherington, Margot Gray, Georgina Hale, Val Hartswell, Jean Hopwood, Marie Louise Hayward, Ken Knight, Rosalind Langdon, David Lorimer, Liz Newnham, Elizabeth Reed, Susie Riechenbach and Josephine Sheridan. I am also indebted to the White Eagle Lodge for the use of its magnificent library and Father Tim Galaghan at the St John's Seminary for his advice on The Affair of the Three Chapters. My heartfelt thanks also go out to my three sons, who learned all about the great British stiff-upper-lip during the long hot summer of 1989, when their mother slaved over a hot word processor instead of taking them to the beach – and my husband Simon, who can no longer look a tin of baked beans in the eye. My appreciation to Irene Earis, who reminded me about Michael, and Ian Wilson for all his advice and giving me access to some of his personal material on the reincarnation debate. I must also extend my thanks to David Roberts, who gave me the courage to write the book that I wanted to, not the one I thought others would want to buy. And last, my deepest gratitude, appreciation and love to Michael Hopwood without whom this book would have been an infinitely lesser one.

'He who thinks and writes about death grows because of it.'

Dmitri Shostakovitch

First Thoughts

As I was putting the finishing touches to my last book, *Romancing the Stars*, the seeds of this one were already beginning to germinate. I wanted to make a departure from one-to-one relationships which had been my 'bread and butter' as an astrologer for some years and expand the field into family relationships; I also wanted to tackle the theme of fate, which I perceived not as a primitive superstition but as a creative principle operating within us all. By early 1987 I had a working title, *Fate and Dynasty*. The dynasty part of the title referred not only to hereditary lines in the conventional sense, but also to past lives, which involve a rather different sort of inheritance. And for this I needed to look into the whole area of reincarnation.

Like many people, I had not been able to resist reading Shirley MacLaine's books on her pioneering forays into the world of the mystical and the divine – rather overblown perhaps, but I was particularly intrigued by the wealth of information she provided about her own past lives. How fascinating, I thought, to put those past lives under the astrological microscope. Thus, one frosty January morning, I made a long-distance telephone call to ask her if she would be prepared to consider the idea. 'Well, it's not new, you know . . . we've been doing this kind of stuff in California for years.' We agreed to discuss the idea again the following month when she would be in England. But by that time I had made my decision. Having experienced considerable frustration with the fragile egos of some superstars when interviewing them for my last book, I decided it might be prudent to leave well alone – especially as this time I would be dealing with some very dark aspects of the psyche. Instead, I decided to jump in at the deep end and launch my own programme of past life regression, using ordinary people, who would want to remain as anonymous as possible.

But where to find a qualified practitioner to regress the subjects? I felt I had to have someone with a medical qualification rather than a lay hypnotherapist – not because he or she would be any better but because past life regression is to a certain extent still in its infancy and considered entirely spurious by the orthodoxy. Thus if there was any negative 'feedback' either from the subjects themselves or critics of the book, I would be in a stronger position to counter them. It was as I was musing to a colleague about this quandary that she reminded me about a mutual friend, Michael Hopwood – a doctor who had been a member of the psychiatric team at Guy's Hospital, London. He was living a mere five miles away and, to my amazement, already using regression techniques in his psychotherapeutic work.

For a nail-biting four weeks I feared that Michael was going to refuse to take on the project, but then he agreed. Fortunately, despite the apparent differences in our temperaments and approach to life, we were astrologically well-suited to work together – we have the same degree of Libra on the Ascendant, our Mercurys are conjunct (to the minute), and both our Moons are in Scorpio. And despite Michael's initial reservations about the project, within a month or two he felt a whole new dimension had opened up for him. As, indeed, it had for me.

I had for many years given reincarnation and karma – and, indeed fate – a wide berth where astrology was concerned; not because I did not believe in such things, but because I felt too many astrologers resorted to them when they had no other answer. Then, in 1982, I was forced to re-examine my stance on these issues.

For eighteen months my husband Simon and I had been trying to conceive a child. It was worrying and upsetting that I kept repeatedly miscarrying. I already had a son by my first marriage and hoped to produce a brother or sister for him before the age-gap widened greatly. During 1981 I looked to the year ahead to assess the various planetary patterns: 1982 promised to be an exceptionally difficult year. While it might have been better to wait until 1983 to produce a baby, the age-gap between my eldest son and any future offspring was increasing all the time, so we forged ahead with our family planning, deciding only to take precautions in October to avoid my giving birth the following July.

July 1982 contained some of the most difficult configurations of the year, including two eclipses which made important contacts to the family's charts. Astrologers have long noted that eclipses tend to coincide with major world events – as occurred in October 1987, during which month a hurricane devastated Britain and there was an international financial crash. And although we twentieth-century astrologers tend to take a less hysterical view of eclipses than our forerunners, we still treat them with some respect.

In the February of 1982 my pregnancy was confirmed. I remained concerned about July's aspects but, in my ignorance, assumed the threat of miscarriage would be over by then. However, at the end of May serious problems developed with the pregnancy – only the skill of a superb physician prevented me from losing the baby – and, after several weeks of bed-rest, Alexander was born – on 9 July. He was just over 12 weeks early and weighed only 2½lbs. He fought courageously for his life from his first tiny breath, our miracle child, and is now a healthy, active and highly intelligent 7-year-old.

This experience was the most transformative of my life. Not only had I been taught a profound lesson about meddling with fate – after all I had done my level best to use my astrological skills to avoid producing a baby in July, but my meeting with Alexander gave me the strongest sensation that this was no new little soul who was entirely unfamiliar with Simon and I. As I approched his incubator, twenty-four hours after he was born, peeping out beneath an enormous woolly hat were two bright eyes that directly engaged mine; then he smiled and I knew it to be a smile of recognition. He was not to smile again for another fifteen weeks.

1982 turned out to be a major watershed. I began to work in a different way with clients, refusing to take on those who simply wanted their horoscope 'done' in favour of those who had problems or seriously needed advice. Reflecting this shift in consciousness, the clients who came to me tended to have extraordinary lives and challenged my skills both as an astrologer and an advisor. I began to read extensively about different systems of metaphysical thought and to practise transcendental meditation. Spontaneous out-of-the-body experiences began to be almost commonplace, as were precognitive dreams.

The momentum of this period of intense growth and change inevitably declined and I was left, somewhat relieved, to get on with it. In a sense this book owes its scope to the roots that took hold during that time. And certainly my reappraisal of fate, reincarnation and karma owes everything to the events and realizations of that period.

By the summer of 1987 *Fate and Dynasty* comprised a detailed synopsis and half a chapter about fate; by the January of 1989 all the research was complete and the regression sessions over. I was ready to start writing. However, by the time I had reached Chapter 3 I realized I was writing a quite different book from the one I had so diligently conceived. No longer was I writing about dynasties and family jinxes, but about the structure of consciousness, near death experiences, astral bodies, morphogenetic fields and the harmony of the spheres.

Indeed, I had hardly written a word about astrology until Chapter 5, although I had made a major inroad into fate. A new title was essential: *The Forces of Destiny* took over.

Synchronicities are not unusual in my line of work. With my last book, while I was writing about the Graeae Sisters of Greek mythology, in my village high street I ran into three of the ugliest old women I have ever seen: one was blind, another on crutches and the third I can only presume was deaf! But I was not prepared for the extraordinary coincidences and phenomena that greeted me during the creation of this manuscript. Prior to putting pen to paper, or rather finger to word processor, I was due to give a lecture entitled 'Fate: The Grand Design' in Cheltenham. As usual, I wrote out the entire text beforehand, even though I do not necessarily refer to it on the day. Finishing work on the lecture one night, I left, as usual, a few notes in capitals at the end to remind me of my train of thought when I returned to work on the text. The following day, when I called up the file on the computer screen, in the middle of my capitalized notes was the phrase GO FORTH IN LIGHT. This, as I well knew, was the ancient name for the Egyptian *Book of the Dead*. But I had absolutely no idea what it was doing in the middle of my notes, for it had no part in the lecture that I was preparing, and I knew without any shadow of doubt that I had not written the phrase. However, it seemed an appropriate and rather encouraging benediction – whatever (or whoever) had engendered it.

Another extraordinary coincidence occurred while I was typing Chapter 4. As soon as I began to write about Kepler's contribution to the harmony of the spheres, strange melodious sounds began to emanate from the water tank in my study – random at first but eventually acquiring some definite harmony and rhythm. They continued eerily for at least an hour, whereupon they stopped as suddenly as they had begun, and I have never heard them since.

Synchronicities of a less exotic nature also occurred. In the late summer of 1988 I organized an open day for all the participants on the regression project, to give everyone an opportunity to meet and have a general interchange of ideas. A few days beforehand Michael telephoned me to ask if he could bring along two more people who had expressed an interest in the project – a writer and broadcaster, Kathy Eldon, and a scientist and author, Roger Coghill. Unbeknownst to Roger, he had been on holiday with my husband and I in August: the only book my husband had taken away with him was *The Dark Side of the Brain* – by Roger Coghill. Simon had enthused over the book for the entire fortnight and informed me that when we returned he would have to contact the author. Within a week of our return, without any contact between them whatsoever, Roger was coming to visit. As we discovered when he arrived, Roger had been trying to contact a certain Simon Best whom he knew to be working on a book on electromagnetic fields. Roger proved to be a storehouse of information, not only on brain function and the electromagnetic spectrum but on Plato, Pythagoras, ancient Coptic texts and sacred geometry! Kathy, for her part, not only became an instant great friend but, more recently, my agent.

In the November of 1988 the Wrekin Trust held a conference on reincarnation where some of the most notable authorities on the subject were speaking. Sadly, Raymond Moody, author of *Life after Life* and other bestselling books on near death experiences (NDEs), was unable to speak; in his place a Buddhist monk talked on the various Buddhist attitudes to death and rebirth. Professor Geddes MacGregor's lecture gave me valuable new insight on Christianity and reincarnation, while Scott Rogo and Ian Wilson proffered some well-researched arguments for and against spontaneous past-life memories and regressions.

Since *The Forces of Destiny* centres on the theme of death and rebirth, I was haunted by the thought that, also in the way of synchronicity, I would have to experience such a process myself, perhaps even face the death of someone close to me. By the completion of the manuscript there had been no great physical loss, but I had experienced the death of an important friendship and the severance of a long-term connection with an organization; both these events – ironically occurring simultaneously though in no way linked – forced me to re-evaluate my life and eliminate those things which were no longer appropriate. As all astrologers will recognize, this is the hallmark of Pluto, the planet of transformation – death and rebirth. Thus when, at the same time, I came across Shostakovitch's prefatory words to a work based on some poems about death, 'He who thinks and writes about death grows because of it', they struck a profound and meaningful chord.

Despite its many and varied themes and its theories about the cosmic principles behind life, *The Forces of Destiny* is fundamentally about death and transformation. As Dr Elisabeth Kubler-Ross, Dr Raymond Moody and others whose work has brought them in touch with the dying have observed, death is not an event to be feared but a transition to another level of consciousness, invariably undertaken in great peace and light. Those who have undergone near death experiences return replenished and revivified, just as those who experience a mystical revelation are also irrevocably changed. Death gives way to a rebirth; the death of old habits, attitudes and feelings makes way for new growth. Although it would seem presumptuous to infer that my writing about death has led to growth, I would suggest that it is virtually impossible not to have one's outlook and value system changed and certainly challenged by involving oneself in the subject – particularly after reading all the uplifting literature on the near death experience. Michael, already a far more proficient student of the psyche and the spiritual than myself, felt his work with the regression project had provoked great personal development, and I came to value his thoughts and suggestions immeasurably over the months of research. Indeed, both of us feel that we must continue with this work – either together or taking our own individual route. Listening to the recordings of the sessions and speaking to the individuals involved about their experiences and subsequent developments in their lives, it was equally impossible not to be won over by their conviction that they had been transformed by their regression. Working with Michael, most of the volunteers were taken through their death (in a past life) and given the opportunity to understand where they went wrong and discover the purpose of that life; in this way they were able to cathect or transmute the residue from these lives. Afterwards, many of them did, indeed, feel reborn. Thus, although my aim in the book has been to try to unite concepts old and new, mysticism and science, and so introduce new avenues of thought to the general reader and some alternative perspectives to the committed seeker, it is the latter part of the book, containing the practice rather than the theory that I hope will open up new territory for astrologers and psychotherapists alike – and even make a chink in the wall of opposition constructed by the hardened rationalist.

I completed the last chapter on 8 August 1989. That night I had a strange dream. I was about to give birth, but the baby was stuck. The midwife, who was a beautiful old Indian woman, wearing a golden sari, came to my assistance. I thought it was going to be a long and painful process, but almost immediately, the baby's head began to appear. I shouted to Simon to hurry or he would miss the birth but he never came. In a matter of instants the baby was born – a most beautiful boy, Caucasian and with a perfect domed head covered in a down of fair hair. I awoke immediately, elated.

The dream was not difficult to interpret. A few days prior to the dream, a friend of mine, Cordelia Mansall had been staying with us. A writer and astrologer herself, she asked if I had finished the book, commenting that she knew from her own experience how difficult it was to finally admit that one had reached the end. 'It's like giving birth, there's always that reluctance to let go of the baby.' Clearly my dream baby was the book, which explained my husband's reluctance to attend the birth – after all he wasn't involved in its creation. The Indian midwife and the Caucasian baby are a perfect symbolism of the infinitely mature East offering its wisdom and skills to deliver this Western infant. I only hope this British astrologer proves to be an adequate mother.

Bramshott, August 1989

I
The Rise, Fall and Rise of Reincarnation

In any attempt to formulate a philosophy of life and endeavour to see meaning in our pilgrimage, these ancient beliefs [reincarnation and pre-existence] cannot be lightly set aside. It is our duty to weigh them carefully, and without prejudice, in order to see if they will illuminate for us tracts of experience which would otherwise remain dark and mysterious . . .

Raynor Johnson, *The Imprisoned Splendour*

On 15th March 1910 a five-year-old girl, Alexandrina Samona, died in Palermo, Sicily. Three days later, her mother, Adela had a dream in which Alexandrina showed her an embryo and informed her not to grieve since she would return to her. Adela could not take the dream as a portent of any note since an ovarian operation some years previously had put pay to the likelihood of any future pregnancies. Nevertheless, intrigued by it, Adela and her husband, Dr Carmelo Samona sought the help of a medium. The medium confirmed that 'Alexandrina' would be reborn before Christmas as one of a set of twins. On 22 November 1910, Adela did indeed give birth to twin girls. Almost as soon as they were born, Adela noticed that one of the babies had two small birth marks in exactly the same place as their dead daughter, so the Samonas decided to name her after their much loved Alexandrina.

From their earliest days the twins' personalities were markedly different, with only Alexandrina displaying the introverted and compliant tendencies of the previous child, even folding clothes and linen in the same orderly way. While these similarities could have been merely coincidental, an incident when the girls were ten made the reincarnation theory distinctly plausible. On being told that the family were about to embark on a journey to Monreale, Alexandrina insisted that she had visited the town once before with her mother and a 'lady with horns'. Yet her parents knew full well that the twins had never been to Monreale. Undeterred, Alexandrina went on to describe the statue on the roof of the church and the 'red priests' they had seen there. It transpired that Adela had taken the first Alexandrina to

Monreale not long before her death, and their companion on the journey had been a woman with some prominent cysts on her forehead. The 'red priests' were none other than some visiting Greek priests in red robes.[1]

This story is just one of thousands, if not millions, of world-wide reports of reincarnation. Some stand up to intense scientific investigation, others do not – of which we will hear more later – but authenticity notwithstanding they all form part of a persistent belief in the concept of death and rebirth: a belief that still finds an acceptable, if not a central place, in virtually all cultures and religions of the world. Though the West has been largely reluctant to accept the feasibility of reincarnation, considering it at best a rather romantic concept to buffer the thought of total extinction and at worst a cultist, 'Eastern' aberration, during this century there has been a gradual but resolute movement toward the re-absorption of such a concept into Western man's philosophy.

For many people the first exposure to reincarnation has been through the somewhat evangelical writings of the actress, Shirley MacLaine. Indeed, to some Ms MacLaine has become a kind of prophetess whose experiences and conclusions emerge as semi-divine revelations in that much over-worked phrase New Age consciousness. But in truth these same ideas have been around for centuries, they're merely experiencing a rebirth in the West – concepts whose time have come. But first things first . . .

ANCIENT RITES

For countless centuries societies the world over have created elaborate rituals for the dead. There is evidence to show that some 60,000 years or so ago, before the last Ice Age, Neanderthal man buried his dead and covered their bodies with flowers. It is even possible that members of a family would have been deliberately sacrificed (or sacrificed themselves) along with the dead person, in much the same way as the ancient Sumerians and Egyptians were to do several millennia later. The common impulse behind these devotions and those of all ancient cultures was a firm belief that some part of the dead person lived on.

The Ancient Egyptians were among many cultures who mummified their dead and afforded them lavish offerings of food, gold and jewels which were deemed necessary for their continued well-being in the life beyond. But though other cultures may also have built fantastic edifices for their dead and compiled complex instructions on the preparation for and the ordering of life in the hereafter, the surviving texts, tombs and pyramids of the Ancient Egyptians are by far our richest heritage.

According to the Egyptian *Book of the Dead*, when an individual died other parts of his being sprang into significance: prayers and ceremonies on the day of burial helped to release the spiritual body (sahu) that could join the soul (ba) and dwell with the gods in heaven. In addition, the deceased had an abstract individuality or personality endowed with all his earthly characteristics (ka)[2] which could unite itself with both the mummified body and the soul. It was primarily for the ka that the offerings (particularly of food) were provided.

The Egyptians were clearly obsessed by death and its processes, to the extent that their earthly life almost seemed a mere preparation for the more important life in the celestial beyond. Indeed, so much importance was placed on establishing a safe passage after death and a sustained heavenly existence thereafter that the Egyptians seemed to have more difficulty in accepting a further return to earth (in another body) than most other ancient cultures. At the time of the VIth dynasty the prevailing view was, 'Thy essence is in heaven, thy body to earth . . .'[3] and there was no possibility, except in the sense of the ka, of returning once more to earth. Yet by the XXth dynasty, the first king, Amonemhat I, was given the ka-name of 'He who repeats births'.

Though the Egyptian *Book of the Dead* itself makes no clear statement on reincarnation, by 500 BC or so, in the heyday of the Egyptian Mystery Schools, the concept had for the most part seeped into the Egyptian's belief system. It is possible that when the Persians occupied Egypt such beliefs, as the transmigration of souls (or reincarnation), were blended with Egyptian concepts, like that of the ka's return.

But while the Egyptians may have encountered some confusion over the eternal return, elsewhere the belief proliferated.

MYTHS AND RELIGION

The origin of the idea of reincarnation is practically impossible to trace, though according to the *Cyclopaedia of Biblical, Theological and Ecclesiastical Literature*: 'Transmigration, dating back to a remote antiquity, and being spread all over the world, seems to be anthropologically innate, and to be the first form in which the idea of immortality occurred to man.'[4]

The cycle of birth and death permeates nature: as a seed breaks through the earth, matures, then withers and dies, so too man 'cometh up, and is cut down, like a flower'; in spring, the earth gives birth only to die in autumn, the sun rises at dawn and disappears at nightfall. Not surprisingly, faced with such awesome dependence on nature and the elements, the earliest societies created powerful myths to explain those things that were effectively beyond their understanding and out of their control. What they also noted was that although nature died it was also reborn: as the sun set, so, in its unalterable course, would it rise again. Even the smallest daisy, once withered, would be reborn.

Myths of all cultures resound with the familiar themes of death and rebirth, often illustrated by a great hero figure, who, after a life of glory, dies yet is transformed to live on eternally: Persian Mithras is one such hero, Greek Herakles, another. The Greek myth of Demeter and Persephone is perhaps the best known allegory of the death of nature in autumn and its rebirth in spring. Demeter is so grief-stricken over the abduction of her daughter, Persephone, by Hades, the Lord of the Underworld, that she refuses to bless the earth and make it fruitful. Only when a compromise is struck whereby Persephone can spend six months on the earth with her mother and six in the Underworld with Hades, does the earth become fertile again, but only for the period of spring and summer.

The theme of death and rebirth was frequently taken onto a cosmic scale in Eastern mythologies, though they were not the only cultures to do so. In Hindu myth, after four declining aeons the world was destroyed by Shiva's dancing upon it; it was then reborn with the smile of the dreaming Vishnu.

Many of the greatest Hindu myths, like this one, originated from the Brahman culture that flourished in 500 BC. The Brahmans were firm believers in reincarnation and since the Hindu religion effectively grew out of Brahmanism, Hinduism has retained the concept of reincarnation at its core.

Over great periods of time, mythical themes and religious beliefs have almost inevitably intertwined. The point at which myth is succeeded by religion invariably coincides with the arrival of a great teacher whose messages contain not only divine truths but fuse with mythological themes – whether such dovetailing is achieved by the great teacher himself or by his followers. By saying this, I am not intending any diminution of religion. Earlier civilizations, whose intuitive sense was probably more developed – and certainly far more valued – than ours, could well have directly perceived divine worlds which enabled them to clearly understand the existence of spiritual hierarchies. Thus a great teacher – Buddha, Zoroaster, Krishna or Jesus Christ – not only personified a myth but, inspired by a direct comprehension of the divine, revealed in his teachings an essential truth.

BUDDHISM

The rise of Buddhism began in India in the mid-500s BC, at about the same time as Brahmanism was at its height. And while Buddhists have long maintained that Buddhism is not a religion based on the sayings of one man who lived in Northern India some 1500 years ago, nonetheless Siddhartha Gautama ('the Enlightened One') who was born in 563 BC, is usually credited with being the founder of Buddhism. Ironically, Buddhism was on the decline in India by AD 500, though elsewhere in Asia, and even in Greece and Egypt, it was thriving. Indeed, the spread of Buddhism to different countries gave rise to subtly different forms of the religion from culture to culture.

Buddhism, in common with Hinduism, Jainism and Sikhism, has the wheel of rebirth as its central tenet: the ceaselessly revolving wheel that keeps the unwary, unenlightened soul in an obligatory and relentless round of births. As the soul returns to yet another life it is given opportunities to right the wrongs of previous lives, thus the conditions of one life are entirely dependent on the actions and behaviour displayed in the one before – as a man shall sow, so shall he reap. This spiritual law of cause and effect manifest through successive lives – karma – forms the key teaching of Buddhism and would be completely redundant if divorced from the idea of a reincarnating ego.[5] The supreme purpose of Buddhism is to achieve liberation from this cycle of death and rebirth by reaching enlightenment and entering Nirvana – a timeless state of perfection free from earthly suffering and desires.

THE GREEK MYSTERIES

The Greek philosopoher and mystic, Pythagoras, is credited with bringing the idea of reincarnation to the West around 550 BC. A century or so later, the Greek philosopher, Plato embodied the theme in some of his greatest works;[6] in so doing he ignited a flame of interest in reincarnation that was to inspire philosophers and writers across the centuries. Plato and Pythagoras were among other notable figures (including Socrates and Aristotle) associated with the Greek Mystery Schools. In effect these schools were direct copies of the earlier Egyptian and Indian Mystery Schools, and like their forerunners, reincarnation was not only taught as a central doctrine, but represented an indispensable grade (symbolic ritual) through which all initiates had to pass before they could be purified and allowed to progress to higher states. Plato's influence, particularly on Western philosophical thought, is almost incalculable; his Academy in Athens, where he taught for nearly fifty years, inspired the great Platonic schools of Greece; almost six centuries after his death the famous Neoplatonic school at Alexandria was founded by Ammonius Saccas. Through its portals were to pass Porphyry, Plotinus, the Emperor Julian, Hypatia and the great Christian Church Father, Origen – of whom we shall hear more later. To all disciples of Platonic thought, the journey of the soul through successive lifetimes as a form of purification was the linchpin of their belief structure.

JUDAISM

By the beginning of the third century BC, while the Mystery Schools were still flourishing in Greece, a group of Jews, the Tanaiim who lived in Jerusalem, became the first kabalists. Their teachings, of which metempsychosis (reincarnation) was an essential part, were incorporated in the kabala by rabbis, during the Middle Ages: these older, secret doctrines of the kabala are thought to represent the hidden wisdom behind the Old Testament. Indeed, some authorities considered that Moses himself transmitted many kabalistic ideas which were passed on by oral tradition, later to be included in the kabala. Certainly, by the second century BC, of the three main schools of philosophy among the Jews – the Sadducees, the Pharisees and the Essenes – the latter two both upheld the concept of reincarnation.

Furthermore, many of the ancient Jews firmly believed in the periodic return of their great prophets: Abel, the son of Adam was, in their opinion, Moses, and the Messiah to come was the reincarnation of Adam who had already appeared as David. The very last book of the Old Testament, Malachi ends with the prophecy, 'Behold, I will send you Elijah the prophet before the great and dreadful day of the Lord.'[7] Elijah, of course, by Malachi's time was long since dead.

THE CHRISTIAN MYSTERIES VERSUS CHRISTIANITY

References to John the Baptist as the reincarnation of Elijah (or Elias, in the Greek form of the name) appear several times in the New Testament.

And as they came down from the mountain, Jesus charged them saying, 'Tell the vision to no man, until the Son of Man be risen again from the dead.' And his disciples asked him, saying, 'Why then say the scribes that Elias must first come?' . . . 'But I say unto you, That Elias is come already, and they knew him not, but have done unto him whatsoever they listed. Likewise shall also the Son of man suffer of them.' Then the disciples understood that he spake unto them of John the Baptist . . . [Herod had already beheaded John the Baptist.][8]

These words, uttered by the Messiah himself, have provoked considerable theological argument. Could Jesus Christ really be referring to the idea of reincarnation, or are these just abstruse metaphors? There is a wide divergence of opinion as to the interpretation of such verses but most orthodox theologians consider that Jesus's words are indeed metaphors, not to be taken literally to mean that Elijah returned to earth in the form of John the Baptist. However, reading Christ's words in the New Testament, 'Ye shall see the Son of man ascend up where he was before'[9] or John the Baptist's words on Jesus, 'He that cometh after me is preferred before me: for he was before me'[10] it is difficult to interpret them as anything other than statements about pre-existence.

Certainly, modern orthodox Christianity does not embrace reincarnation, but prior to the sixth century AD several revered Church Fathers believed unequivocally in the concept, most notably Justin Martyr, St Augustine and Origen. Why, if such hallowed individuals believed in pre-existence, was the concept not adopted by orthodox Christianity? Until the 4th century AD Christianity was by no means a coalescent body of religious thought. Indeed, the more one delves into the history of Jesus's time, with its troubled political climate and its scores of religions and cults vying for ascendancy, the more amazing it becomes that Christ and his teachings survived beyond his lifetime. The New Testament provides us with information about the life of Christ and his sayings, but because the four Gospels differ markedly in their versions of key events, such as the nativity and the crucifixion, establishing the reality of the man and his word is fraught with complications. To throw these issues into even greater confusion, the discovery of ancient texts, including gospels and secret writings, at Nag Hammadi in 1945, revealed an entirely different Christian ethos – of a distinctly Gnostic flavour.

Until the Nag Hammadi discovery, Gnosticism had been largely regarded as a pseudo-Christian religious philosophy with its roots firmly entrenched in Greek philosophy, mystery religions and astrology; but the Nag Hammadi texts showed beyond all doubt that the roots of gnosticism lay in Christian soil. In *The Gnostic Gospels*, Elaine Pagels writes, 'ideas [e.g. reincarnation] that we associate with eastern religions emerged in the first century through the Gnostic movement, in the west, but they were suppressed and condemned.'[11] The authors and proponents of the gospels found at Nag Hammadi 'did not regard themselves as heretics, but as Gnostics – that is, Christians who possess knowledge (gnosis) of Jesus' secret teachings – knowledge hidden from the majority of believers.'[12] Indeed, this concept is clearly stated in the New Testament gospel of Mark, when Jesus says to his disciples, 'To you has been given the secret of the kingdom of heaven, but for those outside, everything is in parables.'[13]

In some of the Gnostic gospels, for example, the *Pistis Sophia*, discovered in the nineteenth century, Christ makes many clear statements about reincarnation which again raises the question, why were such concepts not readily accepted by all Christian groups? One possible reason is that reincarnation was a mystery teaching and given only to the disciples themselves. Another is that among many early Christians the concept of reincarnation paled into insignificance compared with life everlasting (or eternal damnation) promised by the Second Coming – an event they saw as being imminent. The predominant view among believers at that time was that Christ would return to earth soon after his death; hence there was no point in considering further lives in 'mortal sin' since the Second Coming would bring an end to such a process. But the preoccupation with Jesus's return to earth is not entirely responsible for the disregard of reincarnation and, indeed, of the Christian mysteries as a whole.

Many people assume that the much-persecuted early Christians were a unified group. Much persecuted, yes, but by no means unified. Increasingly, from the 2nd century AD, the chasm between those Christians oriented toward the mysteries and those who adhered to the more dogmatic type of Christianity – akin to the religion of the Sadducees – was growing wider all the time. A major nail in the coffin of the Gnostic movement proved to be the Church of Rome which, to further its own interests, positively encouraged any bishop who would brand Gnosticism a heresy. Rome's power to suppress any cult or religion that threatened its autonomy was greatly increased by Constantine, who, somewhat ironically, is considered to be Christianity's great patron.

Two events, some 200 years apart, succeeded in annihilating mystery teachings, with their central tenet of pre-existence from Christianity.

Constantine – ruler of the Roman Empire from 312 AD until 337, played one of the most crucial roles of all in the development of orthodox Christianity. Indeed Constantine's conversion to Christianity far from being a spiritually motivated and deeply felt commitment may well have been a case of divinely inspired expediency! The rifts within the Christian movement were a destablizing factor in the Roman Empire, and Constantine, like any great emperor, was none too happy to have his supremacy threatened by another divine leader – albeit a dead one. By embracing Christianity and ending the persecution of the Christians he calculated that he could bring the movement under Rome's secular umbrella – and keep his power. In order to stabilize the unruly Christian movement, Constantine's first task was to try to unite it. To this end he presided over a meeting aimed at reconciling its divergent aspects. It is from this Council of Nicea in 325 AD that Christianity as we know it today is derived; a meeting that not only established Jesus's divinity by a vote, but hurled the first ecclesiastical boulder of any real weight at the mystery teachings, a boulder that came near to making reincarnation a heresy.

But it took a second synod, some two hundred years later, to effectively rid orthodox Christianity of any vestige of Gnosticism.

Despite Constantine's attempts at co-ordination, the schisms between the various schools of thought rumbled on long after his death. In 553 there was another attempt to make all Christians toe the same line: a council at Constantinople finally anathematized, among others, the belief in pre-existence – or rather this was the intention. After the Council of Nicea the orthodoxy had been deeply anti-Gnostic. Thus it rankled the Church hierarchy that in some quarters Christians enthusiastically followed the mystery teachings of such individuals as Nestorius, Eutyches and Origen. It was with the intention of condemning the teachings of these Church fathers that the Council of Constantinople was convoked. However, because not all the bishops who should have been there were present, nor the pope (Vigilus) himself, the decision to anathematize their teachings on pre- existence could be said to be invalid. Indeed, subsequently the pope only approved some other aspects of this synod.

The orthodox Christian view held today is that at Constantinople pre-existence (as an example of Origenistic teaching) was declared a heresy. But this is by no means a unanimous view. As one Catholic rector put it, 'even if it could be shown that the undivided ancient Church officially forbade belief in reincarnation, the 21st of our Articles of Religion says "General Councils may err and sometimes have erred, even in things pertaining unto God."'[14]

THE CATHARS

If things looked bleak for reincarnation in the west in the sixth century, they had become even worse by the Dark Ages. Indeed, the very name given to this period of history evokes the relentless cruelty, inhumanity and pitilessness of the time. Yet despite the strenuous efforts of the orthodox Christian church, Neoplatonic and Gnostic teachings refused to die. Indeed, it required the full force of the Holy Inquisition to prevent Gnostic ideas from filtering through to almost every level of European society. As the historian Henry Lea put it, Gnosticism 'spread so rapidly and resisted so stubbornly the sternest efforts of suppression that at one time it may be fairly said to have threatened the permanent existence of Christianity itself.'[15] Gnostic ideas that had proliferated in the East were gradually transplanted into central Europe with the advance of commercial trade routes, so that by the eleventh century little Gnostic communities, known as the Albigenses, or Cathars, had sprung up, principally in areas of southern France and Italy. To those who were dismayed by the corrupted life-style commonly found among members of the orthodox clergy, the Cathars' simple way of living and their rich spiritual philosophy must have seemed only too appealing.

The Cathars taught that through continuing cycles of reincarnation the human soul was able to perfect itself; they also believed that Christ came not to die for mankind, but to help man save himself. In comparision to the sin and eternal damnation ethos of the orthodox church, Catharism offered hope. As the psychiatrist and author, Dr Arthur Guirdham states: Catharism 'was a mystical, real, living experience of Christianity as opposed to an avidly theological concept.'[16] It was primarily because of their belief in reincarnation that the Cathars were massacred. The extermination of these medieval Gnostics was so successful that only a handful of records are left to tell the tale.

But what was it about these simple but mystical people that provoked such hatred in the Church? Gnosticism, as it had done before Constantine's time, threatened the orthodox Church, which stood to lose all its power, control and wealth by Gnostic teachings on reincarnation. After all, if the common man could find his own route to salvation through successive lifetimes, what need did he have of the costly rites of passage proffered by the Church?

Despite the genocide of the Albigenses and the subsequent vigilance of the Holy Inquisition, reincarnation and other mystical teachings were kept alive in the west during the Middle Ages – and beyond – by such orders as the Knights Templars, the Rosicrucians and the Freemasons. Of course these groups, with their intricate rituals and mysterious signs, were shrouded in secrecy and beyond the experience of the 'common' man. Thus it took until the nineteenth century and the emergence of the theosophical movement for the philosophy of reincarnation to seep into general awareness.

REINCARNATION REBORN: THE THEOSOPHISTS

Nowadays, the word theosophy tends to conjure up images of gloomy Victorian halls half full of eccentric old ladies absently listening to a frail and elderly speaker. But in the late 1880s the theosophical movement swept across the world like a forest fire, igniting the passions of proponents and antagonists alike. The inspiration behind theosophy was a middle-aged Russian 'aristocrat', Helena Petrovna Blavatsky (or HPB as she was more affectionately known). Together with Henry S. Olcott and William Q. Judge she founded the theosophical movement in New York City in 1875. HPB was an extraordinary and fascinating woman. From a middle-class background in Russia, she married, at the age of seventeen, a man considerably older than herself. The marriage lasted only a few months and, a year later, she began to travel extensively. During her journeys through India and Tibet she studied Eastern philosophy and religion and was one of the first to bring the seeds of oriental esotericism to the West. Her writings, apparently inspired by ancient Tibetan masters, were voluminous and rich in occult detail and cosmic truth. Ironically, the theosophical movement inspired a revival of interest in reincarnation in the *East*; Gandhi himself is quoted as saying, 'Theosophy is Hinduism at its best',[17] and in 1975 the Indian Government celebrated the centenary of the theosophical movement by issuing a stamp with the seal and motto of the society, 'There is no religion higher than truth'. However, HPB considered theosophy to cover a far broader spectrum than Eastern mysticism alone. According to its official objectives, its aims were 'to form the nucleus of a Universal Brotherhood of Humanity without distinction of race, creed, sex, caste or colour'; 'to promote the comparative study of ancient and modern religions, philosophies and sciences'; and 'to investigate unexplained laws of nature and the psychical powers of man.'[18] While nowadays such aims are almost commonplace, in Queen Victoria's day they were astounding; and theosophical teachings not only attracted huge interest and support from the spiritually starved but much derision and opposition from within scientific and ecclesiastical circles.

HPB's first book, *Isis Unveiled*, sold out in nine days; in its massive two volumes, one on science the other on theology, she expounded on the doctrines of reincarnation and karma: 'Karma and reincarnation are in reality the A B C of theosophy.'[19] Blavatsky maintained that to reach the highest level of perfection in the physical world, many lifetimes were necessary, and that those who had achieved it were humanity's greatest teachers: Jesus, Buddha and Krishna were highly evolved souls sent to help mankind in its struggle for spiritual evolution. Blavatsky's case for reincarnation was a forcible one.

> The doctrine of Metempsychosis [reincarnation] has been abundantly ridiculed by men of science and rejected by theologians, yet if it had been properly understood in its application to the indestructibility of matter and the immortality of the spirit, it would have been perceived that it is a sublime conception . . . If the Pythagorean metempsychosis should be thoroughly explained and compared with the modern theory of evolution it would be found to supply every 'missing link' in the chain of the latter.[20]

Of course there were other important and influential theosophists of the time besides HPB: the British-born Annie Besant, for instance, her protégé Krishnamurti, and Rudolph Steiner. Ultimately, both Krishnamurti and Steiner broke away from the main theosophical movement and acquired a huge following of their own, Steiner forming the Anthroposophical Society in 1912.

The nineteenth century saw not only a spontaneous revival of Eastern religious thought[21] with reincarnation as its centre point but a whole new apprehension of the spiritual world: life beyond the veil, as it were. This synchronous appreciation of Eastern mystical ideas in turn provided a new muse for artists and philosophers of the time. D. H. Lawrence employed the Eastern theme to full effect in his short story, 'The Man who came down to Earth'; Wagner composed a musical drama, *Die Sieger* (The Victor) based on a reincarnational theme, Leo Tolstoy, J. B. Priestley, Ralph Waldo Emerson and Jean Sibelius were among many fervent reincarnationalists, so too was the British Prime Minister, Lloyd George and the German philosopher, Hegel.

A SPIRITUAL RENAISSANCE

By the 1960s the dawn of the New Age had arrived with full vengeance; now the occult revival had reached a new audience in the youth of the Western world, and with the passion and enthusiasm of the young, interest in mystery teachings, especially astrology, moved onto yet another level. The 1960s and '70s were the heyday of the Indian guru; this was an era that inspired millions of Europeans and Americans to troop off to ashrams in India to sit at the feet of the enlightened ones and so become enlightened themselves. The evolution of the soul, the purification of the spirit through repeated lifetimes, gave meaning and purpose to fertile young psyches bored and spiritually dissatisfied with the uncharismatic, uninspired Christian Church. The search for expanded consciousness, the desire to access other realities (all too often achieved by taking a shortcut through drugs) gave Western society a new psychedelic ethos – make love, not war – and gave rise to an entire culture. And while the hippies have grown up and learned some salutary lessons from their gigantic leap into inner space, the seeds of the '60s have nevertheless proved fruitful. And though in the materialistic, Yuppy-possesseed but ecology-aware '80s many of those gurus have been seen under a more critical beam of light, some of their teachings are receiving scientific attention, if not some sanction, through progress made in such areas as brain biochemistry and the new physics. The emergence of considerable data on consciousness after death by highly respected doctors and psychiatrists[22] would seem to support many esoteric beliefs, from those held by the ancient Egyptians to those of the nineteenth-century theosophists.

I feel, judging by the huge advances being made on the scientific front at the present time, that by the beginning of the twenty-first century reincarnation will no longer be treated as a fanciful belief but as an unequivocal shared truth. And perhaps it isn't such a wild dream that within our lifetime we shall see the world-wide re-establishment of the Mystery Schools.

NOTES

1. Dr Samona presented his daughter's case (together with depositions from several witnesses) as evidence for reincarnation in the Italian science magazine, *Filosofia della scienza*.
2. The ka relates to the *astral body*, which is fully discussed in Chapter 3.
3. *The Book of the Dead – The Papyrus of Ani* by E. A. Wallis Budge (The British Museum, 1895).
4. McClintock and Strong, *Cyclopaedia of Biblical, Theological and Ecclesiastical Literature*, 'Transmigration': as quoted by Cranston and Head in *The Phoenix Fire Mystery* (Julian Press, 1977).
5. In parts of the East, there remains a belief in the regression of souls into animal and other sub-human form, and vice versa.

6. Among them, The *Timaeus*, The *Phaedo* and *The Republic*.
7. Malachi 4:5
8. Matthew 17:9–13
9. John 6:62
10. John 1:15
11. Elaine Pagels, *The Gnostic Gospels* (Penguin, 1979)
12. Ibid.
13. Mark 4:11 (The King James version)
14. The Reverend Patrick Blakiston in his monthly parish letter (Alvechurch, Worcester), May 1963.
15. Henry Lea, *The History of the Inquisition of the Middle Ages*, Vol. 1 (Russell & Russell, 1955)
16. Lecture: 'Reincarnation and the practice of medicine', March 25 1969 at the College of Psychic Studies.
17. Louis Fischer, *The Life of Mahatma Gandhi* (Harper, 1950)
18. H. P. B. Blavatsky, *The Key to Theosophy* (Reprint of the original 1889 edition, Theosophy Co., Los Angeles, 1968)
19. Helena Blavatsky, *Isis Unveiled*, Vol. 1 (reprint of original version, Theosophy Company, Los Angeles, 1968)
20. Ibid.
21. During the early 1800s the first translations of Eastern mystery teachings were made available in Europe; by the late 1800s and the beginning of the twentieth century *The Sacred Books of the East* (edited by Max Muller) was published. This huge 50-volume work comprised translations of Confucian, Taoist, Hindu, Buddhist, Muslim and Parsi scriptures.
22. See Chapter 2, pp. 33–35.

BIBLIOGRAPHY

Pierre Grimal (ed.), *Larousse World Mythology* (Hamlyn, 1973)

Richard Cavendish (ed.), *Mythology Edited* (Orbis, 1980)

Joseph Head and Sylvia Cranston (eds), *Reincarnation: The Phoenix Fire Mystery* (Julian Press, 1977)

Sylvia Cranston and Carey Williams, *Reincarnation: A New Horizon in Science, Religion and Society* (Julian Press, 1984)

Colin Wilson, *Afterlife* (Harrap, 1985)

Arthur Guirdham, *The Cathars and Reincarnation* (Nevil Spearman, 1970)

Michael Baigent, Richard Leigh and Henry Lincoln, *The Messianic Legacy* (Jonathan Cape, 1986)

Anne Fremantle (ed.), *The Papal Encyclicals in their Historical Context: The Teachings of the Popes* (Mentor, 1956)

Raynor Johnson, *The Imprisoned Splendour* (Pilgrim Press, 1989)

2
Fate and Destiny

> The notion of 'chance occurrence' is an easy refuge for those who seek to exclude from the universe all that is godly and meaningful, all that indicates a purpose behind the living world, in favour of the barren myth that the universe came into existence not through the realisation of a deliberate plan but quite arbitrarily and entirely by itself.
>
> Herbert Fritsche

I cannot remember when the concept of reincarnation was first introduced to me, but I can recall the moment where my passion for mystery and truth-seeking found a focus. I must have been about nineteen when I went to visit Ingrid Lind, the renowned astrologer, at her home in Chinnor, Oxfordshire. Swanlands was an idyllic country house set deep amidst rambling woodlands – a far cry from my rented bed-sit in London, and the perfect setting in which to meet for the first time a Teacher. During that first day together Ingrid introduced me quite casually – since this was an everyday part of life to her – to the power of absent healing, exorcising devils out of a severely mentally disturbed patient, and life in the planetary spheres after death! With my consciousness so inspired, it should have been no surprise when, in the middle of the night, I found myself out of my body – an absolutely terrifying experience because I first became absolutely paralysed, then, after what seemed a never-ending period of intense noise and vibration, I was suddenly floating about on the ceiling. Sheer terror shot me back to earth. After an early morning panic phone call to Ingrid, who treated my experience in the most matter of fact terms, I felt reassured. I had taken my 'psychic initiation test'; from now on it had to be downhill all the way.

Throughout the late 1960s and early '70s, I spent a large part of my time digesting all manner of occult literature and visiting sundry psychics and spiritualists, so that by the time I began my own studies in astrology I was well versed in sifting the wheat from the chaff, the valid from the bogus. Despite Ingrid's conviction about life on the other side and her belief in reincarnation and karma, she was an extremely down-to-earth astrologer who tended to look for practical solutions to life's problems without resorting to flimsy 'spiritual' explanations. She was a huge influence on my life and her commonsense approach to astrology naturally filtered through to me. Thus, paradoxically, far from astrology leading me deeper into the mists of the mystical and the divine, it tended to increase my desire to seek a rational, if not a scientific, basis for zodiacal and planetary effects.

To this end I became quite intolerant of astrologers who used karma and reincarnation to support their arguments. However, as I discuss in detail in First Thoughts, an event in my own life in the early 1980s triggered the start of a radical U-turn, and while I still hesitate before I resort to karmic reasons for each and every life event, my renewed belief in the concept of reincarnation and karma has enriched both my work and my life.

There can be few people who do not question God's infinite wisdom in the face of a huge disaster like the Armenian earthquake in 1988 when over 100,000 people lost their lives, or the Jewish holocaust of the 1940s, or the genocide of the Vietnamese in the 1970s. God certainly moves in mysterious ways when He allows one individual 95 years on earth to find his route to the kingdom of heaven, and another only 19; one to die in a blood-bath, another peacefully surrounded by loved ones. The Bible does at least offer some comfort to children who, in their innocence, go straight to the bosom of Jesus. Faced with such a spectre of a cruel God, I think the Existentialists' attitude has a few points in its favour. To my mind, it makes no spiritual sense whatsoever that a loving God ordains that one individual should be born blind, crippled and in poverty while another should be born whole, beautiful and heir to a royal fortune. No matter how theologically one may try to circumvent this dichotomy with arguments about rich men and needles, in my experience it is far easier to spread goodness, sweetness and light with all one's faculties intact on a full stomach, than when in pain, cold and poor. Whichever way you look at it, the cards are definitely stacked against a disabled pauper. If, however, the disabled pauper has *earned* his afflictions through his own actions (in a previous life) then there is some meaning and purpose to his present struggle and hardship. Likewise, the blessed in health and abundance need fear no guilt, but must struggle to use such gifts wisely. Across the course of many lives, each individual receives its just allotment of pain and pleasure, hardship and ease. Divine justice, or karma, is at work. Armed with such a belief, the conflict involved in the notion of an all-loving but cruel God disappears; what also disappears is the concept that eternal salvation or damnation depends on one life only; we evolve gradually over the course of many lives.

Why, if we can accept that man has a physical evolution, can we not accept that he has a spiritual evolution too? And while a succession of earthly lives designed to lead the individual soul to return to the paradise of the Source may be the way I would look at man's spiritual evolution, there may be those who would consider that each individual, like every cell in an organism, lives and dies as part of a *greater* life cycle; inasmuch as man has evolved from the billions of life cycles of organisms and creatures before him, so does each man in his earthly efforts and labours contribute to the overall spiritual development of man.

Clearly when we are discussing the lot of a man and pondering the whys and wherefores of life's vicissitudes we are talking about fate. Of course, we in the West are often far happier accepting that a situation is God's will, or plain and simple good or bad luck, than using the term fate, with all its connotations of an inexorable force; but in essence they are one and the same. To my mind, the working of God's will or the hand of fate, whichever way one chooses to look at it, is inextricably linked with the action of cause and effect; this is to say that there is a design at work based on the connection between deeds and actions in one life and those in another: 'as ye shall sow, so shall ye reap'. To consider otherwise is to accept that fate is a random force and God is folly.

Of course, finer minds than mine have through the ages grappled with the concept of fate – and have invariably raised more questions than they have found answers. Thus, I do not assume my belief in fate as part of a chain of cause and effect to be 'right'; it is the view that enables me to make a sense of why we are here and why our lives evolve as they do, and for what purpose.

Our dependence on the forces of fate and destiny is little apparent in our sophisticated, materialistic age, but in times past, when man had far less control over his environment and less understanding (in scientific terms) of the world about him, fate played a powerful role indeed. Every ancient culture had a deity of fate, almost always personified as a goddess and usually in triplicate. Most ancient peoples also tended to believe that such deities could aim their arrows of fortune or disaster quite haphazardly on mortals, although they could be appeased by offerings and sacrifices. The Scandinavians took the view that each individual was in the grip of incomprehensible and inescapable forces; in their mythology, fate was personified by three maidens, the Norns – Urdi, Vedani and Skuld – to whom the witches in Shakespeare's Macbeth bear more than just a passing resemblance. The Norns were not only responsible for an individual's fate, but also that of the world, and though no man could change his fate, he could seek omens to give him some idea of what was to come. The triple goddess of fate, whatever the guise – the Weird Sisters, the Morrigan, the Graeae or the Furies – depicted the past, present and future. The three goddesses also represented the three lunar phases – waxing (the youthful maiden); full (the fertile, fecund wife); waning, dark of the moon (the old crone). Life as a mystical thread was spun by the Virgin, measured and sustained by the Mother and cut by the Crone. This significant theme of three can also be found discreetly hidden in Christianity, with the three aspects of Mary and, even more abstrusely, with the Father, Son and Holy Ghost.

The Ancient Greeks, however, did not conceptualize fate simply as a blind, merciless force but as an essential ingredient of cosmic law and order. In one form she was Moira.[1]

Moira, it is true, was a moral power; but no one had to pretend that she was exclusively benevolent, or that she had any respect for the parochial interests and wishes of mankind. Further – and this is the most important point – she was not credited with foresight, purpose, design; these belong to man and the humanized gods. Moira is the blind, automatic force which leaves their subordinate purposes and wills free play within their own legitimate spheres, *but recoils in certain vengeance upon them the moment that they cross her boundaries* [hubris, my italics] . . . She is a representation which states a truth about the disposition of Nature, and to the statement of that truth adds nothing except that the disposition is both necessary and just.[2]

At least this was the view favoured by Anaximander and the Ionian school of Greek philosophy. The more mystically oriented Plato deployed myth to describe a different aspect of cosmic judgement and fate, which enabled him to elaborate on the theme of reincarnation. In his Republic (Book 10) Plato tells the story of Er, who was slain in battle but returned to tell the tale of his journey beyond the gates of death. (I recount this at length since it contains themes to which I will constantly refer.)

[Er's soul] had travelled with many others to a mysterious place of gaping chasms where they were all judged by their conduct in life. The souls of those who were benefactors of others and who were just and pious were allowed to enter a chasm which led up through the heavens. There they benefited from various experiences and sights, and returned cleansed to the place of judgement. The souls of the unjust entered the chasms into the underworld, where they were punished tenfold for their misdeeds, and they too returned cleansed. Some souls proved irredeemable . . . and the mouth of the underworld bellowed in protest when they tried to leave it . . . The other souls now travelled on towards a pillar of light, like a rainbow, which was connected to an enormous spindle that rested on the knees of Ananke (Necessity) and caused eight spheres of the heavens to revolve. Upon each sphere stood a siren, singing a single continuous note, and the eight notes together made a complete scale, a harmony. There too the souls saw the three fates – Lachesis, Klotho and Attropos – the daughters of Necessity, singing of things past, things present and things to come. In the gift of Lachesis *lay their choice of future lives on earth. Choose well, they were told, for you alone are responsible, not God (Theos)* [italics mine]. The various lives, human and animal, of every condition, were laid out before them, and they chose in turn. One soul, in folly and greed, chose to be a great tyrant, only to discover that his destiny was to eat his own children. At this he blamed fortune and the gods, anyone but himself. Souls which had formerly been just from habit, rather than knowledge, also made unwise choices. Er saw many heroes, schooled by hardships, choose lives quite different from their former ones . . . Then each soul came again before Lachesis to be assigned a spirit (daimon) which was to be its guardian in its new life and would give effect to its choice. All drank the waters of the River of Forgetfulness and slept.[3]

The judgement of souls was an equally important feature of ancient Egyptian philosophy. While there were two distinct ways of looking at the soul's return to the Source – the way of Horus with the re-animating of the physical body (see Chapter 1, page 11) or the path of Osiris which involved successive reincarnations – judgement of the individual soul was crucial to both. To the ancient Egyptians, Ma'at was the goddess of truth and justice; she represented the principle of order ruling the cosmos and providing it with the necessary and correct balance. Although Osiris, the great lord of the underworld, was the ultimate judge, Ma'at was also always present at the day of judgement of every soul to ensure that the proceedings were carried out fairly. Ma'at's feather (the symbol of truth) was weighed against the dead man's heart (considered the seat of intelligence) and only if they perfectly balanced each other could the soul pass onto the Osirian underworld. Although the Egyptians considered three deities to rule over fate and destiny, only two were goddesses: Renenet, the great protectress of children and Meshkent who could predict the future of a baby. The god, Shai (who like Meshkent was present as a character witness at the day of judgement), was the god of destiny and had control over a man's allotted life-span and the conditions of his death.

Plato's view of an ordered cosmos where judgement and choice are bound together and with the soul are woven into an eternal pattern of fate and destiny is indebted to the earlier mystical tradition of the

Orphic Mysteries yet, considering the visionary work of more recent mystics, such as Blavatsky and Steiner, not to mention the descriptions of life beyond death of those who have undergone near death experiences, it may be that Plato also relied on his own direct revelations about the nature of man and the cosmos.

It has always seemed curious to me that while we accept from archaeological evidence that ancient civilizations (particularly of the Greeks and Egyptians) were culturally sophisticated, we tend to view their cosmologies as evidence of gross naivety. One only has to examine ancient hermetic texts to discover that the early Egyptians had comprehended certain essential laws about the *physical* universe,[4] theories and findings that have been borne out by twentieth-century scientists. The great thinkers and philosophers of these ancient civilizations considered their knowledge to be so powerful as to be sacred and thus only to be made available to the initiated or the equally elevated in mind and stature. One of the ways they employed to record their knowledge yet to hide it from the uninitiated was to couch the information in metaphors and allegories; thus, the uninformed and unenlightened heard only a story.[5] Myths and symbols were a powerful way of evoking the understanding of great truths; truths that could not be addressed to the reasoning mind but had to be directly perceived by the intuition.

Is it not just possible, then, that Plato's story of Er is not simply an exposition on the workings of fate but the delivery of a fundamental truth about the laws of nature governing the universe[6] as well as a graphic description of the survival of consciousness beyond death? Certainly, this is a line of thought I am inclined to follow.

However, there is an equally strong argument for considering that myths were in no way an attempt to describe a literal truth, but only a way of dealing with the internal chaos of the psyche – making a recognizable drama out of an internal crisis. Indeed, Jungians would consider that the archetypal, mythic themes of 'primitive' man, which formed the basis of his entire belief system, are still alive and well in the psyche of modern man.

> The language of myth is still, as ever, the secret speech of the inarticulate human soul; and if one has learned to listen to this speech of the heart, then it is not surprising that Aeschylos and Plato and Heraclitus are eternal voices and not merely relics of a bygone and primitive era. Perhaps it is now more than ever important to hear these poetic visions of the orderly nature of the universe, because we have grown so dangerously far from them. The mythic perception of a universe governed by immutable moral as well as physical law

is alive and well in the unconscious . . . Fate in the writings of the Greeks is portrayed in images which are psychologically relevant to us.[7]

While Jungian psychology locates these mythic images firmly in the unconscious, albeit recognizing that they are a driving and compelling force, the mystic views them as objective realities. I suspect that they are both right in their own way, merely two routes to the same Source – and I am not the first person to point out that to the ancient Greeks 'psyche' and 'soul' were one and the same.

Theosophy has provided us with an embarrassment of mystical riches and since its rise was synchronous with the development of psychology, perhaps it is true to say that they were but two branches of the same tree – both dealing with ideas whose time had come. The theosophists, as a 'modern' mystical movement, penetrated the veil between life and death and provided a complex archaeology of the soul and the 'other world'. Blavatsky and Steiner shared many of the same views about the soul's experience after death and the relationship between karma and destiny. According to Steiner, a new consciousness that can look back over everything that has been done by an individual during his life comes into play after death. Steiner refers to this period of recollection as the 'kamaloca', a dimension which shares many of the qualities of the Catholic concept of purgatory, and, indeed, many of Plato's 'landmarks'. Throughout the journey (through the planetary spheres) between death and the next life, the soul is sometimes accompanied by beings – not always benign – who take part in the process of judgement and urge the soul in a particular direction. Whether this is on the 'upward' or 'downward' path depends entirely on the soul's accumulated wisdom and karma. After purification, the soul chooses its next life. While Steiner's views about death and resurrection may have radically departed from those of the orthodox Christian Church, he was nevertheless a profound believer in the Christos principle, which he saw pervading life on all levels of consciousness and in all dimensions of experience.

As with so many of the theosophical, or in this case Anthroposophical, concepts, there are strong parallels in Eastern mystical thought. In the *Bardo Thotrol*, the *Tibetan Book of the Dead*,[8] the soul moves through a series of spheres experiencing, albeit on a new level of consummate consciousness, the pain and suffering it has inflicted during the life just past. Eventually after the purgatory of the spheres, the soul 'chooses' the next life:

from now on the body you had in your past life will grow fainter and your future body become clearer . . . The six lights of the six realms of existence will shine, and the one in which you are going to be born because of your karma will shine most brightly . . . Examine where you are going to be born and choose the continent.[9]

Joel Whitton and Joe Fisher, in *Life between Life*, noted the parallels between the descriptions of the *Bardo* and the accounts of between-life states given by patients under hypnotic regression.

The testimony of Dr Whitton's subjects thoroughly endorses the existence of a board of judgement and enlarges considerably on the rather sparse descriptions handed down from the old world. Nearly all who ventured into metaconsciousness [a state of superconscious memory awareness] have found themselves appearing before a group of wise, elderly beings – usually three in number, occasionally four, and in rare instances as many as seven – perceived in a variety of guises. They can be of indeterminate identity or they may take on the appearance of mythological gods or religious masters . . . If there is a private hell in the between life it is the moment when the soul presents itself for review. This is when remorse, guilt and self-recrimination for failings in the last incarnation are vented with a visceral intensity that produces anguish and bitter tears on a scale that can be quite unsettling to witness . . . Any emotional suffering that was inflicted on others is felt as keenly as if it were inflicted on oneself . . . The knowledge of self gleaned from the review process equips the soul to make the vital decisions that will determine the form of its next incarnation But the soul does not act alone . . . The judges recommendations are made according to what the soul needs, not what it wants.[10]

According to Whitton, some of his patients were appalled at the prospect of the next life and had to be 'pushed' into it; his patients also spoke of the existence of a barrier in the between-life state that the soul must cross before coming into birth – the classic River of Forgetfulness.

The amnesia is invaluable in that it prevents endless pining and homesickness . . . and allows the individual to embark on the new life unhindered by confusing echoes of past deeds and misdeeds.[11]

What all these systems of thought emphatically underline is that the soul effectively judges itself; the experiences of the past life give rise to the conditions of the next – destiny fulfilled.

Those who believe in karma have to believe in Destiny, which from birth to death, every man weaves thread by thread round himself as a spider his web . . . it is not karma that rewards or punishes us [nor divine providence that saves us] but it is we who reward and punish ourselves, according as we work with, through, or along with Nature, abiding by the Laws or breaking them.[12]

While conventional Christian thought considered that one lifetime determined man's destiny for all eternity, theosophy propounded that one life was merely one 'day' in the life of the soul.

Thus it [reincarnation] combines strict justice and mercy, in that it allows the Wandering Pilgrim the opportunity of retracing his steps, and of re-entering the Path which leads to perfection. Moreover, the doctrine of karma is not fatalistic – karma is . . . self-conditioning, rather than determining.[13]

A person who is not prepared to admit the reality of karma, of repeated earth lives, can never really accept the fact that a destiny belongs to him . . . He does not know that he himself is the cause of what comes to meet him . . .[14]

If we pull these various strands of myth and philosophy together we should be able to arrive at a point where we can accept fate as a vital force in our lives; the crucial issue being that our fate is not dished out to us by an all-loving or by a cruel God or goddess but something we have engendered ourselves. We create our own fate. Every action is both a result of a former creation and the spark of our future fate. And this is surely not such an ocean of thought away from the psychologist who would consider that we consciously and unconsciously influence the events that happen to us.

If fate and karma supply the reason for who we are and what we meet in life, or as Jung put it, 'fate is what I am, and what I am is also why I am and what happens to me', where, in the great scheme of things, does free will fit?

When I took the diploma of the Faculty of Astrological Studies, I had to discuss in an essay the dilemma between fate and free will. At the time, the issue appeared quite cut and dried to me that while there was a divine plan at work, we also had the God-given ability to exercise free will. I find the issue much more complex now. As an astrologer, one cannot avoid the knotty problem of fate, since a birth chart at almost every level is showing a fated pattern, even if character is the fundamental issue and future 'trends' are avoided; character may indeed be destiny, but how did we come to have such a character in the first place? Is this not also fate?[15] And where does free will come in when an individual is born with deformities or multiple disabilities?

Edgar Cayce in his clairvoyant readings provided us with many ideas on the more esoteric aspects of astrology, and indeed, on almost every metaphysical theme. He did not flinch from addressing the issue of fate and free will, which he saw as working entirely in symbiosis.

> Every person's life is shaped to some extent by karma: his own, that of his associates and loved ones, that of his nation and race, and that of the world itself. But these, singly or together, are not greater than free will. It is what the person does about these influences and urges, how he reacts to them that makes a difference in his soul development. Because of karma some things are more probable than others, but so long as there is free will anything is possible. Thus free will and predestination coexist in a person. His past experiences limit him in probability, and incline him in certain directions, but free will can always draw the sword from the stone.[16]

Fate or free will is another version of the proverbial chicken or egg conundrum. Even if one takes on board the concept of karma, so that an apparently fated experience in one life time has its cause in a former – which, as I have stated earlier, is to my mind the only way one can comprehend the vicissitudes of life – one is still left with the existential problem of how it all began. What was the initial cause that gave rise to the effect? What, if you like, set fate in motion? If we have earned (or indeed chosen) our present life, is it mapped out in its entirety to the minutest detail, or is it just a sketchy outline? According to Dr Whitton, it is the less developed souls who require a detailed blueprint while the more evolved need only a brief outline, 'so that they may act more creatively in challenging situations.' Whitton also maintains that it is possible to be born with no plan at all, in which case 'the soul becomes a reed shaken by the wind – a victim of fate rather than a participant in destiny'. If we accept that we do have free will, how can we be certain that it is operating in any given situation, and not an impulse predetermined in some between life state?

There are no absolute answers to these questions; we can merely feel our way around the issue; it may be that there is no free will as such, and that any change and development through the seemingly eternal cycle of reincarnation and karma occurs as a spontaneous event, in much the same way as a species of plant or animal will suddenly produce a new characteristic. However, virtually all schools of mystical thought have included choice or free will as the catalyst to the soul's evolution, and I see no reason to argue with them. I would like to add, however, from my own experience, that while I cannot be sure how much free will operates in our life, I am persuaded that the more one accesses the intuition the more one's awareness and perception expands, so that in meeting situations, the possibilities of those situations appear to increase. Perhaps this is free will. I am also aware that there are times when one feels entirely swept up by fate, yet the more one has expanded one's inner 'eye' the better one is able to cope with it and find purpose in the experience – and make the appropriate response. As Voltaire said, 'experience is not so much what happened to you, but what you did with what happened to you.'

While the teachings of the spiritualists, Eastern religious doctrine and the writings of ancient philosophers (even the reliability of patients under hypnosis) can be all too easily dismissed by twentieth-century rationalists, it is a little harder to disregard the findings of some present-day, highly regarded medical practitioners. Yet it is with the medical establishment that research has begun to define the nature of consciousness after death and in the process throw greater light on the whole area of reincarnation, karma and fate.

In the early 1970s, Dr Elisabeth Kubler-Ross, while working with terminally ill patients, found that time and again the dying would give similar accounts of their experience of 'life' beyond death. She was not the only doctor to hear such reports. In 1975 an American psychiatrist, Dr Raymond Moody, published *Life after Life*, which became a world-wide best seller. Other accounts were to follow.[17] All these individuals, renowned in their own fields of medicine, were inclined to believe or were convinced that statements from patients about their out-of-the-body journeys after 'death' were true. These were patients who had been pronounced clinically dead and later resuscitated – some of them after several hours, and one man waking up on the mortician's table! These deeply felt accounts of life after death contained similar 'core' experiences, regardless of race, socio-economic group, age or religion. What is also remarkable is that ordinary people, with no grounding in theology, literature or metaphysics, produced accounts which closely parallel the descriptions of the spheres of experience beyond death made by mystics and modern inner-space explorers.

Almost all individuals who died but returned to life reported an initial stage prior to death of *immense peace accompanied by a sense of well being*; this was followed by *separation from the body* where the individual floated above the 'corpse' often observing the frantic attempts to resuscitate 'him'.

> All pain disappeared, comfort seized me. Only my essence was felt. Time no longer mattered and space was filled with bliss. I was bathed in radiant light and immersed in the aura of the rainbow. All was fusion. Sounds were of a new order, harmonious, nameless (now I call it music).[18]

(The parallels to Plato's afterlife are particularly striking here.)

Bang, I left! The next thing I was aware of was floating on the ceiling . . . I'm very nearsighted by the way, which was one of the startling things that happened when I left my body. I see at fifteen feet what most people see at four hundred . . . They were hooking me up to a machine that was behind my head. And my first thought was, 'Jesus, I can see! I can't believe it, I can see! I could read the numbers on the machine behind my head . . . And I thought, 'They gave me back my glasses.[19]

The third state, *entering the darkness* is usually accompanied by a sensation of a high speed journey through a tunnel, eventually emerging into an indescribably *bright and all pervading light* (stage four).

The next thing I remember was being carried or projected very rapidly through what appeared to be a cylindrical void . . . I heard sounds around me . . . they were vibrations . . . more than anything else. As I came closer to [this] light it grew so bright and so all encompassing, I found myself suddenly totally surrounded and submerged in this beautiful light.[20]

This fifth stage of *entering the light* is only as far as most of the clinically 'dead' go. But those who progress further often report seeing a beautiful place in the distance (sometimes deceased friends are glimpsed at this point, though this phenomenon may occur at almost any stage). This place is usually sensed as the boundary which, once crossed, denies the individual a return to life.

Off in the distance . . . I could see a city. There were buildings . . . gleaming, bright. People were happy in there . . . it was wonderful . . . I was told that if I went in there I couldn't go back . . . that the decision was mine.[21]

The understanding that one can go no further is usually sensed to have been 'uttered' by a benign presence, a being of great light, often interpreted as Christ. This being exudes love, complete understanding and an all-pervasive warmth; 'he' stands by while the individual assesses his life – invariably perceived as a series of flashbacks – and either informs him that he must go back or allows him to make the decision to return himself.

My life started to flash before me. I felt embarrassed every time a stupid thing I had done came up. I sensed that the presence was saying, 'Yes, you did these things, but you were learning at the same time.' It was then communicated to me that I should go back. I didn't want to, but I understood that there was still a lot of work for me to do.[22]

> The thought came to my mind, 'Lovest thou me?' This was not exactly in the form of a question, but I guess the connotation of what the light said was, 'If you do love me, go back and complete what you began in your life.' And all during this time, I felt as though I were surrounded by an overwhelming love and compassion.[23]

This is as far as any near death experience takes us, or indeed can take us. And although no one has reported seeing a lady balancing the universe on a spindle (nor, for obvious reasons, a plan for the next life), I think it is the most impressive ratification of the esoteric world view. Though the pragmatist might argue that if there is to be any truth, other than a psychological one, to be found in NDEs all the experiences should tally precisely, it would seem self-evident that free from the world of matter, without our physical senses to guide us, our ability to conceive a form of any sort and make a sense out of the experience must rely on that other amorphous 'body', the mind, with its storehouse of familiar images. I think therefore I am, so to speak.

While the NDEs are unable to support the concept of a plan for the next life, most of the individuals who were resuscitated came back with a newfound resolve and a conviction in life beyond death; some of them also returned with a firm belief in cosmic law and order.

> . . . I know I was sent back because I've got work to do for God. I now know that there are laws governing the universe. God does not break these laws, they are part of his own nature. But when we transgress these laws, suffering and disease follow and the only way to reverse this is to learn to live in harmony with God's laws.[24]

Of course, this idea of transgressing God's law is not a new one. The ancient Greeks believed that if you overstepped the boundaries of your fate – a condition known as hubris – Moira would demand her dues. One only has to look at such present-day morality tales as that of the Marcoses of the Phillipines to see how absolute power can lead to absolute corruption and how in the swell of their overreaching ambition, the tide has turned against the Marcoses with a vengeance. Ferdinand Marcos died from a particularly unpleasant form of cancer, and Imelda, bereft of wealth and influence, must bear the ignominy and increasing precariousness of her position. The hundreds of people imprisoned, tortured and murdered to prop up the Marcos regime, the thousands of poor violated for Imelda's vanity may never themselves see justice done, but Moira is already wreaking her revenge.

How karma came to be set in motion is an even more elusive issue, and one for which once again we must look to myth and metaphor.

And the Bible seems as good a place as any to begin at the beginning. We know from Genesis that God created the first humans, Adam and Eve, and that they lived in a state of grace in paradise. They might have stayed there for all time and had not the wicked serpent tempted Eve to eat the forbidden fruit of the tree of knowledge. In a similar vein we have the story of Atlantis, a vast continent located variously in the Pacific and the Atlantic whose inhabitants were technologically and spiritually highly advanced – godlike, in fact. Through misuse and corruption of power the Atlanteans brought about their own destruction.

In their own way both these stories describe the concept of a state of perfection from which there is a knowledge-inspired breaking of bounds, leading to chaos and destruction. Man, through desire and discontent, breaks God's immutable law and from thenceforward is propelled deeper and deeper into reality, materialism and evil and further and further away from his Source. At some indefinable point man reaches his own nadir and begins the return journey back to perfect bliss. But this time in the light of knowledge, reaching the state of perfection – heaven, nirvanah, whatever – in full consciousness. We can look at this in the sense of individual karma and collective karma, so that each individual through his own efforts to reach full consciousness in turn contributes to the greater mass of humanity's evolution. We may also have a basis for understanding the role of evil here, in that if we accept that the universe is sustained by balance and order, in both the physical and metaphysical context, evil becomes a necessary balance for good; so that the outer journey into hell balances the return to heaven, like a cosmic see-saw. Yet while I might consider that the route to heaven is the only one to aim for, who is to say that hell is not a state of perfection in its own right – pure evil!

One can take this concept of the involution and evolution of consciousness and work it into a design for fate reminiscent of a *cobweb*. The centre of the cobweb represents both the Source, or God, and the beginning of karma. The strands are woven through the action of karma, initially taking humanity away from the centre then ultimately providing the route for it to return. In this way fate is woven by man, yet following a perfect model; all actions interconnecting with one another – a process which is impossible to see at close range, only comprehensible viewed from a distance. It is also possible to take this idea of the cobweb away from the collective and perceive it as an individual creating his own pattern by responding accordingly to his experience. To put it another way, a situation gives rise to a number of options, the action taken then moves the individual along an appropriate path which in turn gives rise to another experience, offering further options and so on. Had the individual taken an alternative course of action in the first place, the path would then have led to an alternative set of experiences. All paths ultimately lead to the centre but some make the journey more circuitously than others. I would see this process as operating in the physical and material as well as in the non-physical realms of experience.

Given that free will may be an illusion and there may be no divine purpose or justice, one could view fate in terms of a *game of chance* – a throw of the cosmic dice determines what happens to you. The game begins at birth and ends at death. No more, no less. Keeping the same idea of the game but amplifying it to a board game of 'snakes' and 'ladders' (reaching the end of the board marking the entry into nirvanah or heaven) permits life to become less meaningless and fate more purposeful. The action of the dice-as-fate is still the essential factor since it has the power to propel us up the 'ladders' and down the 'snakes', but while this process may appear to require no plan or no real effort or skill, the 'player' is not entirely a victim of fate. By developing his intuition, the more in tune he becomes with the throw of the dice-as-fate, thus the more events synchronize with his needs and the better able he is to reach the destination.

We could also draw an analogy of fate's hand in life with the all-the-world's-a-stage-and-all-the-men-and-women-merely-players theme. In this design, life as a *stage*, the play is written – the blueprint already created – the parts are cast. While initially a life script might appear to limit the potential of a player by offering him no outlet for change, the possibilities are almost limitless when it comes to performance. A man brings his unique individuality to his fated role, he also brings his experience (accrued through previous parts) and his particular talents and deficiencies. A fine performance depends on preparation for the part, the understanding, skill and intelligence to make the part work and the sensitivity to respond to co-performers and so contribute to their performances.

Those who are living out their karmic scripts, or have even exceeded them, have an inner sense that life is unfolding as it should. Those who have strayed from the blue print feel, instead, that everything is out of control. Chaos rules. Like actors hopelessly unaware of their lines as they step out into the spotlight, they are forced to extemporise as the drama of life unfolds, yet there are also people who appear to be placed precariously between destiny and fate, between scripting their lives and taking the stage as impromptu players. They have a plan, but the plan is open to an inordinate amount of improvisation.[25]

Through the many avenues of thought, I have endeavoured in this chapter to make a case for the existence and nature of fate and destiny in our lives. Fate, as we have seen, cannot be separated from karma; in this way fate is not something to be feared or striven against, but to work through. We create our own fate. We are our destiny.

NOTES

1. Moira is considered to mean, 'share' or 'allotment' but by some to mean 'fate'.
2. F. M. Cornford, *From Religion to Philosophy* (Harvester Press, 1980)
3. Richard Cavendish (ed.) *Mythology* (Orbis, 1980)
4. See Chapter 4 p. 75
5. Many theologians consider Jesus's parables in the New Testament to contain two 'truths', one for the disciples and another for laymen. The same could be said of the duality of the ancient Egyptian hieroglyphs, hermetic symbolism on the one hand, phonetic script on the other.
6. See Chapter 4.
7. Liz Greene, *The Astrology of Fate* (Mandala/Unwin, 1984)
8. *Bardo* means gap.
9. *The Tibetan Book of the Dead*, translated by F. Fremantle and C. Trungpa (Shambhala, 1975)
10. Joel Whitton and Joe Fisher, *Life between Life* (Grafton, 1986)
11. Ibid.
12. H. P. Blavatsky, *The Secret Doctrine*, Vol. 1 (reprint of original version, Theosophical Company, Los Angeles, 1968)
13. Ibid.
14. Rudolph Steiner, *The Manifestations of Karma* (Rudolph Steiner Press, London, 1969)
15. I will be covering the issue of character, heredity and fate in Chapter 4.
16. Thomas Sugrue, *The Story of Edgar Cayce: There is a River* (Dell, 1970)
17. Among those who have published their findings on near death experiences are: Kenneth Ring, *Life at Death* (Coward, McCann & Geoghegan, 1980) and *Heading toward Omega* (Quill, 1985), Michael Sabom, *Recollections of Death* (Harper & Row, 1982).
18. Margot Grey, *Return from Death* (Arkana, 1985)
19. Ian Wilson, *The After Death Experience* (Sidgwick & Jackson, 1987)
20. Ibid.
21. Raymond A. Moody, *Reflections on Life after Life* (Corgi, 1977)
22. Margot Grey, op. cit.
23. Raymond A. Moody, *Life after Life* (Corgi, 1976)

24. Margot Grey, op. cit.
25. Joel Whitton and Joe Fisher, op. cit.

BIBLIOGRAPHY

John Anthony West, *The Serpent in the Sky* (Harper & Row, 1979)

3
Cosmic Consciousness

> I cannot totally grasp all that I am. But where is that part of the mind which I do not know? Is it outside me? As this question strikes me I am overcome with wonder and almost stupor.
>
> St Augustine

Though there may be some comfort to be found in accepting that we create our own fate, there still remains the mystery of what we can do about it. How can we prevent ourselves from creating further 'bad' karma? If only we knew what lessons we had come to learn. If only we didn't have to drink of the Waters of Forgetfulness, we would remember what *It* was all about! On the face of it, the Ten Commandments should provide all the guidelines we need. But while we know what we *should* do, only rarely do we do it. By and large we are at the mercy of our instincts, our appetites and our self-motivated actions. Thus in taking the path of least resistance we continually meet the same pitfalls and encounter the same problems. Yet it is not without some small voice within doing its best to point us in a more worthy direction. That still small voice is the direct link to the soul, it can tell us all everything we need to know; most of us have become used to calling it the Higher Self.

The Higher Self, the super-self, the transpersonal, the superconscious are all names for that part of our being most in touch with the soul, that aspect of ourselves that has a bird's-eye view of life, as opposed to our normal ground-level perception.

> In the occult sense the concept of the higher self is one that goes beyond the Freudian superego. The higher self is not a 'socialized' self, but the creative, choosing and aspiring psyche, endowed with supraconsciousness, and in this sense is known as the true, transcendental or nouminal self, the self of faith and the higher reason. It is asomatic, acerebral, arational, acausal and symbolic.[1]

Virtually every mystical tradition both past and present has a version of the Higher Self: the Japanese refer to the 'seishin', the Ancient Greeks to the 'nous' and the Haitian (Voodoo cult) to the gros-bon-ange (great good angel) and the ti-bon-ange (little good angel). While the Higher Self is ever-present, our major attention in the here and now limits our access to its resources. Put another way, our normal range of consciousness (essential for coping with everyday life) is largely held in focus by the ego; only by rising above the ego can the faculties of the Higher Self come into play.

One of the major problems facing anyone attempting to bring order and cohesion into the chaos of the ephemeral is that so many of the words common to all esoteric systems vary in meaning from system to system. Three of the worst culprits are the words spirit, soul and ego.

Ego is a familiar word to psychology and metaphysics alike. Where psychology is concerned, ego (Latin, I) is generally used to describe processes concerned with the self and a person's conception of himself; to Freud, the ego was the emotional, 'socialized', thinking and feeling personality, the cerebral self guided by the conscious mind; to Jung, the ego was the centre of an individual's field of consciousness (drawing from both the unconscious and conscious). To occultists like Steiner and Blavatsky, the ego represented man's higher nature, his ability to apply continuity, purpose and choice in his life – factors that differentiated his type of consciousness from that of animals.

To most minds, the soul refers to the constant, divine essence that permeates our being; it is neither psyche nor soma, yet linked to both. In Jungian terminology, the soul is an '"inner personality" . . . the way in which one behaves in regard to one's inner psychic processes.' (In his later years, Jung expanded this view by commenting that the soul was 'the greatest of all cosmic miracles.')[2] The Neoplatonist Proclus considered the soul to be 'an incorporeal, indestructible, self-animating principle, having temporary activity in matter and an eternal existence in the immortal realms.'[3] The soul is created by God, yet it is also intrinsically God 'himself'; every living thing has a soul which is but a facet of divine light.

The line between spirit and soul is a fine one indeed. As far as the spiritualists are concerned, man is a spirit enclosed in a physical body. Jung, on the other hand, considered the spirit to have 'a natural bond with the unconscious'[4] and to comprise the intellect and the soul. Other occult sources conceptualize the spirit as the 'flame' that kindles the lamp of the soul.

As the higher so the lower . . . inasmuch as the Higher Self links to higher states of consciousness, the lower self (the Freudian sub-ego) responds to the lower instinctual forces of the unconscious. Somewhere, fluctuating in between these two levels of consciousness, gaining input from both, we are primarily focused – the small self as opposed to the greater (Higher) Self. It is the (small) self that has the strongest links to the personality – that which characterizes us to our fellow man.

To a major extent, what we refer to as the personality has little in common with the Higher Self and most systems of esoteric and psychological thought consider the personality to be an adjunct of the ego. 'As the sub-ego is related to the unconscious, so the ego or personality is related to the conscious mind or waking behaviour.'[5] The personality (in Jungian terms, the persona) could be likened to the 'actor-on-stage' being the part other people can see, though not the whole production. Paradoxically, though our personality is what registers on the world around us, what is deemed entirely characteristic of us – our uniqueness – is not our true Self at all.

In many ways the self, or the personality, can be seen to be the 'driver' in the 'bus' of the psyche; the driver receives most of his input from his external surroundings, his limited view of the road ahead means he cannot see what's around the corner and his attention is often misdirected by the noise and demands of his passengers (subconscious thought processes and sub-personalities). The driver may think he knows where he's going; he may have a reliable map but he cannot know what experience awaits him. The Higher Self, of course, has the plan and an all-round view, but due to constant interference on the 'intercom', only the occasional garbled message gets through. The driver mistakenly trusts in what he sees and 'knows' to be reality 'out there'; only when he makes contact with the Higher Self, perhaps in meditation, a mystical or near-death-experience does he realize how blind he truly is.

The self, however, is not a structural concept but a dynamic one; a process as well as a pattern. So while for the purposes of explanation I have isolated the Higher Self as a supreme but rarely tapped higher aspect of ourselves and our lower self as the accumulation of our basest instincts and most undifferentiated dimension of our unconscious, in effect there are conduits interlinking the whole psychic organism of the individual.

Certainly the Higher Self, or the expanded, unlimited Self is our route to enlightenment, the key to the transcendental realm. And from the descriptions of those who have nearly died (NDEers), it is the Higher Self as characterized by a sense of expanded awareness and a bird's-eye perception of the world that is released from the physical body at 'death'.

A friend of mine who 'died' during an emergency Caesarean operation, describes how she felt herself 'sucked' out of her body through the top of her head. Finding herself above her body on the operating table, she moved off (floating through walls) in search of her husband; she was able to describe conversations between the hospital staff (which were confirmed later). My friend eulogizes about the clarity of thought and vision in this state and remains convinced that she had at last found her true Self.[6]

At the risk of repeating myself, while I have referred to this sense of finding the Self as contacting the Higher Self, I am only attaching a label to what is essentially a dimension of consciousness as a whole. One of the most illuminating aspects of NDEs is that people describe the experience of finding the Self in different ways. Some individuals on leaving the body perceive that they are still enveloped in a body, while others feel only that they are pure consciousness. While a psychologist would explain such phenomena in terms of the dissolving of the ego boundaries, the mystic would go one step further and propose that the ego had been dissolved in favour of the divine I. The renowned spiritual healer living in Cyprus, Daskalos (also referred to as the Magus of Strovalos) describes the experience of locating the true Self, of super-conscious self-awareness as

> We are outside our bodies while at the same time our bodies are within our sphere of receiving impressions. We can feel everything around us, including our bodies. We are no longer within the material body, but the material body is within us.

Tennyson creates a more evocative picture of the same process:

> All at once as it were, out of the intensity of the consciousness of individuality, individuality itself seemed to dissolve and fade away into boundless being. And this was not a confused state, but the clearest, the surest of the sure, utterly beyond words, where death was almost a laughable impossibility. The loss of personality, if so it were, seeming no extinction, but the only true life.[8]

The very essence of mysticism is that one must seek to express the divine within and overcome the petty preoccupations of the ego. To a certain extent, most schools of psychology would go along with this concept of a higher aspect of man's inner being, accepting it as an amorphous dimension of the psyche dependent upon the physical body for its expression. The big divide between psychology and mysticism emerges when the esotericist deems consciousness to exist in other spheres beyond the physical and to function independently of the body.

As I have already discussed, the Higher Self is the most accessible way of conceptualizing part of a stream of consciousness that flows through our entire being. When 'we' leave the physical body in sleep or at a near death or 'out-of-the-body' experience, some form of consciousness capable of responding to certain stimuli still remains with the physical body. (I shall give some examples of this shortly.) According to most esoteric traditions, the 'body' that leaves the physical behind is the astral body which may or may not take the form of the physical body.

The astral body is a unit made up of sensibilities, memories and thoughts which reflects the condition of the soul. It is the vessel of the soul and the vehicle which keeps the individual integrated as 'he' moves through dimensions of experience in the non-physical realms. To this end, the astral body also becomes the vehicle of the Higher Self, although it is not the Higher Self.

Rudolph Steiner divided man into seven bodies; physical, etheric, astral, ego, Spirit Self, Life Spirit and Spirit Man (Atma). According to Steiner, the *etheric body* is responsible for sustaining the physical body and takes the precise form of the physical body. With his clairvoyant vision, Steiner described the etheric body as 'glowing with a redish-blue light like a phantom, but with radiance, a little darker than young peach blossom . . . it is responsible for nutrition, growth and reproduction.' The *astral body* is 'the seat of all we know as desire, passion and so on . . . [the visionary] sees it as an eggshaped cloud, continually mobile within, which not only surrounds the body but also permeates it.' The *ego body* is the 'I' within; contained within the constantly mobile astral body is 'one small space, shaped like a somewhat elongated blue oval, at the base of the nose behind the brow . . . This is the outer expression of the I or ego.' The more highly evolved morally, emotionally and intellectually a man becomes the more form is given to the remaining three Spirit bodies. Steiner maintained that after the death of the physical body, the etheric body too disappears over the course of approximately three days; the astral body and the ego body remain together as major constituents of the soul and go on to traverse the spheres of the other worlds.[9]

In Carlos Castaneda's books[10] the Yaqui Indian shaman, Don Juan, maintains that the seer sees a nagual (supreme sorcerer) or anyone with supernatural powers as a 'luminous egg' while ordinary people appear as dull grey egg shapes – a clear parallel to Steiner's perception of the astral body. One of the techniques Don Juan enables Castaneda to accomplish is to split himself into two separate selves, to become a 'double man'. It is this second self which has the extraordinary powers; the double who is used in dreaming, who has access to parallel worlds, and the double who must ultimately leave the body behind once and for all eternity, thus outwitting death and presumably avoiding the eternal cycle of rebirth.

The ability to produce the double self, or the astral body, can be achieved by many psychics at will; but for most people the experience is a spontaneous result of trauma or illness. Sir Aukland Geddes (Professor of Anatomy at Dublin University) whose heart stopped beating during a severe bout of gastroenteritis described the separation of his astral body from the physical body in this way,

> as my physical condition grew worse and the heart was fibrillating rather than beating, I realised that the B-consciousness [attached to his physical body in the chair] was beginning to show signs of being composite, that is, built up of 'consciousness' from the head, the heart and the viscera. These components became more individual and B-consciousness began to disintegrate, while the A-consciousness, which was now me, seemed to be altogether outside my body [I was] free in a time dimension of space where 'now' was in some way equivalent to 'here' in the ordinary three-dimensional space of everyday life.[11]

Geddes supplies us with a curious observation here in that he sees the B-consciousness attached to the body in the chair as being derived from the body and dependent upon it, whereas the A-consciousness was more truly him.

The psychic Rosalind Heywood was able to see her physical body clothed in a pink nightie actually tossing and turning in bed next to her husband, while she was simultaneously focused in another body clothed in a white robe. Clearly the body in the bed was alive and kicking and thus also had some form of consciousness; however, Rosalind also observed that the body in the bed possessed a far inferior form of consciousness to that of the 'white' self.

> This White Me seemed just as actual as Pink Me and I was equally conscious in both places at the same time. I vividly remember myself as White Me looking down and observing the carved end of the bed in front of me and also thinking what a silly fool Pink Me looked . . . Pink Me was a totally self-regarding little animal, entirely composed of 'appetites', and she cared not at all whether her unfortunate husband was tired or not . . . She was particularly furious because she knew very well that the White Me was stronger . . . A moment or two later – I felt no transition – White Me was once more imprisoned with Pink Me in one body, and there they have dwelt as oil and water ever since.[12]

From the Steinerian point of view, the inferior 'pink' consciousness was the stuff of the etheric body and the sub-ego, while the 'white' consciousness comprised the astral body and the Higher Self.

Most psychologists and orthodox scientists would positively cringe at the notion that an individual was capable of sustaining consciousness in two 'places' at the same time – unless the individual was hallucinating or a raging schizophrenic! But then the whole area of mind and consciousness and their relationship with the brain is a deeply mysterious one. The majority of scientists and neuro-physicians hold the view that consciousness is a by-product of the brain – what they would term an epiphenomenon – and that without a brain an individual can have no consciousness. The mind, like consciousness, is also considered to be a by-product of the brain. However, no one has yet established how the mind and body interact. Nerve fibres are known to conduct impulses to the brain, but what stimulates thought? Thought is not an activated neuron; consciousness cannot be a mass of vibrating nerve cells. In some quarters, science is gradually shifting its somewhat mechanical view of the brain, and espousing a dualistic interactionist mechanism for the brain-mind whereby the physical brain is conceived as a kind of filter that enables certain types of experience or thought to be constructed while limiting others. (David Lorimer[13] refers to this as the transmissive theory of consciousness, which implies that the brain is a transducer or transmitter of consciousness, but not the origin of consciousness.) The eminent brain physiologist, Sir John Eccles, concluded after years of research that the brain was an apparatus not for generating conscious activity but for responding to the conscious activity of some immaterial agent. And the neurosurgeon, Dr Wilder Penfield, founder of the Montreal Neurological Institute and Hospital, commented in a debate on the relationship between body and mind, 'What is the real relationship of the brain to the mind? Perhaps we will always be forced to visualize a spiritual element of different essence, capable of controlling the mechanism of the brain.'[14] Clearly, 'the spiritual element capable of controlling the brain' must be the Self – the organizing principle in a field of pure consciousness.

With developments in such areas as modern physics and astrophysics, science is having to widen its parameters. At one time there appeared to be no way in which matter (i.e. brain) could interact with the immaterial (mind). But since matter can no longer be viewed as solid but regarded (at the sub atomic level) in terms of energy, there is now a basis for such an exchange: the interaction between mind and matter can be interpreted as an interchange between mind and energy – the organization of energy by mind.

The esotericist, however, has no need to wrestle with the mechanics of the brain-mind-consciousness interchange: to the mystic, consciousness is primary, consciousness animates the body and the brain is simply the transmitter. In a sense our experience of life is an experience in consciousness – the world exists (stands out) because we are conscious of it. Consciousness exists at all levels and within all dimensions; but whereas the scientist reasons that the physical gives rise to the psychic, the mystic believes that the soul stream of consciousness is the essence of life.

Given the mystical view that consciousness is the wellspring of life, all occult disciplines have elaborate constructs of how consciousness and subtle energies combine to produce the interconnecting network of the physical and non-physical bodies. And though at first these ideas may seem far-fetched, in the light of modern physics, the ancients and mystics aren't looking quite so ridiculous.

Mystics through the ages have all shared a single view, that man is not merely a physical body with a mind dependent on the brain for its existence, but a soul connected to God which permeates all aspects of the individual's being and is *not* dependent on the body for its existence. Mystics of all races and creeds are also united in believing that man is made up of several layers, or bodies, and that these bodies are gradually built up from psycho-cosmic energies before being manifested as flesh and blood in the physical body. This process is perceived as part of a continuing cycle such that after the death of the physical body the soul gradually sheds its cosmic substances as it returns to the innermost spiritual planes; the soul then begins another outward journey into the physical world, drawing to itself the appropriate energy patterns.

Theosophy teaches that the divine spark (spiritual monad) stems from the Monadic sphere from which also emerge the impulses that form man. The monad passes through five worlds before entering the physical; the higher worlds of the Spiritual, Intuitional and Emotional are where the human ego (in this case, the ego representing the handmaid to the soul) are developed and will, wisdom and intellect acquired. The lower worlds of the mental and astral (and the physical body) are where the personality is created.

In almost all mystical systems it is considered that the various bodies are formed as the soul passes through five or seven dimensions. These dimensions – all with different names and attributes depending on the belief system – are not only psychic realms where different aspects of consciousness are acquired, but fields of energy; energy patterns that create form in both its subtle and gross state. John Davidson discusses this complex concept at length in *The Web of Life*.

In its descent, the soul first encounters the Universal Mind, where the qualities and attributes of energy and matter as they appear in our familiar physical world are first manifested. Sanskrit, as well as modern mystical understanding, talks of three sets of energy plexi [networks] related to qualities within the vibrational fields of existence. These qualities are also known as the tattwas, roughly translatable as the elements [akash (ether), air, fire, water and earth] . . . all energy substance is of the tattwas. This we *experience*, through our physical form, not only as the material phases of matter, but also as the energetic substrate of our emotions, our sensory perceptions and our motor responses.[15]

These five tattwas (the elements so familiar to astrologers) are the material essence of form, 'the weaver and integrator of this fabric is our soul'; the life-giving maker of the pattern is prana, which means life energy or life breath.

Flowing like a complex wave through water, prana flows through the tattwas in their subtle state, creating the energetic blueprint out of which the gross physical body is formed. This subtle blueprint has been called the etheric body and contains within it six major centres of resonance [chakras] five of which relate to the energetic density and quality of the five tattwas in their subtle form . . . [the sixth centre acting as a higher control point][16]

To add to the complexity, when prana comes into contact with each of the tattwas, its vibration is subtly modified, thus creating five pranas. These five combined energy systems (tattwas and pranas) provide the 'raw material' of the supersensible organs of the astral and etheric body; in this way the chakras act as 'junction boxes' from which the energies can be distributed to the psychic bodies and to the physical body.

Because of the life-giving qualities of the pranas related to the . . . consciousness within, [the] chakras are more than just primary nodes in a wave form, but are spinning wheels of organisational power.[17]

To simplify matters a little, consciousness (as the expression of the soul and spirit – life-energy) combines with the subtle essences of the elements to create a psychic, hologram-like image of the body which is ultimately (with the aid of the oscillating chakras) brought forth into the physical. The vital energy points (chakras) in the system are crucial to the psychic and physical well-being of the individual; they are also intricately involved in the formation and organization of the body and its functioning in life. What is also extremely interesting here for astrologers (and which I will expand on in the next chapter) is that the elements, the essential building blocks of astrology, are seen to form a vital part in the psycho-physical formation of the individual.

Steiner also believed that something wove the body, or rather bound it together, 'All the physical organs are maintained in their form and shape by the currents and movements of the etheric body.'[18] This concept of energy forces shaping the body, holding it together and breathing a life-force into it sounds fanciful to say the least, but modern physics, on the frontier between metaphysics and science, is coming up with some remarkable new models that are but a whisker away from demonstrating how such esoteric processes could work.

As yet, however, even with the recognition that matter is but matrices of energy, there is no single comprehensive model in modern physics that would explain the interaction of subtle and gross energy fields nor account for the form-creating principles of the tattwas and pranas. But there are frameworks that could deal separately with different parts of the jigsaw puzzle.

One of the great mysteries about the body is just how a single cell, 'a relatively homogeneous shell of material', can organize itself to form a particular part of the body. Grappling with this mystery in the 1950s, the late Alan Turing postulated that through the chemical process of cell division, waveforms are emitted that control structural development. Rupert Sheldrake has expanded this theme in *A New Science of Life*, with his theory of morphogenetic fields. Briefly, Sheldrake's theory is that the exact shape of living things – from a hydra to a whale, a garden snail to a human being – is not dependent on DNA and information transmitted from cell to cell, but a response to a previously shaped field. (I will be looking at the part genes play in the process of inheritance in the next chapter.)

> Biological morphogenesis can be defined as the 'coming into being of characteristics and specific form in living organisms'. The first problem is precisely that form comes into being . . . new structures appear which cannot be explained in terms of the unfolding or growth of structures which are already present in the egg at the beginning of development . . . developing systems proceed towards a morphological goal, and . . . they have some property which specifies this goal and enables them to reach it.[19]

What Sheldrake has done for the metaphysical point of view is propose a framework based on scientific processes which allows for some other *unseen* principle to be involved in the formation of the body. He does not take the step of proposing that the unseen principle at work is composed of elemental energy patterns that depend on a life breath to weave them together, nor is he positing that consciousness is the architect of form; rather he resorts to the theory of morphic resonance: that new forms capture the correct structure from 'echos' of previous systems. By failing to incorporate the function of the tattwas and pranas, though at the same time drawing heavily from Yogic ideas to which he was exposed during his time in India, Sheldrake, so John Davidson maintains, has effectively missed the essential metaphysical point of morphogenetic fields. I might also add that John Davidson may also have missed the metaphysical point (though this could well be because I couldn't see the wood for the trees in his thesis) that if consciousness does indeed create form and the Self is the organizing principle in a field of consciousness, then it is we who create ourselves!

Nevertheless, Sheldrake has provoked science to look beyond its well-defended frontiers – indeed John Maddox, editor of the prestigious British scientific journal *Nature*, called it 'A book for burning!' But like all pioneers, Sheldrake clearly drew some of his inspiration from other sources.

Before Sheldrake's work on morphogenetic fields, an American Professor at Yale University, Harold Saxton Burr had proposed the concept of a biological shaping field. Burr, together with F.S.C. Northrop, conducted experiments with plants and embryos that suggested that all living organisms possess an organizing electric field (L-field) – which is not dependent on local conductivity variations nor on ion currents in the tissues. Burr was convinced that electromagnetic fields had shaped all the various forms of life on earth. By the 1970s the Russian scientist Aleksandr Dubrov, in *The Geomagnetic Field and Life*, had put forward a new theory of evolution in which all life forms have developed as a result of geomagnetic (earth) forces.

Yet even before the 1930s, scientists had toyed with the idea of an electric, or rather magnetic, shaping principle at work within living organisms. As far back as the eighteenth century, Chladni was using sand sprinkled on a vibrating plate to show that by altering the frequency different patterns could be created. From this simple experiment he was able to show that *form was a function of frequency*. Newton himself posited that there must be a 'subtle . . . vibrating . . . electric and elastic medium'[20] to account for such disparate phenomenon as repulsion, attraction, sensation and motion. More recently, the artist and scientist, Hans Jenny has been able to demonstrate that just a single audio frequency of sonic or magnetic energy can produce complex forms.

This foray into the environs of morphogenetic and electromagnetic fields seems to have led us far and away from the initial premise that consciousness and the Self choreograph our being, but as I see it, these concepts are poised to unite science and metaphysics in a new paradigm of scientific enquiry.

To a non-scientist like myself, it would make a certain sense that the only known energy force we can compare to the sort of subtle energies proposed by mystics, would indeed be electromagnetic. (And by this statement I am not inferring that electromagnetic energies *are* etheric forces). Whereas the forces of gravity are too weak to be responsible for the structure and organization of living organisms and nuclear forces are too short in their range of action, electromagnetic forces are just right. We know that the body generates its own electric and magnetic fields; we also know that electromagnetic phenomena are the primary forces involved at the cellular molecular control level. As Cyril Smith and Simon Best document in *Electromagnetic Man*, man is orders of magnitude more sensitive to coherent electromagnetic fields than has previously been realized. The authors also point out that the research of quantum biologists is showing that Nature is making use, in her regulatory and communication systems, of the entire frequency range of the electromagnetic spectrum with varying degrees of precision.

Man is essentially an electromagnetic system: as such, he is able to respond, or rather resonate, with certain electromagnetic frequencies occurring naturally in the world around him. Furthermore, the geomagnetic field has co-existed around the earth since the time of its formation so it seems self-evident that it must have played some part in the creation and moulding of living organisms.

Thus, in scientific, causal terms we have three major pieces of the puzzle as to what forces shape our being. We know that sound, or acoustic frequency, plays a part in the creation of form; we understand that electromagnetic frequencies are used in regulating and communicating within living systems, and we have Rupert Sheldrake's theory of morphogenetic fields to account for how the structure and shape of living organisms are inherited and transmitted from cell to cell.

It takes an intuitive musician and mathematics graduate to find a model that embraces them all – and show how the psychic and the physical can interconnect. In *Mind, Body and Electromagnetism* John Evans discusses the chakras and their relationship with the neuro-endocrine system; he compares the patterning effects of the chakras' rotational movements to the concept of 'spin' in particle physics, thus finding a way of objectifying the chakras and demonstrating their effect on the development and maintenance of living organisms. Evans also makes a very sound case for the brain being generated by three major oscillatory centres – two frontal and one posterior – correlating to the physical (lower conscious), the emotional and the higher conscious. He presents a series of fascinating computer-derived graphics generated by the electrical activity and associated waveforms along the spine, which brilliantly capture the lotus/mandala-like composition of the chakras, which then develop into the familiar structure of the pelvis, spine and skull. In this way, Evans dramatically conveys how the psychic and the physical come together, how the psyche inspires soma. The pictures

> confirm the general idea that *it is possible* that the cellular material of the body is patterned by means of electromagnetic waveforms with a definite ordering of frequency along the central axis . . . If our reasoning is correct, then beneath the outer physical appearance of things, there exists a composite and homogeneous system that, on the one hand, generates the infinite variety of physical effects; and on the other hand, coordinates with the psychical aspects of mind, emotion, instinct and sexual activity. Putting this slightly differently, we might say that, from a common frequency pattern, there is on the one side the same basic physiology common to all life; and on the other, the endless diversity between individuals through interaction with differently evolved psychical forms.[21]

This latter statement about a common frequency pattern nevertheless allowing for diversity through different psychic structures is especially interesting in the brain-mind-consciousness debate. Marine biologists have long been fascinated with the brain of the dolphin; since the dolphin's brain is far larger than man's it is naturally assumed that it must be superior and that dolphins are in effect a superior form of life. But if we adopt the theory that consciousness creates form, we can conceive that a dolphin's consciousness, no matter how evolved and no matter how efficient its organ of transmission (the brain), is nevertheless an 'animal' consciousness and thus not in the same category as a human's.

Over the course of this chapter we have looked at consciousness, its synergy with the soul and its expression through life; I have discussed the mystical view of the creation of form and presented some alternative scientific concepts that could support these esoteric views. I would like to conclude by throwing in my own 'wild card' based on the concepts of etheric forces, the chakras and electromagnetic fields.

One of the most recent and important discoveries in connection with electromagnetic fields is that water has been found to 'remember' the electromagnetic fields to which it has been exposed. Since the human body is roughly 65 per cent water, this means that any change

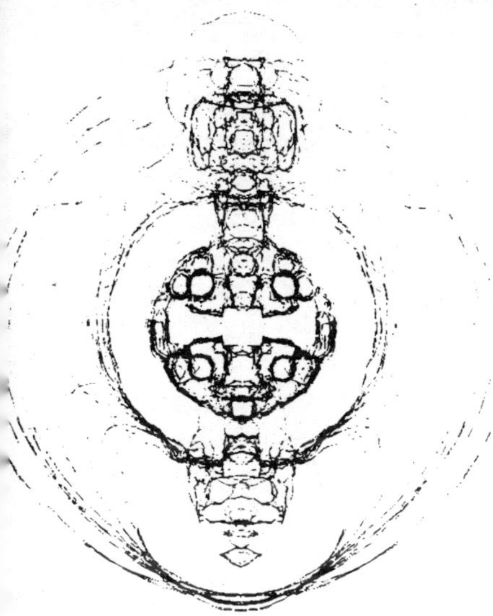

Fig. 1

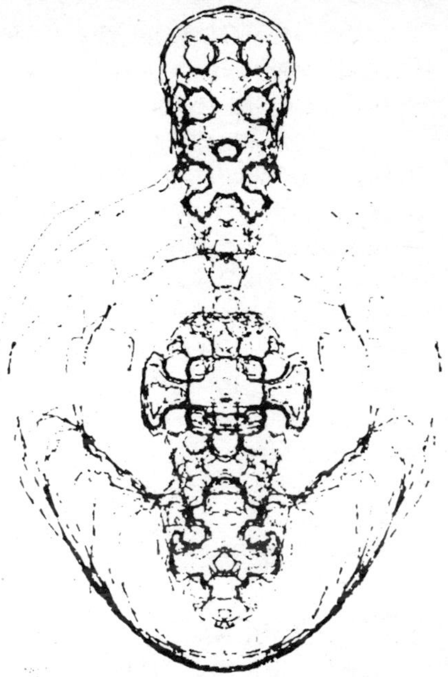

Fig. 2

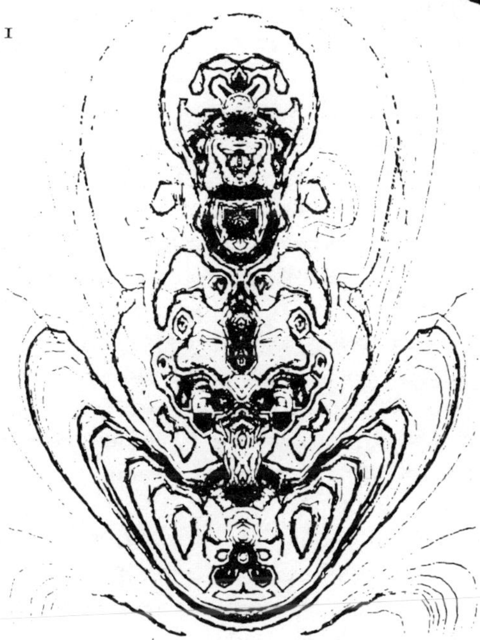

Fig. 3 *Figures taken from* Mind, Body and Electromagnetism *by John Evans (Element Books, 1986).*

or effect in the body's electric field is registered and transmitted to the rest of the system. No matter how great the amount of water, the 'message' will be relayed throughout. Placing on one side the huge impact this knowledge must make on the understanding of how, say, homoeopathic treatments can work, the implications for the process of evolution are enormous. (The recent pioneering work of the French scientist Professor Jacques Benveniste is most important in this respect). While John Evans has pointed out that 'the very creation of *primitive* [my italics] life-forms may be controlled through the interaction of the earth's electromagnetic field and water', I would suggest that this interaction is the basis of all life-form.

If we return to the esoteric view, the Divine Spark, embracing soul and consciousness, gathers to itself increasingly denser substance in its descent into physical being; from a whirling mass of elemental energy, the ether-ic body is woven and through the agency of the chakras, psyche merges into soma – the soul/consciousness as ever the architect. The finer, subtle energies of the psyche are composed of emotions, memories, instincts and mental models – a karmic heritage and essentially the Jungian collective unconscious; they are imprinted on the ether (the mystical, as yet scientifically unproven element) and so enter into the very fabric of the physical body through the chakra interchange. The concept of attributes of the psyche imprinting themselves on ether is not such a quantum jump away from seeing how an emotional charge can imprint itself on the psyche via the electromagnetic field of the body; and if water can 'remember' frequency, no matter how great the volume, it should follow that frequency is stored and transmitted even as water evaporates into steam and ever finer, subtler levels of energy. In this way the electromagnetic field becomes the ultimate translator of energies between the physical and the non-physical.

Clearly, I may not impress the hard-line materialist with this tentative hypothesis, but it might well provide a springboard for others more equipped to deal with such concepts from the scientific standpoint.

In the preceding chapter on fate, I attempted to explain that ultimately we create our own fate; in this chapter I have endeavoured to show that consciousness does indeed influence form and that essentially we – in the sense of our purest essence – create ourselves.

Through the fission of heavy elements, or the fusion of light elements, some of the mass-energy concentrated in atomic vortices can be released to generate those cosmic or spatial energies in which we are all immersed. Thus East and

West can agree that we form part of an energy complex of infinite diversity where the energies of space merge into the energies of matter; and in our own bodies, there is a gradation from the most subtle low-frequency electromagnetic vibrations to the gigantic protein molecules containing many thousands of atomic units. This type of energy conceptualisation is a powerful and unifying view, helping us to see ourselves, not as lonely individuals whiling away the time on a deserted space-ship called earth, but as receptors of the cosmic energies from furthermost points of space every moment of time . . .[22]

NOTES

1. Benjamin Walker (ed.), *Encyclopaedia of Esoteric Man* (Routledge & Kegan Paul, 1977)
2. C. G. Jung, *The Soul and Death* (Routledge & Kegan Paul, 1960)
3. *Encyclopaedia of Esoteric Man*, op. cit.
4. Jolande Jacobe, *The Psychology of C. G. Jung* (Routledge & Kegan Paul, 1968)
5. *Encyclopaedia of Esoteric Man*, op. cit.
6. While sceptics might assume the brain starved of oxygen would produce such hypnagogic effects, the theatre team ensured that oxygen was pumped into my friend's system throughout the emergency. Furthermore, mountaineers who experience oxygen starvation at great heights report being anything but clearminded.
7. Kyriacos C. Markides, *Homage to the Sun: The Wisdom of the Magus of Strovolos* (Arkana, 1987)
8. W. T. Stace *Mysticism and Philosophy* (Macmillan, 1961)
9. All quotes are taken from a lecture given by Rudolph Steiner in Stuttgart on 22 August 1906. *At the Gates of Spiritual Science* (Rudolph Steiner Press, 1970)
10. Carlos Castaneda has written eight books to date on his experiences of Shamanism. These include *The Teachings of Don Juan: A Yaqui Way of Knowledge*; *A Separate Reality: Further Conversations with Don Juan*; *Journey to Ixtlan: The Lessons of Don Juan*; *Tales of Power*; *The Second Ring of Power*; *The Eagle's Gift*; *The Fire from Within* and *The Power of Silence: Further Lessons of Don Juan* (Simon & Schuster)
11. Colin Wilson, *Afterlife* (Harrap, 1985)
12. Rosalind Heywood, *The Infinite Hive* (Pan, 1964)
13. David Lorimer, MA is Director of the Scientific and Medical Network, Chairman of the International Association for the Study of Death, and UK Director of the International Institute for the Study of Death.
14. *The Encyclopaedia of Esoteric Man*
15. John Davidson, *The Web of Life* (C. W. Daniel, 1988)
16. Ibid.
17. Ibid.
18. Rudolph Steiner, *An Outline of Occult Science* (Theosophical Publishing Society, London

19. Rupert Sheldrake, *A New Science of Life* (Paladin, 1987)
20. From an article by Leonard J. Ravitz, 'History, measurement, and applicability of periodic changes in the electromagnetic field in health and disease' from the Yale Scientific Magazine 1944; 18:5–6.
21. John Evans, *Mind, Body and Electromagnetism* (Element, 1986)
22. Ibid.

BIBLIOGRAPHY

Richard Seddon (ed.), *Rudolph Steiner: Essential Readings* (Crucible 1988)
John Eccles, *Brain and Conscious Experience* (Springer, 1966)
Aleksandr Dubrov, *The Geomagnetic Field and Life* (Plenum Press, 1978)
Cyril Smith and Simon Best, *Electromagnetic Man. Health and Hazard in the Electrical Environment* (Dent, 1989)
David Conway, *Secret Wisdom: The Occult Universe Explored* (Aquarian Press, 1987)
Lewis Spence, *An Encylopaedia of Occultism* (Citadel Press, 1960)
Charles T. Tart, *Transpersonal Psychologies* (Routledge & Kegan Paul, 1975)
Roger Coghill and Harry Oldfield, *The Dark Side of the Brain* (Element Books, 1988)

4
The Harmony of the Spheres

> Whether we attribute any significance to these cycles [of the planets] or not, we are still faced by the inescapable harmony produced by their combination. These perfect and everchanging octaves fill one equally with awe at the subtlety and perfection of the cosmic order, and amazement that human perception should remain unaware of it.
>
> Rodney Collin, *The Theory of Celestial Influence*

In earlier chapters I have mentioned the concept of the soul moving (after the death of the physical body) into the innermost spiritual planes before embarking on a return journey back to the physical. Almost all mystical traditions consider these spheres to be the planets in our solar system. That is to say, the seven planetary bodies Sun, Moon, Mercury, Venus, Mars, Jupiter and Saturn, enclosed by an eighth sphere – the belt of the fixed stars. These are the heavenly spheres Er beholds on his arrival in the afterlife.[1] The Persian cult of Mithras believed that the soul descended at birth through the planetary spheres, accumulating impurities as it went. Life on earth, according to Mithraism, represented a term of trial where, through moral effort and revealed wisdom, the soul earned its right to pass once again (after death) into the realms of light, shedding any impurities as it transited the planetary spheres.[2]

Around 5 BC, the Babylonian astrologer-priests applied this mystical concept of the soul's journey through the planetary spheres directly to astrology. In the process they became the first mystics to extend astrology's influence beyond the destiny of nations to the fate of the individual. The Babylonian astrologers maintained that the planetary pattern at the moment of birth portrayed the nature of those cosmic forces operating within the individual. According to the neoplatonist, Macrobius, as the soul approached incarnation it acquired specific attributes from each of the planetary spheres – Saturn provided, 'reason and understanding', Jupiter endowed the 'power to act', Mars generated a 'bold spirit', through the Sun 'sense-perception and imagination' were received, from Venus the soul was given the 'impulse of passion'. Mercury engendered the 'ability to speak and interpret' while the Moon offered the 'function of moulding and increasing bodies'.[3]

Rudolph Steiner wrote and lectured extensively on life in the planetary spheres after death. He also considered that the planetary sojourns enabled the soul to transmute its karma; he further believed that an individual's birthchart described the nature of his experience of the planets. Steiner, like Blavatsky, asserted that after death, the soul and ego enter the realm of *kamaloca* (or kamaloka to Blavatsky); here the soul undergoes a second life-review[4] after which the ego is shed and the soul can proceed into the spiritual world of *devachan* and on through the planetary spheres.

> [In kamaloca] One feels oneself drawing away from the earth. The earth is far away below one, and journeying into the spirit world one feels that one has reached the sun. Just as during earthly life we feel ourselves linked to the earth, so now we feel at one with the sun with its whole planetary system . . . the sensation of the sun is not one of being surrounded by streaming physical light, but of dwelling in the pure light of the spirit.[5]

Since the moon is the nearest planetary body to the earth, it is here that the karmic process begins. The soul submerges itself into the moon's 'consciousness' experiencing in an emotional and intellectual sense the results of its actions towards others in the preceding life; in this way the soul not only leaves a residue of its emotional and intellectual past on the moon but gathers new emotional and thought 'material'.

Steiner also perceived that the planets played host to other beings and that the experience of the soul's interaction with the various planetary populaces also added to its karmic inheritance. To Steiner, the journey after death was just as much of a learning and developing experience for the soul as life on earth – and fraught with such pitfalls as being lead astray by mischievous elementals[6] or downright evil entities.

From the Moon, the soul journeys to Venus – this time immersing itself in Venus consciousness – and from there to Mercury and so on. Steiner, in placing Venus before Mercury appears to have taken no account of the natural planetary sequence as we understand (and perceive) it to be. But Steiner is clearly following the more mystically oriented, ancient Egyptian view of the cosmos in which Mercury (from the heliocentric standpoint) is nearer to the Sun than Venus.[7]

The renowned psychic Edgar Cayce was another who spoke of the the soul's journey through the planetary spheres after death.

> The solar system is a cycle of experiences for the soul. It has eight dimensions, corresponding to the planets [the sun through to Saturn and the fixed stars]; they represent focal points for the . . . environments in which the [essence of the planetary] dimensions can express and materialise themselves . . . This

[earth] is the third dimension, and it is a sort of laboratory for the whole system, because only here is free will completely dominant. On the other planes, or dimensions, some measure of control is kept over the soul to see that it learns proper lessons.[8]

Cayce, like Steiner, maintained that the experiences of the soul and its progress, on earth and in the planetary domains, leaves its imprint on the 'consciousness' of the planets, which is how the planets influence our life on earth.

Our astrological influences from the planets, or dimensions, we have inhabited will be good or bad, weak or strong, according to the experiences we have had there, and how we handled our problems.[9]

Steiner and Cayce pay scant attention to the planets beyond Saturn – Uranus, Neptune and Pluto. While this may be due in part to the lack of understanding about the nature of these outer planets (Pluto, of course had not been discovered in Steiner's lifetime and Neptune was a comparative newcomer) it was more a case that the arrival of further planets upset the mystical significance and the divine harmony of the eight planetary spheres.[10] In this way many mystically minded individuals of the day tended to avoid incorporating them in astrological interpretation and treated them somewhat as beleaguered outposts of the solar system. However, with the likelihood of further planets to be found beyond Pluto[11] it may well be that Uranus marks the beginning of another eight-fold system. Already in more esoteric astrological circles, Uranus is considered to represent the higher octave of the Sun, Neptune the higher aspect of the Moon and Pluto the higher resonance of Mercury. I shall be covering this in more detail in the next chapter.

Also, significantly for astrology, Steiner teaches that the experiences in the planetary dimensions are interrelated such that the soul's experience on say the Moon is not viewed in isolation from his experience on Mars. In this way, the angle (or aspect) formed between the Moon and Mars in the birthchart describes how the two dimensions operate together – whether in conflict or harmony. 'When the Moon stands in a certain relationship to Mars . . . [they] work in conjunction upon the man and bring about what this combined influence is able to achieve.'[12]

Steiner believed that the human being responded to the planetary and zodiacal patterns because he was constituted of the very stuff of the planets and stars.

That we appear as a human being, that we are inwardly able to have karma imbued with cosmic forces, depends on the fact that we received certain forces from the whole cosmos during a certain period between death and a new birth . . . We bear the whole cosmos within us when we incarnate again on earth.[13]

Of course, Steiner's views are not original. This concept of the cosmos reflected within man dates at the very least from the 2nd century BC. Yet it is still today the astrologer's greatest, but often least understood, maxim, 'As above, so below'.

Astrologers tend to use this phrase in general to describe the marrying up of heavenly events with earthly matters, but its real significance lies steeped in hermeticism. To the hermetic savants, the archetype of the physical body was constructed from the fixed stars – the clusters of stars that form the familiar zodiacal constellations. Man (microcosm) reflects the stars (macrocosm): 'As above, so below'. The hermeticists 'wrapped the primitive, erect cosmic man . . . about the path of the Sun with the top of his head touching the soles of his feet at O Aries . . . his heart lies in Leo, on whose breast shines the bright star, Regulus'.[14] This is the origin of the concept of Aries ruling the head, Pisces the feet, Leo the heart, and so on. The ancient hermetic astrologers, in keeping with the mystical teachings on the voyage of the soul through the planets, asserted that in the eighth sphere of the fixed stars the soul, in collaboration with higher spiritual powers, creates the zodiacal blueprint for his physical image. The planetary sojourns with their karmic inheritance form the 'inner' man. This concept is inherent in Cayce's pronouncements on astrology.

The stars [constellations] represent soul patterns, not experiences. The twelve signs of the zodiac are twelve patterns from which the soul chooses when coming into the earth plane. They are like races . . .[15]

To the hermeticist, the soul's choice of image – its particular 'pattern' – is reflected in the sign on the Ascendant (the rising sign) of the birthchart. In this way, the Ascendant becomes identified with the earth-linked personality of the individual.[16]

While Steiner may have felt a strong sympathy with the hermetic view of the image-making function of the constellations, he also felt that the choice of zodiacal and planetary patterns was linked to the horoscopic pattern at death; in other words, since the horoscopic pattern at death was at the same time that of the birth into the spiritual realms, each pattern had a bearing on and a connection with one another. According to Steiner, as the soul prepares to return once again into the physical life, 'there remains an endeavour to enter into this same constellation, to do justice once again to the forces it received at the moment of death.'[17] Steiner maintained that in his experience, the charts of death and subsequent rebirth showed a 'remarkable correlation'. (In Chapters 5 and 8 I shall be looking at some of Steiner's ideas through the work of Robert Powell.)

Thus, it is in the outer reaches of the fixed stars, the eighth heavenly sphere, that the soul experiences the 'call' to return to the physical world, to acquire a personality and undergo further opportunities for growth. From the bliss of the heavenly state (*devachan*) the soul must gradually return through the planetary spheres absorbing its karmic residue.

> As we move out beyond the Saturn sphere our state of consciousness is changed. We enter into a kind of cosmic twilight . . . Now for the first time the powers of the whole cosmos can work upon us . . . when the forces . . . stream into our being from the whole of the starry realms, as it were. Then we begin to draw together again, pass through the different spheres . . .[18]

On the threshold of the physical world, the soul meets the seeds of its new earth life in *kamaloca*. It was here, after death, that the previous etheric body disintegrated; now the soul and ego must acquire another etheric form. In Yogic philosophy, this is the point where the *tattwas* combine with the *pranas*[19] and the *skandhas* – the karmic components of the personality – to weave together the psychic body that is 'father to the man'.

The *tattwas*, as I discussed earlier, are none other than the elements – air, earth, fire, water (and ether) which play such a fundamental part in astrology.[20] Maharaj Sawan Singh (one of India's greatest spiritual teachers) not only teaches that both mind and body are created by the finer essences of the elements but, focusing on the karmic 'material' of the tattwas and skandhas, he correlates each element with specific lessons that must be learnt – fire with anger, earth with attachment, air with greed and water with passion.[21]

The four elements with their karmic components also demonstrate a clear parallel with Jung's four psychological types, fire (intuition), earth (sensation), air (thinking) and water (feeling). As the Jungian psychologist and astrologer, Liz Greene points out: 'This basic structure of four is the cornerstone of astrology, in which it is reflected by the four elements: air, water, earth and fire. That this structure is archetypal and inherent in all human beings we know from the work of depth psychology . . .'[22] In the same way that the voyage through the planetary spheres provided a basis for understanding the nature of the planets and the zodiac and how they function in a birth chart, the appreciation of the psychic body-building role of the elements offers deeper insight into the dynamic force of the elements in astrology.

From the esoteric point of view, we enter the world programmed by our karmic inheritance; even our hair colour, the shape of our face has been formed through psycho-cosmic processes before sperm meets egg so to speak. This, quite naturally, is not the view of mainstream science, which is that we are who we are is entirely a result of genetic inheritance. Certainly genes are the vehicles of inherited characteristics and the chemical basis of genes is DNA (deoxyribonucleic acid). But while DNA with its hereditary code is the life-giving ingredient of each cell, there are other unknown factors that influence the development of the characteristics of each cell and ultimately make us unique – not merely clones of our parents and forefathers.

I have already discussed the role morphogenetic fields play in the shaping of living things, whereby an organism develops according to a pre-shaped field – responding to a resonance, as it were.[23] While it may or may not provide a scientific model for explaining how we become who we are physiologically, it certainly gives us a mechanism for the way in which aspects of the psyche, such as memory, instinct and talent are acquired. Adopting the concept of resonance, instincts, memories and abilities could be transmitted across time in the same way that a vibration from a particular note will be picked up endlessly by those of the same frequency. Memory, for instance, is not considered by all neurosurgeons[24] to be stored in the brain, though some American neurophysiologists have suggested that RNA (ribonucleic acid and, like DNA, present in every cell) might act as a memory molecule.[25] The zoologist, Sir Alister Hardy proposed a parallel stream of information to the one in the DNA code – a 'psychic stream' of shared experience – every bit as vital to survival and development of living organisms.[26]

This concept of a 'psychic stream' of shared experience is not so far removed from Jung's theory of the collective unconscious – the infinite pool of experience containing the imprints of countless generations of man's ancestral experiences which is deeply embedded within man's consciousness and thus shared and responded to by all.

Jung, of course, was far more the mystic than the scientist: while he founded a psychoanalytic school as renowned as Sigmund Freud's, he expanded the territory of the unconscious far beyond the libido and childhood memories and impressions. He sought his inspiration in ancient hermetic texts and mystical literature – indeed he culled the term 'archetype' from the *Corpus Hermeticum*.[27] Jung also saw in astrology a remarkable and revealing symbolic map of the psyche. Since Jung's death in 1961, Liz Greene, the astrologer and Jungian analyst has greatly enlarged on Jung's ideas and in the process has emerged as one of the prime movers in the alignment of astrology with psychology. Liz Greene, like many psychologists, would argue that the rich variation in the psychological make-up of each and every one of us militates against a mechanistic view of the individual: 'If we were wholly the product of our heredity, conditioning and environment, children born into the same circumstances would be exactly the same psychologically – which of course they are not.'[28] But while psychologists might recognize that man is something other than the sum total of his physical parts, quite how he acquires his psychic inheritance remains a mystery, unless, of course, one is prepared to explore the possible explanations offered by concepts of morphic resonance or RNA acting as a psychic molecule within the hereditary stream.

As one might expect, Steiner and Cayce, as examples of mystical thinkers in general, approach the issue of heredity quite differently.

> Choice of incarnation is usually made at conception, when the channel for expression is opened by the parents. A pattern is made by the mingling of soul patterns of the parents . . . A soul whose own karma approximates these conditions will be attracted by the opportunity presented. Since the pattern will not be exactly his own, he must consider taking on some of the karma of his parents . . . in order to use the channel. This concerns environment, companionship with the parents and certain marks of physiognomy. [Other important considerations are] coming situations in history, former associations with the parents . . . [other] souls it wishes to be with . . . The body is formed in the womb according to the pattern made by the mingling of the life forces of the parents, each with its respective pattern . . .[29]
>
> on rebirth the individual has to bring with him forces ['planetary' and karmic] which, once he has connected himself with the stream of heredity, enable him to fashion plastically his corporeal form . . . What is provided by our ancestors in the physical heredity stream only corresponds to the individuality inasmuch as we are attracted by the mixture in the hereditary stream . . . [formed by] the nature of our forefathers.[30]

Broadly speaking from the esoteric point of view, the supersensible forces (planetary, karmic, elementary, etc.) that constitute our very essence must find a sympathetic and appropriate set of physical circumstances to be born into. In this way there are two separate chains of the past that make us who we are – the genetic inheritance from our ancestors (which may or may not include such things as memory) and a karmic inheritance constituted of the soul's accumulated experience.

If we inherit some things directly from our parents and ancestors, yet fashion other aspects of our being according to our own nature, might this effect not show itself astrologically? Could we not inherit some planetary patterns and zodiacal areas from our family yet present others suited to our own karmic requirements?

For at least 2,000 years, from the time of Ptolemy, a belief has proliferated that the horoscopes of parents and children display similar characteristics. In the early seventeenth century, the mathematician and astronomer-astrologer, Kepler made the strong assertion, 'There is one perfectly clear argument beyond all exception in favour of the authenticity of astrology. This is the common horoscopic connection between parents and children.'[31] Then in 1919 the French astrologer Paul Choisinard announced that he had statistically proven the laws of astral heredity – that children tended to be born with the Sun, Moon, Ascendant and Midheaven in the same zodiacal position as their parents. Ask any of today's astrologers who see many hundreds of charts in the course of a year if they notice any similarity between the charts of family members and virtually all will answer a resounding, yes. In my own family for instance there is a pronounced Mars-Saturn theme and a predominance in the cardinal signs; that is to say a 'hard'[32] angle between Mars and Saturn occurs in almost every chart[33] and most of us have a greater number of planets and angles in cardinal signs (Aries, Cancer, Libra and Capricorn) than any of the others. However, put to the acid test with statistical analysis, the heredity effect appears to be an illusion.

In 1966 the French statitician Michel Gauquelin published his book *Planetary Heredity*.[34] He was unable to support Choisinard's statistical findings (which Gauquelin concluded were based on faulty procedures); thus he failed to find parents and children presenting similar Sun and Moon signs or the same sign on the Ascendant or Midheaven. However, he did find another effect: children born of a parent with a particular planet rising (on the Ascendant) or culminating (on the Midheaven, the 'peak' of the chart) tended significantly to have the same planet in the same area of the horoscope; if both parents had the same planet at the same point in the sky, then the effect was even greater.[35] Somewhat disappointingly for astrologers and puzzlingly for Gauquelin, his replication of this study in 1984 failed to corroborate the findings of the previous experiment despite using a sample of 33,000 parent–child comparisons. Nevertheless, two aspects of Gauquelin's research did throw some fascinating light on astrology.

In the course of his experiments (in both the 1960s and the '80s) Gauquelin established that the planetary heredity effect was only present when birth had occurred naturally – without induction or surgery of any kind. The significance of this observation for astrology is noted by the British astronomer Percy Seymour in *Astrology: The Evidence of Science*:[36]

> This [planetary effect only applying to natural births] strongly suggests that the planets are actually, in some way, influencing the natural timing of birth, making it more likely that a person of a certain type will be born at one particular time than another. This work, together with his [Gauquelin's] earlier work, seems to suggest that for people with different genetic constitutions, different planets will act as the trigger for the moment of birth, and that these genetically inherited characteristics can also play a part in determining success in different walks of life.

Ironically, Gauquelin considers that his original findings of the planetary heredity effect eliminate astrologer's precepts that the birthchart is a determining factor in the destiny of the individual and that 'only genetic factors are determinant, and the planet no more than a minor participant in the birth process.'[37] However, adopting all the more esoteric themes discussed so far in the book, especially the concept that the soul must find a sympathetic and appropriate breeding ground for itself, Gauquelin's findings positively support astrology's fundamental principles!

A second factor to emerge out of Gauquelin's experiments was that the planetary heredity effect was far more noticeable when the magnetic field of Earth was highly disturbed. While Gauquelin himself could not explain why magnetic disturbance should enhance the planetary heredity effect. Seymour was able to account for this phenomenon with his theory of planetary resonance. In supporting his theory of a geomagnetic-planetary link to personality, Seymour also looked to the work of the Austrian scientist, Birzele, who found that the similarity between personality and characteristics of a child and one of its parents was linked to the similarity of geomagnetic activity close to the birth of the child and the parent. Seymour's work allows for both a hereditary link to personality and a planetary one.

Briefly, Seymour's theory rests on the proposition that the planets resonate with the Sun's magnetic canals; in turn those resonances are pitched (via solar wind) into the Earth's magnetic field which, as I have explained in Chapter 3, is responded to by the electromagnetic sensitivity of the nervous system in human beings – and indeed all living things. Seymour proposes that the nervous system not only acts as a 'radio receiver' for geomagnetic waves which subsequently affect the way our systems develop and organize themselves[38] but that every nervous system has its unique receptivity to certain frequencies due to its 'geometry, physical dimensions and proportions of the body in which it is embedded'. And this, in part, is subject to hereditary factors in both a physiological and psychological sense.

Seymour also makes a good case for how a baby triggers its own birth due to its cosmic attunement: at conception the hereditary code is transmitted to the embryonic cell, providing all the information it needs for physiological and psychological development. Thus the embryo is already predisposed to 'receive' certain resonances[39] by the inherited 'wiring' of its nervous system. (Seymour considers this a function of the personality.) The baby responds to these planetary resonances, or 'chords', throughout its development in the womb; when the phase relationship between the various planetary 'chords' is in tune with the baby, then it is born. While these 'chords' may be struck several times during the pregnancy, only when the baby is biologically ready to be born can the nervous system release the necessary hormones for labour to begin. In this way, the planets trigger the birth process.

> The tuning of the nervous system aerial is determined by the genetically inherited personality of the individual, and this tuning also determines the time of birth. This means that the cosmos cannot alter our inherited characteristics but, by causing the actual moment of birth, the state of the Solar System at that time is in fact *labelling* these character traits.[40]

Seymour has provided a very workable model for the way in which planets forge a link with human destiny. However, to my mind there is a fatal flaw in his proposal that the tuning of the nervous system depends on the *genetically* inherited personality of the individual. I have already presented an alternative psychological and mystical view of the role of the personality[41] and the way supersensible forces, including planetary and zodiacal, fashion the psychic structure of the individual prior to the physical. Thus, as I would see it, the planetary patterns from the moment of conception synchronize with the individual, and, throughout gestation resonate with his psychic and physical being, so that his birth is not only triggered by the appropriate planetary 'chords', but he enters the world at a time that astrologically reflects precisely who he is – his fate, his destiny, his karma.

Seymour might well have subtitled his book, 'the music of the spheres', for, with his proposals, he has shed new light on the elusive quest for the theory of celestial harmony.

> It is as if the whole solar system – the Sun, Moon and planets – is playing a complex symphony on the lines of force of the Earth's field . . . the womb is no hiding place from the all-pervading magnetic field of Earth so the 'tunes' of the 'magnetic symphony' of the solar system which we receive can become part of our earliest memories. It is there that some of the magnetic 'music of the spheres' becomes etched in our brains. When the 'orchestra' of the solar system 'plays our tune' on the magnetic field of Earth, at a later stage in our life, it evokes those memories and our response can influence the way we react to a given situation.[42]

The concept that the universe is full of sound and vibration and that this somehow connects everything with everything else has been embraced by mystics through the ages, but perhaps the name most synonymous with 'the music of the spheres' is that of the Greek philosopher Pythagoras. By noting that the vibrations (and therefore the different notes) of stringed instruments depended on the length of a string. Pythagoras was able to link length (distance) a quantitative experience, with sound (resonance), a qualitative experience. Pythagoras went on to show that the intervals on a musical scale could be represented as simple ratios; he then applied these ratios to the distances between the planets and theorized that in moving around the Earth (in the 6th century BC, of course, the discovery that the planets revolve around the sun had yet to be made [43]) they made a kind of music. Pythagoras was more than just a mathematician and a philosopher, he had studied the Egyptian mysteries and was an adept of the Orphic mysteries. Thus it is almost certain that he had already been exposed to the mystery of number and harmony of proportion – the ancient Egyptians clearly built the great pyramids according to divine geometric proportions – and was merely applying Greek logical thought to Egyptian mystical teaching.

Some two thousand years later, Kepler had a revelation that Pythagoras was right. Kepler, of course, like his mentor, the astronomer, Tycho Brahe was a hermeticist and thus exposed to similar mystery teachings as Pythagoras. Kepler was convinced that there was a divine musical proportion encoded in the solar system. By associating the same principle of length and vibration in music (a string twice the length of another will have half the vibrations and produce a note exactly one octave apart) with the relative distances of the the planets and their speed in orbit around the sun, he thought he had found the real harmony of the spheres. Sadly, he was mistaken; intuitively he had captured a fundamental truth, but the theory was wrong – it was an idea whose time had not yet come. One or two of Kepler's theories, such as the concept that a system of rays propelled the planets around the sun and some of his ideas on magnetism, also proved to be muddled glimpses of later scientific discoveries. It seems that, like Tycho and Pythagoras before him, Kepler tried to bring mystical knowledge into scientific reality, yet for him the effort proved frustrating and sometimes unworthy: 'I have robbed the golden vessels of the Egyptians [a direct reference to Egyptian mystery teachings], to make out of them the tabernacle for my God . . .' [presumably, science].[44]

More recently, the renowned British astrologer, the late John Addey, used the concept of resonance to develop his theory of harmonics in astrology. Using again the analogy with a string of a musical instrument, which plucked at different intervals along its length will yield different tones, he was able to show that when the cycles of the planets are treated in the same way, their different qualities emerge. (Addey applied the same concept to the cycle (or circle) of the zodiac and the aspects.) Addey's work expanded and refined Gauquelin's findings that certain planets tend to be found in specific areas of the horoscope (reflecting the daily cycle of the planet from the point of view of the earth) according to the personality and profession of the individual. But Addey was also able to augment Gauquelin's findings by showing that certain types of personality are associated not with one harmonic of a particular planet, but with a set of harmonics. In other words, Addey was able to show that a planet manifested a specific tone or quality according to the harmonic it expressed in a birth chart. Addey also applied harmonic wave theory to the zodiac, so that the first harmonic of the zodiac circle can be seen as one cycle of 360, the second harmonic can be viewed as two cycles of 180, the third harmonic may be represented as three cycles of 120 and so on. In this way, each harmonic chart describes the essence and qualities of a particular number. (I will cover the mystical nature of numbers shortly.)

Through his work on the harmony of cosmic periods, Addey was essentially expressing another version of the harmony of the spheres, and while he was a scientist by profession, he was a philosopher at heart. He impressed on all those who heard him lecture the role number and harmony (or more precisely, harmonic relationships) play in the shaping of life and the spirit.

Another scientist to shed light on the harmony of the spheres, albeit by refraction, is John Evans. In *Mind, Body and Electromagnetism* Evans has combined his skills as an academic and a musician to link acoustic frequency and colour vibration:

Through our understanding of the electromagnetic nature of light, together with our knowledge of wave motion, frequency, harmonics, and resonance, we can relate simply any octave of frequencies to any other octave, including audio vibrations to the colour spectrum . . . we can divide . . . [an] octave of colour at will into regions that can correspond directly to any given musical or sonic divisions

Evans is, as I understand him, not suggesting that electromagnetic resonances have colour, merely that they can be seen in terms of a similar ratio. However, Evans quotes extensively from the writings of the sensitive, Eileen Garrett, who *does* see the electromagnetic field (certainly surrounding the body) as comprised of light and colour:

The movement of this [electromagnetic] energy is not visible to ordinary sight . . . I first see . . . movement which bursts into curving rays of light and colour. Some of these seem to split from the original parent rays, and moving out, form themselves into lines of light which proceed to develop an animated fourfold movement. These vivid lines take on a swaying rhythmic motion as they interlace in light spirals throughout space. From these, more lines are continuously born which tumble into place and create simple forms . . . Globules of colour emerge from these light forms and contain, I believe, the original pattern and essence of all life . . . This magnetic field in which he [man] dwells can be likened to the shifting radiance of a rainbow.[45]

It seems all too easy to me as a non-scientist to perceive this harmony of the spheres, not only as a pulsating system of sound but also a 'symphony' of colour. And that if all of us were blessed with extrasensory vision and hearing, we would know it to be the truth.

The late Rodney Collin explored the 'harmony of the spheres' in his book, *The Theory of Celestial Influence*. And while his scientific theories of planetary resonance and acoustic and colour harmony have to some extent been eclipsed by more recent researchers, such as Seymour and Evans, his work is magnificent from the mystical point of view. Collin follows in the footsteps of Pythagoras and Kepler by establishing a harmonic series of intervals between the planets, this time generated by each planet's conjunctions with the sun: one, a minor cycle when the planet conjuncts the sun in a single orbit (which will occur at different points in the zodiac each time) and a major cycle when the planet and sun meet again at exactly the same point in the zodiac. Collin, like Seymour, perceived that the motion of each planet in its daily waxing and waning cycle and its orbit around the sun emits a certain note 'or an energy transformed for a certain purpose, this note, or energy will be subject to two variations within its cycle. First . . . a variation of *volume*, depending on distance. Second . . . a variation of *pitch* depending on relative speed.' It is impossible here to do sufficient justice to the richness of Collins' theories; suffice to say that his arguments for a universe created and sustained on the principle of harmonic relationships, whether octaves of colour, sound or whatever is deeply convincing.

> . . . the planets, in their quality as refractors or transformers of the life force stand for form, colour, quality and function. And we . . . see how by this harmonic law of their succession one form must in time give way to another, one function to the next. We have, in fact, found the archetypal pattern for the development of all progressions. Every sequence in time or density – whether the audible notes of musical scales, the visible colours of the spectrum, or the tangible growth of organic forms – follows this octave ratio.[46]

Collin draws attention to the fact that of the planets, only those up to Saturn are visible to the naked eye – Uranus, Neptune and Pluto are not. And while the planets up to and including Saturn have orbits around the sun which can repeat several or many times in the span of a human life, the cycles of Uranus (84 years), Neptune (164) and Pluto (248) do not. Collin therefore concludes that the 'visible' planets up to Saturn represent one octave while the 'invisible' planets form the beginning of the next, 'in the same way that the traditional "visible" colours form one octave of vibrations [the visible light spectrum] . . . further "invisible" ultra-violet radiation [marks] the beginning of a second.'[47]

Taking this theme to its logical conclusion, one octave represents the extent of man's consciousness in the sense of what he can perceive; the second octave is a higher vibration which we can only appreciate if we have radically altered our state of consciousness. This is why the true nature of existence can only be apprehended by mystics or, perhaps, just glimpsed by those who have undergone a near death experience.

Plato describes the divine harmony of the cosmos in many of his works. In his *Republic*, he talks of 'the pillar of light like a rainbow' connected to an 'enormous spindle on which revolved the eight heavenly spheres'; on each sphere stood a 'siren, singing a single continuous note which with the other notes made a scale, a harmony'.

The eight notes of a musical scale (octave), like the octave of colour present a natural order and a harmony; to the initiate, the mystery and significance of the eight-fold series was contained in the number 8 itself.

Mysticism teaches that number is a cosmically charged force. According to the *Sacred Science of Numbers*, God is a number endowed with motion and each and every number has a definite vibratory rhythm, or keynote that also emanates a specific colour. Plato, Pythagoras, Kepler, Tycho, Blavatsky and Steiner would all have been aware of the mystery of number and therefore the cosmic significance of eight. The number eight presents an image of the lemniscate – the eternal and continuous spiral motion which is the supreme signature of the universe (Fig. 4) This is beautifully portrayed by Figure 5, which shows the solar system in time. With its positive and negative forces, 8 symbolizes the current of the life force itself. And it surely can be no coincidence that the double helix construction of DNA – the essence of life –takes the form of the number 8 (Fig. 6). Mercury's staff, the caduceus, with its intertwining serpents provides yet another image of the double spiral (Figs. 7 & 8). The vibratory power of the number 8 contains the secret of balance and harmony. The two halves of the number also represent the earth and the four elements uniting the higher planes of the spiritual – one octave with another. Also significant is that the eighth planet in the solar system is Uranus, the *higher octave of the Sun*: Uranus is often known as the 'awakener' and 'he' is associated, among many themes, with electricity. Eight is both the end of an order and the beginning of another.

Since eight plays such a significant part in the cosmic scheme of things, it is somewhat puzzling to find that neither Addey, nor David Hamblin (who has developed many of Addey's concepts) sees much of value or interest in this harmonic chart. In terms of harmonies, a stretched string vibrates first around its midpoint, then at the midpoint of its half distance and then similarly again: eight alone of the simple prime numbers yields integers when divided twice – hence the unique quality of the octave. No other prime number divides itself in such a way and retains its integrity. Symbolically, eight effectively contains everything vital to manifestation within it. As eight represents the ending of one octave and the beginning of another, the eighth harmonic chart (resonating as it does with Uranus) must reveal to us what we have to bring into manifestation, before we can attain the spiritual 'fruit on the tree' implicit in the 9th harmonic.

We can begin to comprehend the notion of number having power if we consider that a number can also express itself as a wave pattern

Fig. 8 *Early Sumerian version of the caduceus. Taken from a Dictionary of Symbols by J. E. Circlot (R.K.P. 1971).*

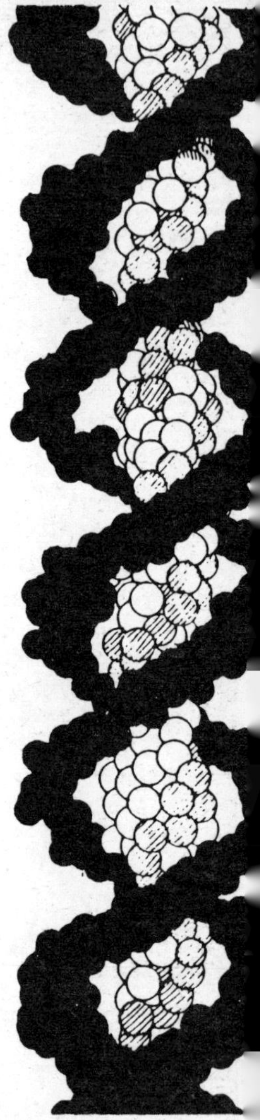

Fig. 6 *(Right) The DNA spiral. Figures taken from* Astrology and the Art of Healing *by A. T. Mann (Unwin, Hyman 1989).*

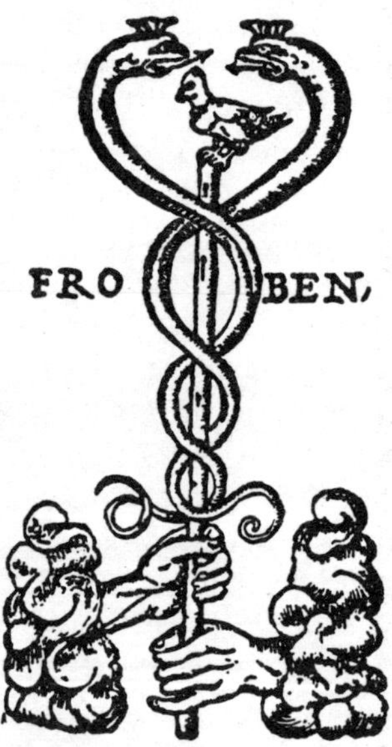

Fig. 7 *(Above) The Caduceus.*

Fig. 4 *The Egyptian snake of time. Taken from* Time *by Maurice Nicoll (Stuart and Watkins, L 1952).*

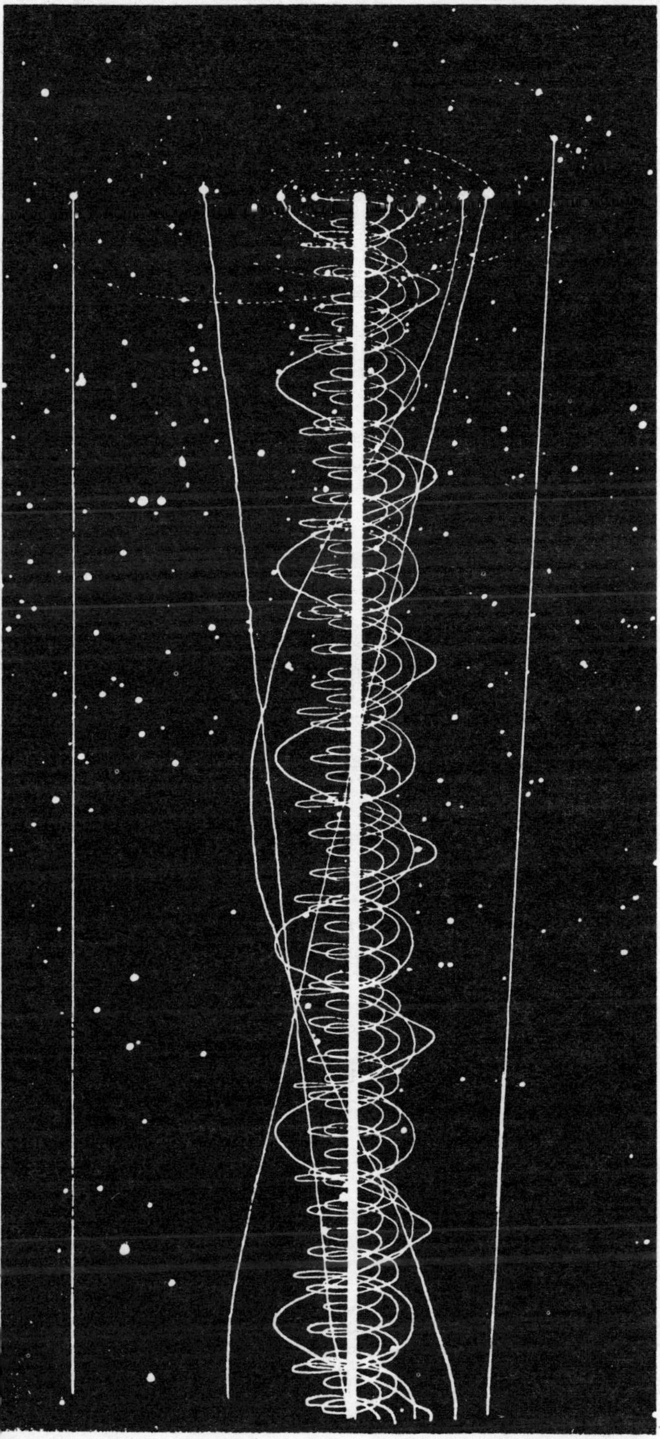

Fig. 5 *The solar system in time.*

permeating an energy system. Thus, any energy arrangement or pattern gains its structure from the frequency that is generated through it, and in this way we can perceive that a light wave or an acoustic wave will differ in quality according to its frequency. Eight has a unique quality, a tone and colour.

Number, harmony and proportion have been thought by many, including Pythagoras, of course, to hold the key to the universe. Indeed, many researchers, John Michell (*City of Revelation*) and Gordon Strachan (*Christ and the Cosmos*) among them, have gone to great lengths to convey this concept by pointing out the sacred geometry encoded in mystical texts, including the Bible. Resonance in light and sound is everywhere and, at the same time, in everything, forming itself into patterns, or structures. Seymour has already mentioned the importance of the 'geometry' of the nervous system, the body's physical dimensions and physical arrangements. Cayce hints at this in his mysterious statement that the body is formed in the womb according to its pattern: 'This is the metaphysical symbolism of the 47th problem of Euclid, the Pythagorean theorem . . . [at conception] the pattern . . . begins to work its way through the body.'[48]

'In the beginning was the Word, and the Word was with God, and the Word was God'. This is the enigmatic opening to the gospel according to St John. With the concept of acoustic vibration this statement at last makes some sense. But John continues: 'In him was life; and the life was the light of men. And the light shineth in the darkness; and the darkness comprehended it not.' Might this vibration also be light? After all, what we perceive as light is the vibration from the *visible* spectrum only.

Helena Blavatsky in *Isis Unveiled* refers to,

> Light – the first mentioned in Genesis is termed by the kabalists . . . the Divine Intelligence . . . Light is the first begotten, and the first emanation of the Supreme, and Light is Life, says the evangelist [John]. Both are electricity – the life principle, the *anima mundi*, pervading the universe, the electric vivifyer of all things. Light is the great protean magician, and under the Divine Will of the architect, its multifarious, omnipotent waves gave birth to every form as well as to every living being. From its swelling electric bosom, springs *matter* and *spirit* . . .

In the way of synchronicity, while I was researching this part of the book Michael Hopwood introduced me to Roger Coghill.[49] Roger, a classical scholar, astounded me by insisting that the familiar translation of John from the original Greek is wrong. He then proceeded to retranslate the opening verses. Not 'In the beginning was the word' but 'In control was a logical system': *En archay ane ho logos*. Not 'And the word was with God' but 'And this system was non-material': *Kai ho logos pros ton Thelon*. Not 'And the word was God' but 'And this system controlled everything': *Kai Thelon ane ho logos*.

It gave birth to every single thing: and without it no creature could be brought to life. It was the origin of organic life, a kind of light within man. But this light shines outside the visible spectrum, and therefore cannot be perceived in what we call darkness.[50]

Roger went on to explain that John had become known as 'the Divine' purely by mistake; in truth, he was a dowser, a diviner. To support his theory, Roger pointed out that the Greek word, Baptidzo, does not mean to baptize, but to find the source of water. It could well be, that the very symbolism of baptism, one of the key axioms of Christianity, has been completely misunderstood. Instead of a simple, uneducated holy man, John as a Gnostic,[51] and living towards the end of the first century BC, would have been steeped in hermetic traditions. He would have been exposed to all the mystery teachings which not only revealed that the planets orbited the sun but that a light shining beyond the visible spectrum – an octave invisible to the human eye – was responsible for (organic) life.

Just how knowledgeable these hermetic savants of the first century BC were can be judged by their explanation of the distribution of matter throughout space.

In the beginning of time the great invisible one had his hands full of celestial matter which he scattered throughout infinity; and lo, behold! It became balls of fire and balls of clay; and they scattered like the moving metal into many smaller balls, and began their ceaseless turning . . .[52]

Blavatsky, who as we know, culled all her theosophist doctrine from the mystery teachings, clearly understood that John was referring to electromagnetism. And she expands on the subject of forces, electromagnetic and otherwise, with great eloquence, which belies the fact that in the late 1880s knowledge about the electromagnetic spectrum was virtually non-existent.

From its [Light's] primordial point gradually emerged into existence the myriads of worlds, visible and invisible celestial bodies. It was [in the beginning] that God, according to Plato, 'lighted a fire, which we now call the sun', and which is *not* the cause of either light or heat, but merely the focus, or, as we might say, the lens, by which the rays of the primordial light become materialized, are concentrated upon our solar system and produce all the correlations of forces . . .

Music is the combination and modulation of sounds, and sound is the effect produced by the vibration of the ether [the fifth element]. Now, if the impulses communicated to the ether by the different planets may be likened to the tones produced by the different notes of a musical instrument, it is not difficult to conceive that the Pythagorean 'music of the spheres' is something more than a mere fancy, and that certain planetary aspects may imply disturbances in the ether of our planet, and certain others, rest and harmony. Certain kinds of music throw us into a frenzy; some exalt the soul to religious aspirations . . . there is scarcely a human creation which does not respond to certain vibrations in the atmosphere.[53]

In view of present research and understanding of the cosmos, Blavatsky's theories may appear somewhat unsophisticated; but her heart, or rather her intuition, was definitely in the 'right' place. And despite the controversy and ridicule she generated in her lifetime and beyond, her writings have often proved to be farseeing and accurate.

In my own experience as an astrologer, there are two concepts that strike a chord of truth within me: one is planetary sojourns – that our experience of the planets and 'stars' is deeply etched in our soul and our consciousness; we are the 'stuff' of the solar system. The other is the music of the spheres. I consider that within these two concepts, approached by both the mystical and the scientific route, the true nature of astrology is to be found.

A friend of mine, with no grounding in philosophy or metaphysics, had a near death experience as a result of a violent accident. He told me that he was propelled out of his body 'at the speed of light' and 'shot' straight into space with the earth far beneath him.

It was the most spectacular and extraordinary experience of my life . . . the thing I remember most vividly was this amazing sound: at first like a low 'Omm . . .' [reminiscent of the Buddhist mantric chant] then gradually I was aware of other sounds . . . beautiful, angelic, harmonious. I realised that the music was everywhere . . . the whole universe was full of sound . . . everything was moving and turning making beautiful sounds.

I believe he is talking about the music of the spheres. And while few of us are fortunate enough to experience the celestial harmony first hand, there is a huge body of esoteric teaching and some scientific research to show us that he and Pythagoras are right.

NOTES

1. See Chapter 2, pp. 26–7.
2. Richard Cavendish (ed.), *Mythology* (Orbis, 1980)
3. The neoplatonist, Macrobius (circa 400 AD) in his work *Commentary on the Dream of Scipio* 1, xii, 13–14, trans. W. Stahl (New York, 1952). Quoted in Robert Powell, *Hermetic Astrology* (Hermetika, Kinsau, West Germany, 1987)
4. The first life-review – that described so often by those who have undergone near death experiences – is believed to occur just before the loss of the etheric body.
5. A lecture given by Steiner on 26 November 1912.
6. Elementals are the spirits that inhabit the astral realms: salamanders are fire elementals, sylphs are air, undines are water and gnomes are earth.
7. The ancient Egyptians were a solar-conscious people, thus the natural order of the planets was taken from the point of view of the sun.
8. Cayce's friend, Lammers, recounting Cayce's clairvoyant pronouncements on the nature of astrology. See Thomas Sugrue, *The Story of Edgar Cayce: There is a River* (Dell, 1970).
9. Ibid.
10. See section on the mystery of number, p. 71.
11. The planetoid (or comet) Chiron was discovered in 1977 and astronomers believe there is now pressing evidence to support the existence of a planet beyond Pluto.
12. Rudolph Steiner *Life Between Death and Rebirth* (Anthroposophical Press inc. New York, 1968)
13. Ibid.
14. Robert Powell, *Hermetic Astrology* (Hermetika, Kinsau, West Germany, 1987)
15. Cayce's words from *There is a River*.
16. In *Hermetic Astrology* Robert Powell elaborates on the true meaning of the Sun, Moon and Ascendant in a birthchart.
17. Rudolph Steiner, *Life Between Death and Rebirth* (Anthroposophical Press inc. New York, 1968)
18. Ibid.
19. See descriptions of the *tattwas* and *pranas*, Chapter 3, pp. 47–8.
20. Astrology includes only the basic four elements – fire, earth, air and water: ether can be seen to represent the sum total of all the elements – the fount from which all the elements spring.
21. Stephen Arroyo, *Astrology, Psychology and the Four Elements* (CRCS Publications, 1975)
22. Liz Greene, *Relating* (Coventure, 1977)
23. See Chapter 3, pp. 49–50.
24. Rupert Sheldrake in *A New Science of Life* (Paladin, 1988) quotes

Beloff (1980), who proposed that the mind interacts with the brain in the retrieval of memories.

25. Benjamin Walker, *Encyclopaedia of Esoteric Man* (Routledge & Kegan Paul, 1977)
26. Sheldrake, *A New Science of Life.*
27. Jolande Jacobi, *The Psychology of C. G. Jung* (Routledge & Kegan Paul, 1968)
28. Liz Greene, *Relating* (Coventure, 1977)
29. Cayce's words from *There is a River.*
30. Rudolph Steiner *Life Between Death and Rebirth* (Anthroposophical Press inc. New York, 1968)
31. Kepler, *Harmonice Mundi* (1619) (trs Arthur Koestler, *The Sleepwalker*, Penguin 1973)
32. The 'hard' aspects in astrology are 0° (conjunction), 45° semi-square, 90° (square), 135° (sesqui-quadrate), 150° (quincunx) and 180° (opposition).
33. My grandmother: Mars conjunct Saturn
    My father: Mars square Saturn
    Myself: Mars conjunct Saturn
    My eldest son: Mars square Saturn
    My middle son: Mars conjunct Saturn
    My youngest son: Mars square Saturn
34. Michel Gauquelin, *Planetary Heredity* (ACS Publications, 1988 French edition, 1966)
35. The effect was most marked for the Moon, Venus, Mars and Jupiter – in that order of significance – but the effect disappeared for the Sun, Mercury, Neptune and Pluto.
36. Percy Seymour, *Astrology: The Evidence of Science* (Lennard Publishing, 1988)
37. Michel Gauquelin, *Planetary Heredity*
38. See Chapter 3, p. 51.
39. The tidal effects of the planets, due to gravitation on the magnetosphere generate a set of notes, or 'chord', which is related to the planetary day (the time taken by a planet, viewed from earth, to rise, set and rise again) of each planet.
40. Percy Seymour, op. cit.
41. See Chapter 3, pp. 42 and 54.
42. Percy Seymour, op. cit.
43. In the Egyptian astronomical system, the planets were considered to circle the sun, although, in turn, the Sun and the planets were thought to orbit the earth.
44. Kepler, *Harmonice Mundi* (trs Arthur Koestler, *The Sleepwalker*, Penguin, 1973)
45. Eileen Garrett, *My Life as a Search for the Meaning of Mediumship* (Rider & Co, 1939)
46. Rodney Collin, *Theory of Celestial Influence* (Robinson & Watkins, 1973)

47. Ibid.
48. Cayce, op. cit.
49. Roger Coghill is co-author with Harry Oldfield of *The Dark Side of the Brain* (Element, 1988)
50. Roger Coghill, *The Teachings of St John the Dowser* (unpublished)
51. See Chapter 1, pp. 15–17.
52. Hermes, Kadmus Thuti, the thrice great Trismegistus quoted in *The Hermetic Book of Numbers*, Helena Blavatsky, *Isis Unveiled*
53. Helena Blavatsky, *Isis Unveiled* Vol. 1 (reprint of original edition, Theosophy Co. Los Angeles, 1968)

BIBLIOGRAPHY

Corrine Heline, *Sacred Science of Numbers* (New Age Press, 1971)
John M. Addey, *Harmonics in Astrology* (Fowler, 1976)
Colin Wilson, *Starseekers* (Granada, 1980)
John Evans, *Mind, Body and Electromagnetism* (Element, 1986)
David Conway, *Secret Wisdom* (Aquarian Press, 1987)
Gordon Strachan, *Christ and the Cosmos* (Element, 1985)
John Michell, *City of Revelation* (Abacus, 1972)

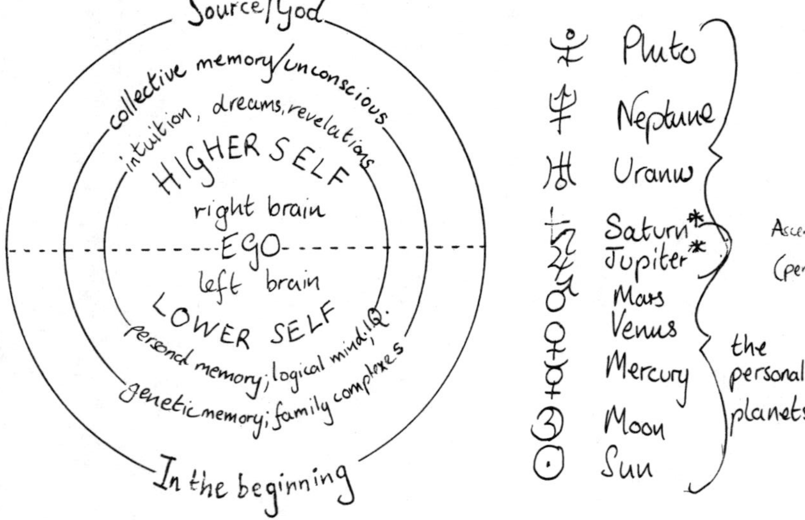

Fig. 9 *Map of Consciousness. The upper and lower hemispheres represent the higher and lower levels of consciousness with the EGO – focussed in the here and now and the physical world – forming the boundary between the two. The upper and lower hemispheres also represent man's divine heritage versus his ancestral lineage. In essence, there is no real separation between the two spheres – they are but two poles of the continuum of consciousness.*

*Saturn and Jupiter are not personal planets in the strict sense of the term, nor are they trans-personal. Saturn, and to a lesser extent, Jupiter form the planetary mid-ground between the two groups.

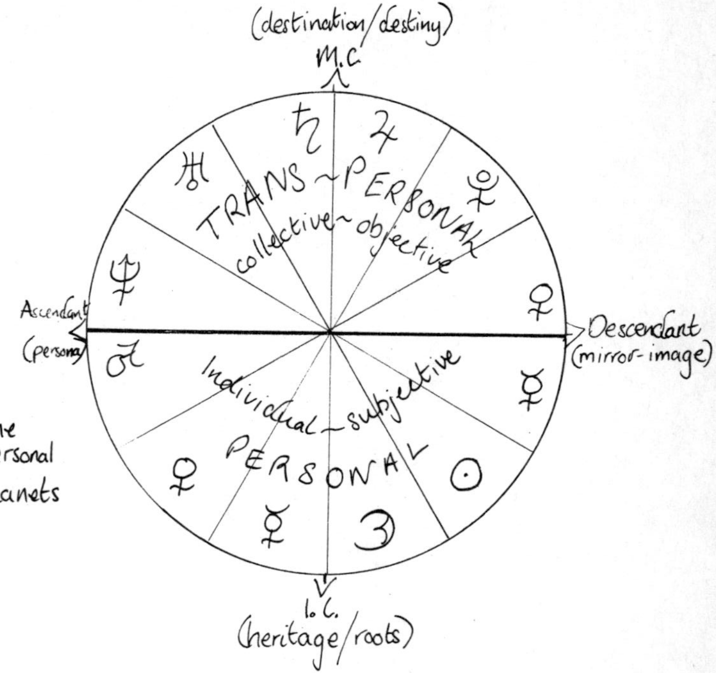

Fig. 10 *The Horoscope. The upper and lower hemispheres of the horoscope, as in the map of consciousness, represent the collective versus the personal and the higher and lower expressions of fundamental themes. Appropriately, the planetary rulers of the 6 houses in the lower hemisphere are the personal 'planets' while those in the upper are (with the exception of Venus and the 7th house) the trans-personal planets. Just as there are conduits linking the HIGHER SELF and the LOWER SELF, there are channels between the transpersonal and the personal spheres of experience (the houses) of the horoscope.*

5
Astrology, Reincarnation and Karma

> What happens to a person is characteristic of him. He presents a pattern and all the pieces fit. One by one, as his life proceeds, they fall into place according to some predestined design.
>
> C. G. Jung

To the layman, astrology is, by and large, a fortune-telling device. But to the initiated and the informed, astrology is a meaningful system of correlations. To the 'man in the street' a horoscope is a mystical something that can tell him what the future holds for him. To the astrologer, the birth chart is a map that reveals who the individual is and where his journey might take him.

The deep misunderstandings about the real value and nature of astrology can best be illustrated by the following story. In my work for a popular British glossy magazine, I began to incorporate a regular section on the way astrology could be used to help with typical life problems. At first the dilemmas were relatively 'light', but within a few months I tackled a more challenging issue. I discussed the fact that some situations in life are unalterable, and that one must simply accept matters for what they are; in this way acceptance becomes the catalyst for resolution. This proved too much for the features editor. 'What use is astrology if it can't tell you what to *do* about a situation? Why would anyone go to an astrologer to be told that he must just accept things the way they are!' This, from a well educated and worldly individual, demonstrated some widely held, deeply ingrained attitudes about astrology, reflected in and reinforced by the media. First, astrology must only lend itself to the lighter side of life. Second, astrologers must supply active, not passive solutions, stressing the 'positive'. And third, that the concept of acceptance cannot be seen as a solution in itself.

Astrology, however, is not about supplying instant solutions that leave the individual ignorant of the deeper issues within a situation, but about showing a route whereby he can gain insight and understanding about himself and his life. Astrology allows the individual to take a bird's-eye-view of a situation so that it can be seen in a larger context; in this way problems become not merely something to solve, but something to learn from. Of course the concept that one can learn something from every experience will have a very hollow ring to it when an individual is facing the death of a beloved child or the terror of an invasion of his country by a ruthless aggressor. The only thing an individual can learn from such traumatic circumstances is how to survive, how to live with and through the pain. And perhaps, his only comfort lies in the belief that a situation is part of a purposeful design and that the acceptance of such a burden expiates some ancient transgression.

To the astrologer and the psychologist alike, an event does not exist in isolation from the individual. There is always a reason for the most 'out of the blue' occurrence; something always to be gained from the most unwanted experience. I have already discussed at length the idea of the 'hand of fate' being simply the effect of a past action, an experience designed by us in a forgotten time. Thus, in a birth chart, an event such as becoming a celebrity may be portrayed by a transit of Jupiter to Venus in the first house of the horoscope – and may indeed represent the karmic harvest of a previous life's action – but it is how the individual reacts to such a dramatic change of fortune that is the crucial issue. Does the experience go completely to his head so that he throws his weight around (a Jupiterian proclivity *par excellence*), thus alienating many of his old friends and thrusting his value system into total disarray? Or does he become bigger in psychological stature through the broadening of his horizons. 'Experience is not what *happened* to you but what you *did* with what happened to you.' While Jupiter is considered to be the 'Greater Benefic' and the symbol of expansion and success, it can also breed chronic megalomania and the tendency for power to corrupt absolutely. It was clearly no accident of fate that many of the Nazi generals of the World War II had Jupiter prominent in their birth charts.

Astrologers are apt to point a finger, usually at Saturn or one of the outer planets, as the doyen of karma or the harbinger of fate. But in light of the voyage through the planetary spheres, we can perceive that all the planets contain the seeds of our karma, or fate – none more so than another. However, in order to separate the sheep from the goats, as it were, the major life events from the minor, it is Jupiter, Saturn, Uranus, Neptune and Pluto that are associated with the greater life events and generate the most far-reaching effects.

The planets up to Saturn make several circuits of the birth chart in an average life span of 70 years, and even Saturn, with its 29-year cycle manages two. Thus, it is as if the planets up to and including Saturn represent those things we can consciously attune to and express, while the outer planets Uranus, Neptune and Pluto epitomize a more rarefied, super-conscious and less individualized experience. In this way, the outer planets represent the larger, collective forces at work in our destiny – those things that characterize and influence a generation – and those events we experience as *force majeure*. One of the ways we are put in touch with these subtler, yet ultimately more powerful, forces is through their position in the twelve houses of the horoscope (the diurnal circle) and the aspects they make with the 'personal' planets.[1]

From the esoteric point of view, because we have absorbed the very essence of the planets in our soul's journey through the planetary spheres – they are imbued with our past experience and provide the nucleus for our future – the natal chart (the birth horoscope) becomes an expression of our karma or our fate. As the planets move in their orbits around the Sun and in turn circle the birth chart, events are triggered that provide us with opportunities to meet our fate – fulfil our karmic potential. From the psychological point of view, the planets symbolize dimensions of consciousness or archetypal forces that dwell within the psyche. As the planets transit the chart, outer events and inner processes occur that synchronize with the various planetary themes. But whether one perceives a planet to be a 'living' expression of certain principles or simply a symbol for certain psychic processes does not detract from the essential experience proffered by that planet.

Certainly in regard to key psychological processes and/or karmic events, the transits of the outer planets are crucial. The cycle of each planet has a particular seed pattern contained within it. Saturn, for instance has a cycle of roughly 29 years which yields four major 'stations'; one at seven years, another at 14, a third at 21 and finally its return to 'base' at 29. At these stages of life in particular, the individual is presented with Saturnian issues that demand to be resolved and, in the process, maturity and wisdom acquired.

In times past every student of astrology was taught that Saturn was the 'Greater Malefic' (Mars being the lesser); 'he' was associated with all manner of doom and gloom and responsible for all types of suffering from disease and famine to material loss and ignominy. However, over the past twenty years, the more psychologically-oriented astrologer has come to view Saturn rather differently. Liz Greene, in her seminal book on Saturn,[2] refers to this planet as the Dweller at the Threshold, 'the keeper of the keys to the gate . . . [through whom alone] we may achieve eventual freedom through self-understanding.' In many ways, Saturn is the personification of the

Jungian shadow – the dark side of our nature, those qualities within us which we consider inferior or 'bad' and consequently highly threatening. Although we tend to repress our 'bad' qualities, they don't obligingly vanish, instead they magically appear in other people and situations 'out there'. Unable to recognize and deal with our own darkness we project it onto the world and his wife.

This concept of the unrecognized, unwanted darkness within our psyches is one way of perceiving Saturn, another is through his role as Lord of Karma. Jeanne Avery believes that Saturn relates to certain decisions made in a past life that are 'engraved on the personality'. She refers to Saturn as,

> one key to the understanding of the karma or major lesson to be resolved in present-day existence . . . the placement of Saturn in the natal chart is a major indication of just how that lesson is to be resolved and through which department of life we may expect to have the greatest level of responsibility and the greatest level of stress . . . It can be likened to a knot in the thread of consciousness that must be untied at some point to avoid a continuous repetition of the same old mistakes . . .[3]

Clearly, Saturn, both in its natal positioning and its transit of the chart, hardly presents the image of a country picnic. However, this planet is not entirely a repository for all our 'bad' karma, nor a haven for every *bête noire*; Saturn also becomes the agency through which we can experience our greatest sense of achievement and truly make our mark in life.

As far as I am concerned, I have experienced no greater sense of achievement than in giving birth to my three sons. And where is my Saturn? In Cancer, of course – *the* sign of motherhood.[4] But pregnancy and motherhood have been fraught with Saturnian difficulties, frustrations and setbacks. I have had a history of miscarriages and spent several weeks of two pregnancies in hospital. Through the nature of my work, I have never been a full-time 'mum' – in a sense I have been unable to enjoy the fruits of my labours, except in a somewhat limited form. Saturn's position in Cancer in the ninth house of the horoscope also provides me with a different opportunity to 'make my mark' in searching for and defining a spiritual philosophy – and writing about it. The publication of each book – the birth after a painful labour – provides yet another source of deep satisfaction and sense of achievement. I received notification that I had passed the Diploma exam of the Faculty of Astrological Studies on the day my first son, Jamie, was born; and the publication of my first book,

Synastry, in July 1982 coincided exactly with the birth of my second son, Alexander. Indeed, the saga of this latter pregnancy was the personification of Saturn in so many ways, it is worth looking into at greater depth.

At twenty-one weeks of pregnancy I went into premature labour. After an operation that was, according to my obstretrician and the nursing staff, nothing short of a miracle, the birth process was halted. However, because of the delicate state of the pregnancy I was rendered completely bed-bound for several weeks – unable even to pick up an item that dropped on the floor beside me. During this time, Saturn edged relentlessly towards my Ascendant through the latter part of the twelfth house – an area synonymous with institutions of all kinds including hospitals. My condition eventually necessitated a transference to a top London hospital, thereby removing me from the loving support of close friends and family. There, a week later, on the day following a lunar eclipse that precisely contacted Mars and Saturn in my natal chart, Alexander emerged tenuously into the world – a full two and a half pounds in weight and 27 weeks and five days gestation. By this time I weighed only 98 pounds and had lost the use of my legs. Alexander – a tiny spark of creation – was fighting for life in an incubator. The weeks that followed presented new dangers and anxieties, new separations and conflicts. And all the while Saturn ticked slowly towards 'nine' (the Ascendant point) on the cosmic clock.

Without insight, this period of my life, and indeed the family's, might simply have been something to get through in the hopes of never meeting anything else like it again. However, the experience developed real meaning viewed through an astrological lens. Saturn certainly provided me with several great lessons. I finally understood what it was like to be weak and helpless – a state exacerbated by the indifference and a degree of psychological cruelty I experienced from certain nursing staff at the hospital in London. In that emotionally and physically vulnerable state, I discovered the stuff I was made of. I had to find dignity in the most reduced of circumstances without any of the usual 'props' at my disposal. And in so doing I found a new strength and maturity. I also discovered who my real friends were and the depth of the love between my husband and I. The marital cords, which had they been weak and insubstantial, Saturn might have sundered were instead strengthened through adversity.

In the psychological sense I had confronted some of the substance of the shadow symbolized by Saturn. Until this period of my life I had despised weakness in others and had always thought myself supremely in control of my destiny. With Saturn's transit[5] the sense of powerlessness I had always feared was thrust upon me, yet I had coped. I didn't like it, but I understood it. And I now had compassion for it.

Examining the experience from a karmic point of view enriched matters even more. Saturn's position in the natal chart indicated that a major lesson would have to be learned in connection with procreation. For my first son, Jamie, although there were no complications in pregnancy or the birth, there was considerable trauma during his early years through the break-up of my first marriage. With my third son, Dominic, while he arrived into a happy and stable family, there had been many anxious moments during the pregnancy, and the birth itself was a nightmare. However, during neither of these pregnancies were there any Saturnian transits to contend with. In 1982, as Saturn formed a 90° angle to its natal position, a pivotal experience occurred; an experience made all the more powerful and transformative by a transit of Pluto to my Ascendant. (Pluto, as I discuss later, is the planet synonymous with death and rebirth, a process I was made acutely aware of as Alexander courageously hovered between life and death in those early weeks of his existence.) Also, with such powerful transits reflected in Alexander's natal chart, he not only has a strong destiny of his own to fulfil, but he clearly manifests a major karmic link to both his parents.[6]

Saturn in a birth chart may show us where our Achilles Heel lies, but it also presents us with the tools to make our mark. Through past experience we have earned our Saturnian lot and we must make of it what we will. Saturn at each stage in its cycle provides us with a test. We, as the alchemist, through the light of self-discovery have within us the ability to transmute Saturn's lead into gold. At each Saturnian station in life, the events that occur, both great and small, offer us that chance.

Robert Powell is one astrologer who considers Saturn to be a key factor in the process of reincarnation. In *Hermetic Astrology* Powell draws on Steiner's teachings and the work of Guenther Wachsmuth[7] and Willi Sucher[8] for his 'laws of reincarnation'. Using Steiner's premise that the soul seeks a similar astrological pattern to be reborn into as the one at death, Powell has theorized that the angular relationship between Saturn and the Sun in a birth chart is representative of the angle at death of the previous incarnation. He provides many impressive examples of this effect including charts of Haroun al-Rashid (a calif of Baghdad, 786–809 AD), Francis Bacon (1561–1626) and Bertrand Russell (1872–1970), maintaining that they were one and the same soul.

Powell's work leads us into the dense and labyrinthine world of hermetic astrology, and while I find a certain sympathy with many of its principles – indeed, I am convinced there must be an astrological continuity between one life and the next, which I will explore in Chapter 7 – I am not entirely happy with the concept of reincarnational *laws*, nor the evidence used to support them. Powell does not expand on why the combination of Saturn and the Sun is so crucial, one can only surmise that the personality of the soul (as described by the Sun) and the nature of cosmic and karmic law (as represented by Saturn) have an intrinsic relationship with each other and that this is expressed and reinforced by the angle between them at birth and death. I also disagree with Powell in his assumption that the sidereal zodiac viewed from the heliocentric point of view is the only astrological medium through which to perceive the spiritual nature and purpose of the individual. In my experience, the planets, their aspects and their positions in the zodiacal and the diurnal circle are capable of being interpreted at any level of manifestation, and the karmic inheritance and purpose is entirely implicit in the tropical, geocentric-based chart.

Beyond Saturn's boundaries the laser-like influence of Uranus reigns supreme. If Saturn presents us with obligations and duties, Uranus urges us to break free of earthly restrictions. Revolution – the keyword principle of Uranus – is a weighty, if somewhat abstract theme for an individual to identify with in terms of his character and his destiny. However, if we conceive Uranus as the higher expression, or octave, of the Sun, we find a route to appreciate the meaning of Uranus in a personal sense: as the Sun represents self-expression and the individuality, Uranus symbolizes the Higher Self – that spirit of awakening that urges us to change our circumstances, to take that uncompromising step into the unknown and so bring forward a new dimension or expression of our Selves. Uranus puts us in touch with our Unlimited Self. It manifests like a thunderflash and is the experience of 'eureka' in every man's humdrum existence.

The outer planets can be seen as consciousness-raisers in that their intrinsic natures can only be perceived as man's awareness increases to accommodate them. The discovery of Uranus (1781), for instance, synchronized with major revolutions in industry, culture and society, Neptune's existence was first noted at a time when Spiritualism and the great romantic movement was sweeping the globe (1846) and Pluto was discovered in 1930 as the world plummeted into a Depression and fascism began to take hold on a global scale. The position of an outer planet in a zodiac sign may cover a span of several years, thus imbuing a large group with certain characteristics and specific political or cultural events to live through; yet an outer planet also provides a route toward an individual destiny within a collective fate.

Liz Greene makes the point[9] that we are all subject to the vicissitudes of collective fate and the only way to avoid being swept up by an 'eruption' of the collective is to stand firm in our individuality.

> Otherwise there is no way in which the eruption can be channelled without you becoming a victim of the collective. Then you are blindly carried along with it, and because it is blind and undirected consciousness it doesn't reason politely and set up careful standards to assess who should pay and who shouldn't. These eruptions run like a torrent, with a ruthlessness that one finds only in blind nature but not in the reflective mind of an individual. One finds it in the natural side of civilized man, the collective instinctual side of him of which he is largely unaware. The collective doesn't theorise. It flows toward its goal in the same way that a baby is born. If you're caught by it, then you must go along with it, and there is no guarantee of the outcome. You might have a Renaissance . . . or you might have a Nazi Germany.

Uranus has an 84-year cycle and spends approximately seven years in each sign of the zodiac. Thus its quarter stage at 21 coincides with Saturn's three-quarter point, making for a period of tremendous cross-conflicts. As Saturn presents the individual with a set of circumstances that threaten his Achilles Heel, and makes him feel very insecure, Uranus challenges him to find a new route for his self-expression. In my own life at this period I broke my contract with the Royal Ballet Company – a career I had nurtured since the age of five – following a very dispiriting experience in the ranks of the *corps de ballet*. By way of another example of Uranian 'revolution', a British Independent Television documentary filmed a group of children at the age of 7, 14, 21 and ultimately at 28. At 21, as Uranus squared its natal position, all the 'children' seemed to have become out of kilter with themselves, which was expressed in their appearance, their attitudes and their occupation; at this stage of life, aspects of their personalities emerged that made them seem almost completely different people.

The Uranus opposition at approximately 42 years of age has been identified as the astrological mid-life crisis. The pressure to 'do something' before it is too late is the impulse behind the often explosive events that occur at this time.

A friend of mine, 'Peter' and his wife, 'Jane' provide classic examples of this syndrome. Jane, a strongly Capricorn lady was the archetypal 'perfect wife and mother'; Peter, another Capricorn figure, was a top executive in a shipping company. They had two 'perfect' children, a 'perfect' house and a 'perfect' life-style. Prior to marriage, Jane had been a high-flying journalist with a brilliant career behind and ahead of her, but in typical earthy fashion, she had put her career 'on ice' and dedicated herself to the home and family.

At the age of 40 Peter suffered a heart attack and subsequently underwent 'bypass' surgery. Jane was not unnaturally concerned about his future prospects especially since Peter's father had died of a heart attack at 42. I noted that Uranus was appropriately in full flight at the time of Peter's heart attack triggering his natal Mars; however, the Uranus opposition had yet to come the following year – and for both of them.

An astrologer could be forgiven for anticipating that the Uranus opposition might indicate a turn for the worse in Peter's condition – and certainly this period was likely to prove a volatile one on all levels. But since Uranus was situated in his seventh house of relationships and Jane's natal Venus (symbolic of love) was also involved in her Uranus opposition, it crossed my mind that the Uranian upheaval was more likely to centre itself on the relationship *between* them.

Some months later, I met Peter at a dinner party. During the course of the conversation he mentioned to me that he had had a rather extraordinary experience and wondered if I might be able to explain it. At the edge of sleep one night he was astounded to find a figure of 'light' at the end of the bed. The figure was an old man with piercing blue eyes and a shock of blue-grey hair: he spoke to Peter gently and told him quite plainly that Peter had the power to heal and he should use it. He then promptly disappeared.

The old man clearly had a Merlin-like quality about him, and was thus an essentially Uranian figure.[10] It could well have been that in that strange half-awake-half-asleep state, Peter had tuned into an archetype and given it a separate reality – literally giving flesh and bones, life and voice to Uranus and the Higher Self. Alternatively, the old man could have been a visitor from another dimension. But whether the Uranian figure was a message from the unconscious or an emissary from the astral plane, the experience evoked a profound change within Peter.

Together with the orthodox medical help he was receiving, Peter began to explore alternative health measures. He drastically altered his eating habits and started to derive enormous benefits from meditation. Through this holistic, mind, body and spirit approach to his health, and indeed his life, Peter changed dramatically. Gradually, he realized that he had little in common with his 'city' colleagues and preferred the company of more spiritually minded people. Before long, he had become an active and much valued member of a local healing group which in turn acted as the springboard for greater things. Over the past few years, Peter has become affiliated to many 'New Age' concerns, organizing lectures and promoting New Age concepts.

Jane, for her part, gradually began to see how frustrated she was in her role of mother-nurse so when she was asked to edit a new county magazine, she accepted wholeheartedly. As their lives began to move in separate directions with different interests and different friends, the almost inevitable occurred. Peter and Jane found themselves with little to share but the children and the furniture. And as Uranus reached its opposition in both charts, they decided to end their marriage – but not in an orthodox way. Instead they divided their large house into two separate flats and, despite the occasional financial hiccup, they have found the new arrangement suits them both.

Another curious feature of this story is that Jane eventually developed a passionate interest in philosophy, largely through her relationship with a Norwegian lecturer – ten years younger than herself. Thus Peter and Jane in their different ways had both experienced an awakening from Uranus. And while Peter's awakening was inspired by a heavenly presence, Uranus for Jane manifested through her new, and very different, lover.

The electric sphere of Uranus is light years away from Neptune – at least in terms of astrological interpretation. If Uranus enters our consciousness like an electric storm, Neptune glides into our experience like some ghostly galleon emerging through a misty seascape. If Uranus, as the higher octave of the Sun, can be interpreted as the Higher Self, then Neptune, as the higher expression of the Moon, can be perceived as the God within us, that which transports our ability to love and feel into the selfless love exemplified by Christ's sacrifice on the cross for mankind. Yet like all these high octane energies, Neptune has difficulty manifesting its divinity within man, and all too often emerges instead as chaos and disillusion.

From an esoteric standpoint, it is as though the outer planetary essences become more and more diluted and less and less able to be integrated as the soul descends through the planetary spheres into human experience. From the psychological perspective, as the ego assumes more and more of a dominant role, the more it inhibits access to the dimensions of consciousness symbolized by Uranus, Neptune and Pluto. Only when the individual is able to sustain a higher level of awareness can he successfully respond to their higher nature.

While Neptune's aspects in a natal chart – particularly the 'hard' angles[11] – are *a priori* indications of illusion, deception and betrayal, ironically, Neptune presents us with a route to the truth. Neptune invites us to perceive how illusory our material reality is; thus through peak Neptunian experience, where one feels at one with the universe, we can contact the God within us and know the truth. We and the universe are one.

Neptune's 164-year cycle proffers two major junctions, one at approximately 41 years of age and another at its halfway point when the individual is around 82: these points can coincide with the Uranus opposition and the Uranus return respectively and when they do, the individual invariably encounters mayhem! One of my clients who consulted me at the time of Neptune's square to its original position presented the classic Neptunian 'symptoms' of confusion and misdirection. As I was describing the nebulous facets of Neptune, her face lit up. 'Does this dream I had recently have anything to do with Nepune?' she asked. 'I was driving my car through a dense forest. Gradually, little tendrils of mist began to form themselves into a thick fog. I put the headlights on, but it made no difference. I had to stop the car. When I got out and lifted the bonnet, to my great consternation, I found that the headlamps were facing *into* the car.'

Prior to this time, my client had been a maths teacher, but various staff changes at the school where she taught and her failure to get an anticipated promotion began to make her question whether or not she wished to continue teaching for the rest of her life. At the same time, she had fallen deeply in love although there was no future in the relationship since he was 'very married'. The dream presented my client with a perfect image of Neptune – the fog, the inability to see the wood for the trees, and the 'message' that she must look within herself for the way through. While, in this case, there was no peak transcendental experience, my client discovered a route in astrology itself. She eventually gave up teaching and is now a practising astrologer.

Neptune's position in the natal chart shows the route to God, or rather the route to the divine within us. Neptune demonstrates our capacity to experience ecstasy through whatever pathway is most accessible to us; on a higher level this may prove to be art, love, music or mysticism and on a lower rung, drugs and other forms of sheer escapism. In the karmic sense, Neptune provides us with opportunities to sacrifice ourselves or give up something we are deeply attached to. Ingrid Lind wrote to me concerning the transit of Neptune to my

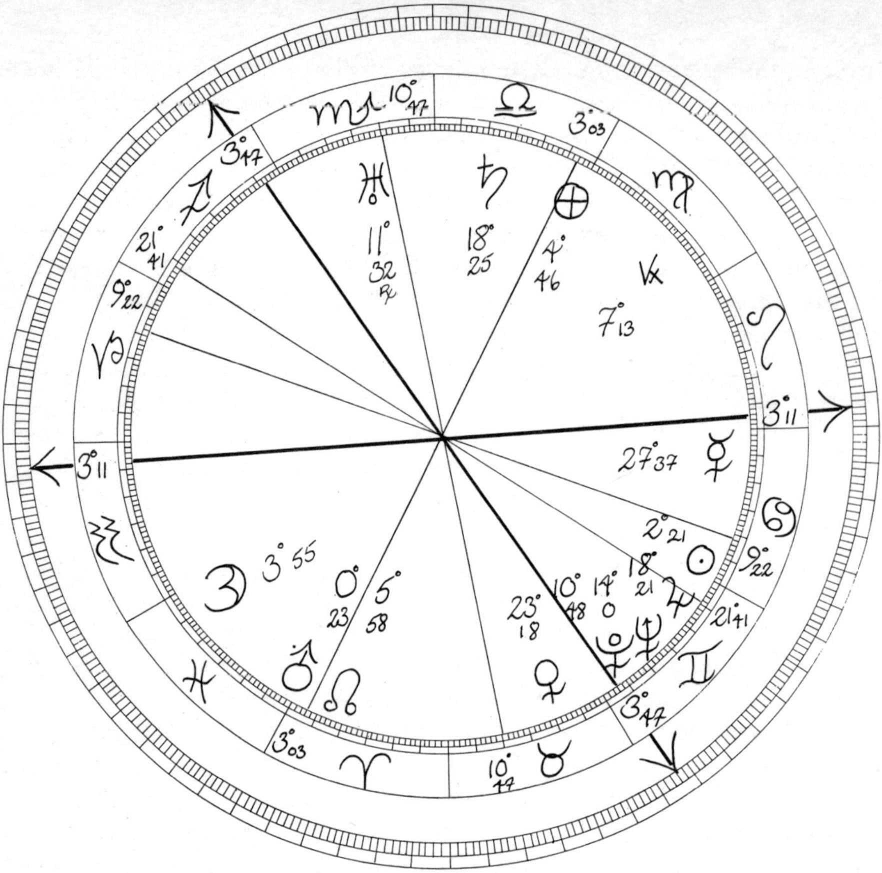

Edward VIII

23rd June 1894 : 22hrs. 0' g.m.t. : 51°N26' : 0°W16'

Fig. 11

Moon, 'Neptune is much in the picture at this time [some two years ahead] which may involve you in some act of renunciation – the giving up of something dearly prized.' This was the period I hung up my ballet shoes for ever. Clearly resonating to a strongly placed Neptune in my natal chart, some years earlier I had taken the theme of renunciation for a choreographic competition in which a nun was tempted by the devil to give up her love for God. The title I gave the ballet was 'The Renunciation'. I think it won third prize.

Neptune's position in the natal chart of Edward VIII provides a major indication of the sacrifice he was forced to make – that between the throne and the woman he loved. In Edward's chart, Neptune is placed in the 4th house of home and family (and his heritage) and forms the centrepiece of a triple conjunction with Jupiter and Pluto. Neptune in the 4th house is by no means the best of positions, for although this placing can produce an individual who considers his spiritual beliefs to be the root of his existence, and therefore he is in essence a born mystic, because of the sheer difficulty in working with Neptune in the material world, this fourth house situation can indicate a lack of definition and therefore security in family life and, at worst, can effect an erosion of the family line. In 1936, the year of the abdication crisis, Neptune, which had moved to the 7th house of relationships, squared natal Neptune and Jupiter while transiting Saturn in Pisces also squared natal Neptune and Jupiter. Although there were other highly significant transits and progressions at the time of Edward's abdication, there is no doubting that the moment had come, from both a psychological and karmic perspective, for the sacrificial potential of natal Neptune to be released.

Liz Greene makes the point that John Kennedy with his Saturn –Neptune conjunction at the zenith of the chart, the Midheaven, was 'a collective sacrifice'.[12] I think this also very much applies in Edward's case, especially since Pluto is closely conjunct Neptune and opposing the Midheaven.[13] The concept of a collective sacrifice is an interesting one. Edward's renunciation of the throne struck a deep chord within the collective psyche of the British nation and indeed the world, and Edward may have seen himself as the Royal Family's sacrificial lamb, or almost certainly as the innocent victim of gross prejudice and bigotry. The constitutional crisis generated by Edward's abdication could well have brought to an end the monarchy as an institution. As it was, the force of destiny brought a new branch of the royal line into prominence and in the process probably ensured its survival.

While Edward may not have been a 'born mystic', it is possible that another member of the royal family with Neptune in the fourth house could be – HRH, The Prince of Wales. Indeed, one biographer[14] was moved to remark that in his opinion, Charles had the makings of a saint. Certainly Charles has displayed many of the tendencies of a modern-day mystic with his contemplative nature, his concern for the ecology and his identification with the suffering and decline of the inner cities. His close friendship with the writer Laurens van der Post has introduced him to mystical concepts and to the teachings of Carl

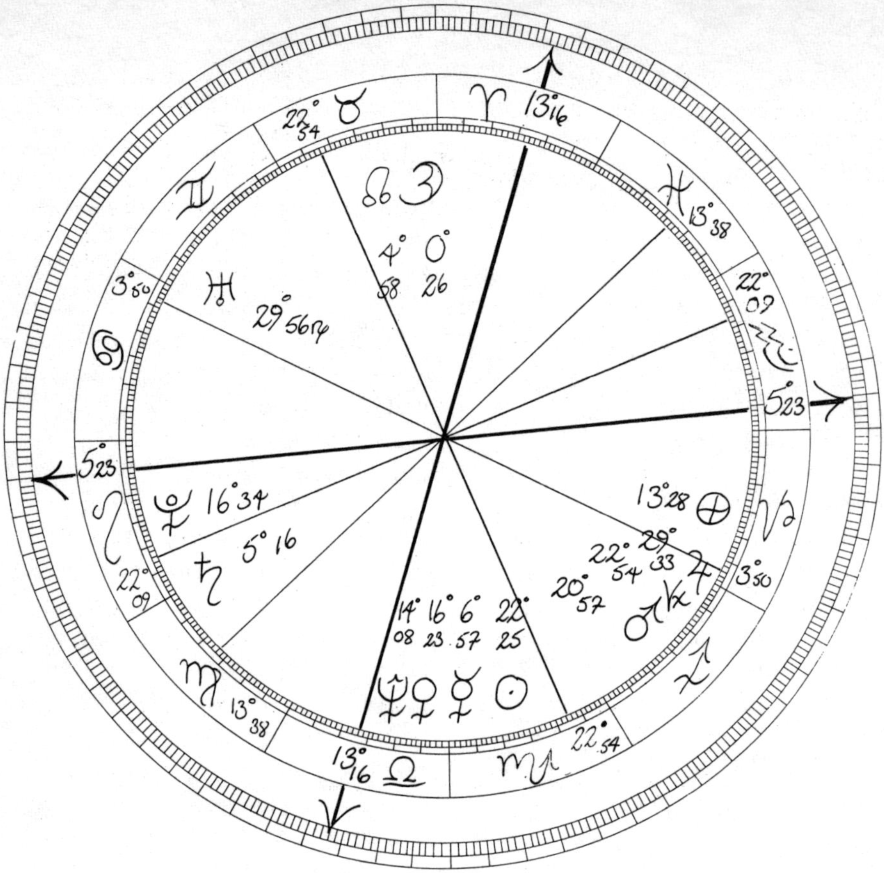

H.R.H The Prince of Wales

14th November 1948 21hrs. 14′ g.m.t. 51N 30 : 0° W10

Fig. 12

Jung. (Ironically, and somewhat disappointingly for modern astrology, unlike Jung who considered astrology to be a profound and meaningful symbolic system, Charles appears to have, as yet, found little of value in the subject.)

Charles is typical of the 'outer planetary' person in that he has the outer planets in key positions in his chart, forming major 'hard' aspects to the personal planets. Neptune, for instance, is closely conjunct Venus and the IC.[15] Pluto, with its transformational signature, is rising toward the Ascendant and in square aspect to his Sun in Scorpio – a Pluto-ruled sign – and Jupiter and Uranus form a tight opposition (within minutes of each other) which contacts his elevated[16] Moon in Taurus and his Mars. On the one hand, given his inclination toward all things spiritual, there is every possibility that Charles can tap the higher level of experience offered through these planets; on the other, he must surely bear the cross of a powerful collective destiny.

Just how this collective destiny may manifest remains to be seen. Will the potential of the Venus–Neptune conjunction be released in a similar sacrificial way as Edward VIII? Will his marriage to the Princess of Wales prove the source of a constitutional crisis? Could the inherent turbulence of such a strong Pluto be made manifest in a transformation of his role? I would like to think that the collective unconscious is ready to respond to the higher nature of these planetary archetypes, in which case we shall see through Charles the emergence of a spiritual, artistic and ecological Renaissance.

Since the 8th harmonic chart is synonymous with the concept of manifestation – what the individual has to bring into existence – I wondered if Charles's 8th harmonic would throw any further light on how aspects of his destiny would be made manifest. I was looking for any strong configurations and particular degree areas of the chart that would reinforce significant natal points. The Ascendant of this harmonic chart at 13° 43 of Capricorn forms an exact square to his natal MC–IC axis; Pluto at 12° 31 Aries in the 8th harmonic is in square to the Ascendant–Descendant axis and conjunct his natal Midheaven. In the 8th harmonic chart the Midheaven cuts through the seventh house of relationships; also in the seventh house (and near to the Midheaven) is Neptune which forms a close opposition to Mercury. Other significant points are a Sun–Moon opposition and an exact Jupiter–Uranus conjunction[17] 60° away from the Sun. To my mind, the reinforcement of the Neptune link to relationships suggests that one of the major life issues for Charles – what he must make manifest – is to bring the highest, most selfless quality of Neptunian love into his close relationships. To this end, he might have to give up 'something dearly prized'. The Sun–Moon opposition also presents a similar relationship theme and shows that he experiences a great polarity between the masculine and feminine, yin and yang, and that the circumstances of his life will force him to confront this division in order to find a harmony between the two.

This seventh house Neptune theme can also be extended to incorporate his relationship with his people, thus, as with his intimate

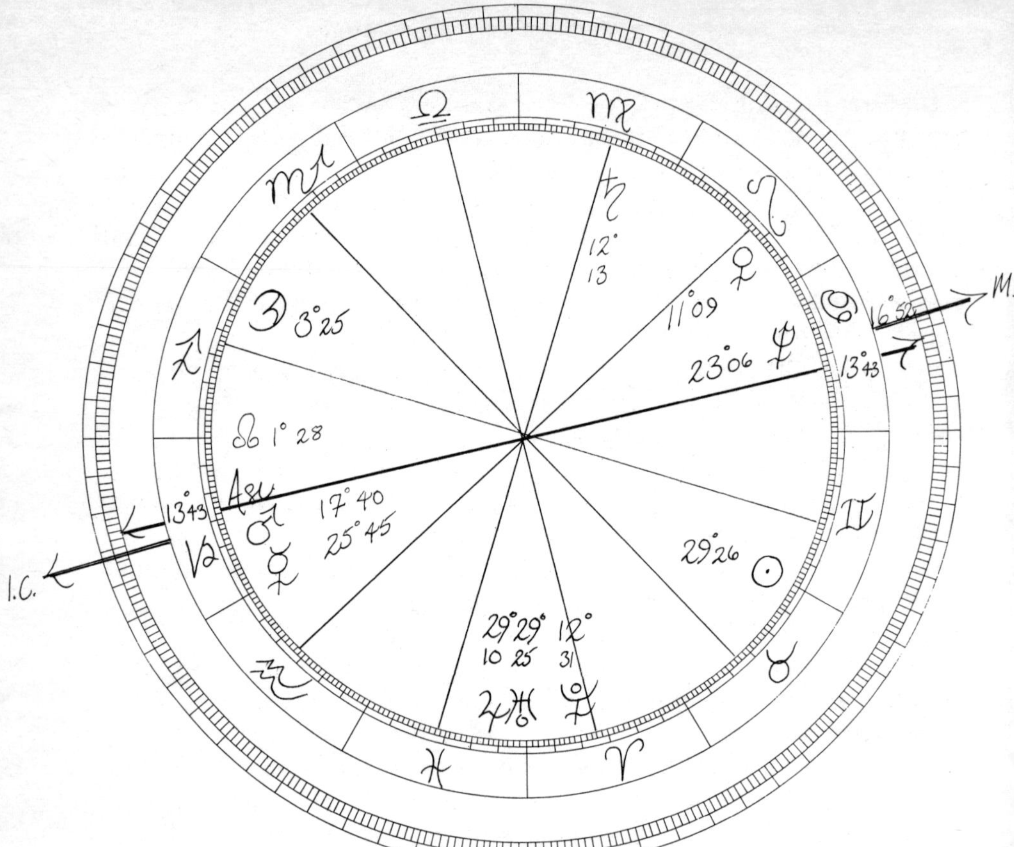

H.R.H The Prince of Wales

8th Harmonic

Fig. 13

partnerships, not only is the potential for selfless service shown, but also the prospect of sacrifice, betrayal and disillusion. The powerful interplay of the Midheaven in the natal chart and the Midheaven – Pluto combination in the 8th harmonic cannot escape significance especially as this same degree area is strongly featured in all the charts for Great Britain;[18] Charles's life direction, his place on the world's stage, as portrayed by the Midheaven are the setting for an inescapable Plutonic task. Charles bears the collective destiny of the royal family firmly on his shoulders – will he make or break it? Will Pluto's transformational theme result in the 'death' of the monarchy or its rebirth into a more appropriate form?

One of the most encouraging signs that Charles's destiny should lead to an enhancement of the monarchy rather than its downfall, is that unlike Edward VIII's chart, Charles's natal horoscope demonstrates powerful links with Great Britain's charts and, not unnaturally, those of the royal family. Neptune has held a significant position in many of the royal family's charts across the generations: King George V, the 'sailor king' had this planet rising, and so does the present Prince William. And while, in keeping with the Great Britain chart of 1066, the middle to late Aries–Libra axis, and the late mutables have been a stronghold of the royal family since Queen Victoria's time, it is only since George VI and Queen Elizabeth, the Queen Mother that 22° of the fixed signs (or thereabouts) has sprung into significance.

In my experience, all families, and certainly all great dynasties, present similar planetary patterns and degree areas through the generations. The Onassis family is no exception. Aristotle Onassis fathered a dynasty that has all the trappings of an archetypal Greek tragedy about it. Appropriately enough, Pluto constantly emerges as a major theme in the family's charts.[19] Fate struck its first blow for Onassis when his mother died when he was only 12. His first wife, Tina, died of suspected barbiturate overdose some twenty months after their son and heir, Alexander, was killed in an air-crash at the age of 24; Ari's long-time mistress, the great opera singer, Maria Callas died of a heart attack (some say, a broken heart because Aristotle married Jackie Kennedy, ironically a refugee from another fated dynasty) and his daughter, Christina, who had led a deeply unfulfilled romantic life dogged by constant weight problems, died when she was only 37, leaving her four-year-old daughter, Athina, the lonely heiress to a massive fortune. Truly the stuff of Pluto.

Pluto is the most remote planet in our solar system; it presents an enigma to astronomers and astrologers alike. Is it small but extremely dense? Or is our perception of it distorted because its surface is covered in ice thereby reflecting the sun and rendering the planet itself invisible? This mystery impresses itself on the nature of Pluto as an astrological symbol. Pluto, like its mythological equivalent, the lord of the Underworld, moves in mysterious ways; while Pluto's realm hidden from the warmth and light of the sun was a place of death and anguish, there were immense riches to be found in its environs; so too in the Plutonic world of the unconscious, the ancestral vaults of the psyche, rests a great heritage of treasure.

If, within the boundaries of Uranus we access the Higher Self and if, through Neptune's mystical realms, we locate the spirit of the Divine, in Pluto's dimension we meet Universal Will. Liz Greene conceives Pluto as the symbol of Moira[20] within the human soul: '. . . Pluto represents a force in the collective psyche as well as in the individual; an impersonal order, a Moira that reminds us perpetually of the limits of nature which we transgress at our peril.'[21] While I have maintained that the whole chart is karma, or fate, if there is one facet that represents a *force majeure*, an expression of a law that we simply cannot violate, then it is Pluto.

Pluto's immensely slow orbit takes roughly 248 years to circle the zodiac; thus no one has yet ever experienced a Pluto return. However, due to the changes in its motion and its elliptical orbit that permits it to spend some thirty years in Taurus yet only thirteen in Scorpio, it is entirely possible for us to live through the Pluto opposition. (If I am hale and hearty by the age of 83 I shall experience mine!) On average, the Pluto square occurs when people are in their late forties and, since this planet is synonymous with death and rebirth and the fertility cycle, one of the most common manifestations of this transit is the onset of the menopause. This is often the time in life when we become acutely aware that we are not immortal; youth is definitely over, and death an inevitability that is now not quite so far away. And while women receive nature's confirmation that they are no longer 'ripe', men also sense a change of rhythm in their sexuality. However, the 'death' of fertility also marks the beginning of a new stage in life that has its pleasures and its rewards.

Since Pluto takes on average some twenty years to move through each sign of the zodiac, it carves its signature on an epoch. For instance, in 1939 Pluto moved into Leo where it remained until 1958. This period was charactized by a world war brought to an end only by the dropping of first atomic bomb on Hiroshima – a quintessential expression of Pluto and Leo. The essential component of the atom bomb is Plutonium and its explosive effect mirrors the fusion that occurs on the sun (The Sun rules the sign of Leo); on the day the bomb was dropped, the Sun in Leo was in close conjunction to Pluto. Pluto in Leo epitomizes the power of the sun to create and sustain life as well as its awesome powers of destruction. Liz Greene makes the point that those born with Pluto in Leo (a sign synonymous with self-involvement) represent 'the so-called "me" generation . . . [who] have made a god of individualism and the right for individual expression and destiny . . .'[22]

Since November 1983 Pluto has been passing through its own sign of Scorpio where it will remain until November 1995. Now, in 1989, we can see some of the effects of this transit. On the negative side, AIDS is a classic Plutonic disease – a virus thought to be spread through sexual activity and initially in the West rampant in the homosexual community. (Pluto–Scorpio and the 8th house of the horoscope symbolize such taboo aspects of life as sex and death.) The crucial factor about AIDS in connection with Pluto–Scorpio is that it is a disease whereby the immune system (the body's defence system) breaks down; in a sense the body self-destructs. In keeping with *Moirian* cosmic law, many strongly religious individuals believe AIDS is God's way of punishing humanity for its decline in sexual morality. On a positive note, 1989 saw a scientific breakthrough by a British and US scientist, Pons and Fleischman who have apparently succeeded in creating fusion in a test tube, thus providing a potentially safe source of power generation and solving the major problem of nuclear waste. And although British scientists have subsequently failed to replicate this experiment, with Pluto remaining in Scorpio until 1995, there is still time! The spectre of the death of the earth itself has become a frightening reality as Pluto reaches the halfway point in Scorpio. Already we have the emergence of a hole in the ozone layer caused by man-made chemical pollutants. The devastation of trees in the Amazonian Basin has contributed to the so-called 'greenhouse effect' whereby scientists agree that the earth is gradually heating up – hence the already noticeable changes in the world's climate. Ultimately this process could cause the ice flows to melt with disastrous global consequences. Almost daily we hear of the extinction of whole species of flora and fauna – and all of them provoked by man himself. Our ability to self-destruct has never been greater or more apparent. We have, indeed, created our own fate, and Moira in the guise of Pluto is ensuring that judgement is passed on us.

Of course, this is not the first time Pluto has passed through its own sign. The Renaissance was at its height when Pluto was in Scorpio between 1490 and 1502. More significantly, perhaps, Pluto occupied Scorpio from 10 AD until 22 AD, a period which saw the rise and fall of Jesus Christ, and brought into mass consciousness the concept of death and resurrection. It is thus no mere coincidence that the 1980s have seen a burgeoning interest in reincarnation and that with increased occurrence and awareness of near death experiences has given rise to organizations and publications for the study of this phenomenon. Cryogenics, the science of freezing an individual who has died so that when a cure for their fatal demise has been found he can be revivified, is a growing business in many parts of the world. There are many people who believe that a new spiritual leader will arise before the end of the century; some even declare that Christ himself will return to Earth.

Death and rebirth, fate and transformation are Pluto's domain. Yet, like Neptune and Uranus, its higher potential is difficult to manifest unless we experience a massive expansion of consciousness. When Pluto reaches a point in the chart, or we are born with this planet in a prominent position, we might aspire to access its transformative properties but all too often we experience only its remorseless dark power.

One of the keyword principles for Pluto is *elimination* – a process that is difficult to relate to unless you have undergone the awesome experience of having something literally stripped from your life. The ill-fated, ex-President of the United States, Richard Nixon, had the 'misfortune' to reap the worst effects of natal Pluto in his tenth house; he fulfilled the destiny Pluto offered through its elevated position in the chart by becoming arguably the most important leader in the Western world at the time; but he was brought down by the Watergate scandal, which implicated him in wholesale political corruption. He must live every day of his life in the knowledge that he was the first American President in history to resign.

Liz Greene makes the point in *The Astrology of Fate* that Pluto's contact to the personal planets can often manifest as a family tie or inherited condition that binds the individual to an ineluctable role or task.

> I believe these differing faces of bondage are purposeful, in the sense that Moira is purposeful. Something is taken away, so that another thing may grow in its place. The seeds of this bondage generally lie several generations back, so that the sins of the parents are well and truly visited upon the children; and it becomes the children's task to attempt some kind of understanding. If one does not take up this challenge, then there is only black despair and a rage against life . . . when Pluto is strongly marked in the birth horoscope, the individual is faced with the task of redeeming or carrying something for the larger collective . . . put another way, he is faced with the expiation of ancestral sin, and must become a bridge over which something ancient and undifferentiated and outcast may walk to find a welcome in consciousness. Collective fate here intrudes upon the life of the individual . . .

Food for thought indeed, when one considers the positioning of Pluto in the charts of both Prince Charles and Edward VIII. Edward's

Pluto was not only conjunct Neptune, but conjunct the IC; it was also square the Moon – the primary symbol of the feminine. Charles's Pluto is rising to the Ascendant and square the Sun. In Edward's case, he bore an albatross of a mother complex on his back and ultimately wreaked his revenge on his emotionally distant mother by failing to honour his heritage; in so doing he became the agency of a constitutional crisis that rocked the world. With the Sun (the primary male symbol in the horoscope) in aspect to Pluto, Charles has more of a father problem to contend with, which in turn has seemingly caused him to anguish over his patriarchal role as future King. While the transit of Pluto to Edward's Mercury (conjunct his descendant) in 1936 coincided with his abdication and later marriage, we have to wait until 1992 for Pluto to reach the conjunction of Charles's Sun to discover what fate Charles must encounter and in turn what influences the collective must contend with.

That Pluto is in some way symbolic of inherited conditions and that the 'seeds' of 'bondage' may lie several generations back is not the easiest of concepts to swallow until one starts to explore the possible reasons why. Pluto as a symbol of the unconscious finds sympathy with virtually all astrologers: indeed Pluto's discovery in 1930 synchronized with the rise of depth psychology. What is 'unconscious' can loosely be divided into three categories – that which is *personal* and derived from our unique experience into which is filtered a stream of parental complexes, family neuroses and our racial and religious ethos which in turn is fed from the great pool of the *collective* unconscious. To my mind, memory is closely linked to the unconscious – after all what is unconscious is technically what we have chosen to forget, or are unable to remember or interpret. And if our unconscious can be seen to connect with that infinite realm of the collective, why not our memory too? From a certain perspective they are one and the same thing. We carry imprints of our ancestors' past within our psyche and despite their invisibility, they still drive us in the form of compulsions, phobias and presentiments. While the psychologist accepts that the psyche is a storehouse for unresolved conflicts which may indeed have a hereditary origin in that such compulsions or neuroses run in families, I am suggesting, from a more esoteric standpoint, that some of these conflicts are the result of incoherent memories of past events – past events implying, not only personal past lives, but those of our ancestors. In this way, Pluto as the symbol of that which is buried, that which is unconscious also becomes the route through which we can discover our past and so account for our fate. Pluto represents that which binds us to our destiny both in the sense of our genetic inheritance and our parental debt and in the esoteric sense of the unbreakable bonds of our karma.

Pluto as the higher octave of Mercury takes Mercury's principle of communication and thought way beyond intellectual enquiry and the process of everyday thinking and decision-making into the realm of memory and the power of thought to create form. As Carl Jung himself pointed out, 'When the alchemist speaks of Mercurius, on the face of it he means quick-silver, but inwardly he means the world-creating spirit concealed or imprisoned in matter . . .'[23] It is not simply by chance that Mercury figures in myth, such as Toth (scribe to Osiris), Loki (the foster-brother of Odin) and Hermes, conveyer of the souls of the dead to Hades, are all linked to the Plutonic underworld realm. The two snakes on Mercury's staff represent Kundalini, the serpent that lies sleeping at the base of the spine which when aroused (through psycho-sexual processes) rushes up the spinal column to bring enlightenment.

These connecting principles between Mercury and Pluto serve to illustrate the point that the Mercurial world of thought leads to the Plutonic realm of the unconscious with its haunting 'shadows' and echoes of the past. In an altered state of consciousness, achieved through meditation or hypnotic regression for instance, the individual using Mercury, the communicator, as his guide can dip into these memory vaults and so bring into the light of consciousness issues that have lain at the root of many of his problems and complexes. (I shall be taking this theme further in Chapter 7). In this way Mercury, as the astrological principle of the logical mind, leads to Plutonic enlightenment.

Enlightenment is the essence of kundalini, and those who have experienced it are left, at the very least, with an improved functioning of their mental skills. However, in the main kundalini catapults the individual into a higher state of consciousness which, even after the intensity of the experience has dissipated, can subsequently be accessed at will. Certainly, kundalini is a transformative experience of the highest Plutonic calibre after which the individual is never the same. His super-conscious awareness brings new understanding and deeper meaning to life, and he may well develop extraordinary psychic and healing powers. Kenneth Ring in *Heading toward Omega*[24] draws many parallels between kundalini and the near death experience (which also subsequently transforms people's attitudes to life) and postulates that kundalini underlies the NDE, or that NDEs lead to an increased potential for kundalini. Clearly a NDE is the quintessential Plutonic event. Based on the assessment that eight million Americans (at least) have had near death experiences,[25] Ring has produced a highly thought-provoking hypothesis that the effect of so many transformed individuals on the planet will lead to a mass heightening of consciousness.

> May it be that NDEers – and others who have had similar awakenings – collectively represent an evolutionary thrust toward higher consciousness for humanity at large? Could it be that the NDE itself is an evolutionary mechanism that has the effect of jump-stepping individuals into the next stage of human development by unlocking spiritual potentials previously dormant?[26]

Pluto in Scorpio, as I have already discussed, portends awesome possibilities for humanity, but perhaps none so potentially transformative as the evolution of a higher level of being. Pluto symbolizes death and rebirth – a process we experience daily as the cells in our bodies die and are renewed and, on a larger scale, when something is eliminated from our lives necessitating new growth elsewhere. Pluto represents the forces in life over which we have least control, yet ultimately those through which we have the most to gain.

Pluto's position in the natal chart depicts the area of life where we experience our greatest sense of *force majeure*. Contacts between Pluto and the personal planets link ordinary human activities and processes, such as thinking, relating, acting and feeling with an ineffable force. Sometimes this force is experienced as a collective impetus and sometimes as an ineluctable role or task thrust upon reluctant shoulders. Transits of Pluto, like natal aspects, to the personal planets and angles[27] are often encountered as irrational compulsions toward certain actions or a powerful drive to fulfil some goal, or a series of events over which the individual has no conscious control nor any part in their inception.

The charts on pp. 104 and 105 belong to a husband and wife, 'Elvira' and 'Miguel'. Miguel was an Italian recording star with a fan club of adoring teenagers and mums. He met Elvira holidaying in Rome at a night club where he was appearing. It was a classic case of love at first sight, made all the more intense by the overwhelming differences in their backgrounds. Despite the largely unspoken but loudly felt objections from both families to the match, eventually Elvira and Miguel were married in 1980. A much wanted son, Andreas arrived some four years later. But by 1986, the marriage was in troubled waters. Unfortunately, almost as soon as they were married, Miguel's popularity began to wane until, by the arrival of Andreas, instead of working in front of the microphone he was stage-managing small time cabaret shows. Then in

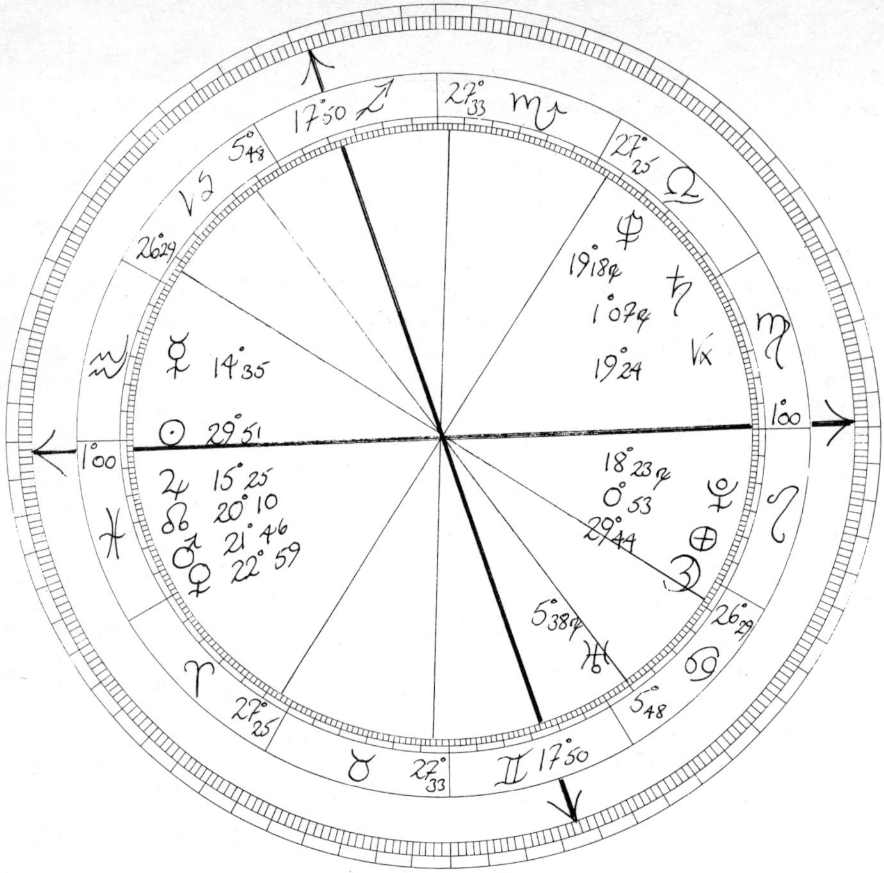

Elvira

February 19th 1951 : 7hrs 30 am. G.M.T. : 50°N22; 4°W10

Fig. 14

1986, the organization he was working for became involved in a massive fraud case and, before he knew where he was, Miguel had been made the scapegoat and thrown into gaol.

Poor Miguel had unwittingly fallen foul of the Mafia. His employers, in the pay of one of Italy's most powerful godfathers, had assumed that Miguel would have neither the courage, nor the funds to fight the case. However, almost immediately, Elvira and Miguel decided that his name must be cleared and they set about finding the best lawyer to

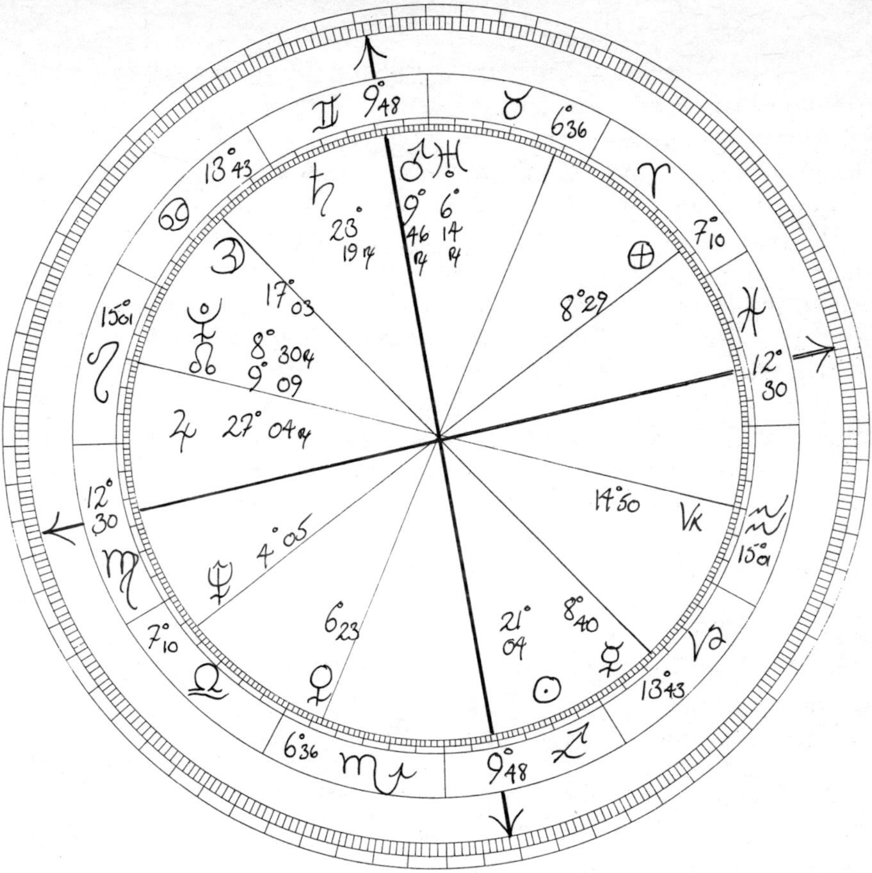

Miguel

December 13th 1943 : 23hrs. 55 L.T. : 39°N34; 2°E39

Fig. 15

defend him. As soon as the powers that be learned of Miguel's decision to defend the case, they began to pursue him mercilessly – threatening phone-calls, a bungled kidnap attempt on Andreas and finally a successful attempt to frame Miguel for the theft of some jewellery. The costs of Miguel's case soared out of all proportion until Elvira's parents could stand aside no longer. They mortgaged the family house to raise enough capital to bail Miguel and their daughter out of their difficulties. And for their reward the Mafia paid them a visit too –

ransacking their house and warning them if they interfered again they would be subject to even greater personal damage.

Almost four years later, the turmoil has not yet ceased. Miguel no longer faces a gaol sentence since the court proceedings were mysteriously dropped. But he is a broken man. Elvira has threatened to leave, but she feels 'something' compelling her to stay. They have been told by a highly regarded medium that they are the victims of a curse and feel they have no other recourse but to try to lift it through the appropriate channels. So far their efforts have been unrewarded.

The Mafia, fraud and black magic are Pluto's territory indeed. Yet at first glance, Elvira's and Miguel's charts do not look unduly dominated by this planet. (Of course, there are many other planetary factors relevant to this tale, but since Pluto is the theme we want to focus on, I shall tend to leave them in the background.) In both charts, Pluto is involved in a finger-of fate configuration[28] whereby one personal planet acts as the focus for two outer planets; in Miguel's case Mercury becomes the focus for Pluto and Uranus and, for Elvira, the Sun is aspected by Pluto and Saturn on the one hand, and Mars by Pluto and Neptune on the other. In Elvira's chart, Mercury, the ruler of her seventh house of relationships is in opposition to Pluto, while Miguel has Venus in Scorpio square to Pluto.

Miguel's father died when he was a child (a factor reflected by the Sun–Saturn opposition straddling the MC–IC axis) and he was brought up by a possessive, overprotective mother. Moon in Cancer – virtually unaspected – and a Venus–Pluto square speak volumes about female domination. In Miguel's case the passion of Venus–Pluto is expressed in a powerful sex drive, returned in equal force by Elvira's Mars–Pluto quincunx. Yet, despite his sexual prowess, he feels fundamentally robbed of his power and authority by women. Like many Latin men, while strutting around like a macho-peacock, he is reduced to the status of a little boy in the presence of his mother and his wife. Elvira for her part, has supported him valiantly out in the world with his battles with authority, but quietly castrated him in the intimacy of their married life. Consumed with the dark, savage power only a woman betrayed by her man in his failure to lead and dominate can be, she has retaliated by reducing him to an emotional and psychological eunuch.

Charm and good looks have been Miguel's passport to success in life and, although he was not actually guilty of fraud and embezzlement, he was guilty of naivëté and carelessness. I do not know what Miguel has done to deserve such a fate, but I do know that he has felt in the grip of forces totally beyond his control. As the women in his life continually robbed him of his authority, so in a greater sense Moira took away his power, stripped him bare and left him like a flailing Phoenix struggling under the weight of the ashes.

Elvira, with a similar Plutonic legacy, was well met by Miguel. Like many strong animus-dominated women, she had a proclivity for gentle and vulnerable men. On the face of it, she had all the ingredients of worldly success, intelligence, wit and an ability to charm and influence any one she wished. Yet, there was a fundamental flaw. She had never truly fulfilled her bright potential; it was only in comparison to her partners, who could never equal her radiance, that she seemed to be the one with all the right qualities. Either through an Aquarian perversity to carve her own path, even if it meant going against a favourable grain, or through an underlying lack of confidence in her ability to express her potential, she had repeatedly encountered men and situations that militated against her fulfilling any of her great expectations. Also, on the surface, Elvira's childhood seemed happy and 'ordinary' – a much-loved only daughter of two exemplary parents. Yet, underneath the aura of family unity and harmony, there lurked an indefinable darkness.

Elvira cannot relate to any such 'darkness'; she only remembers a happy childhood and has all the evidence before her that her parents are there when she needs them. And yet . . . it is apparent that Elvira feels she has to put a continent between her and her roots; unconsciously she wants to build a 'new' life away from the constraints of her past. But distance in physical miles cannot sever the psychological or karmic bonds that bind Elvira to her parents. And even if she could divorce herself from the problem with her mother and father, she has only to meet it in Miguel.

History repeats itself, patterns repeat themselves. Elvira, with her Sun and Mars, both the focus of outer planet-dominated fingers-of-fate, would appear to have her personal power and will thwarted by greater forces, whether this manifests as collective events, or authority figures. Since the Sun and Mars are the primary masculine symbols, it is likely that this frustration of power is wielded by or experienced through the men in her life. I suspect that this conflict over power and dominance is a theme familiar in her own parents' lives. Thus despite her father's winning ways and successful career, he is held firmly by the balls by his wife. And for very different reasons, Elvira's father has betrayed or failed her mother and she has exacted her quiet revenge. I would also hypothesize that this ménage à trois has its origins deep in a distant past and that, while there has been no incestuous relationship in fact between Elvira and her father, that the aura of longing and betrayal hangs heavily, but unconsciously, over them all. Even if her parents have avoided the hidden issues that gnaw away at their own relationship, they have been well and truly forced to confront it through their daughter's marital traumas. And they have paid a heavy price in terms of emotional pain and financial and material loss.

During the past four years there have been several major transits of the outer planets to both Miguel's and Elvira's charts. But, perhaps the most crucial, at least for Miguel, is the transit of Pluto to his Venus in Scorpio and his natal Pluto which has brought out the inherent potential of the natal square. Miguel has experienced the dark night of the soul; the power of the feminine has all but crushed him; dark forces may have been employed against him and, whether or not this is true, this is one of the only ways he can make any sense out of his demise. All this is symbolic of Pluto. That Pluto also represents the 'seeds' of 'bondage' may well indicate that Miguel is the precipitating agent in a drama that has its origins in another time. In this meting out of cosmic justice, all the *dramatis personae* must play their part although unlikely ever to know why these events have happened to them. Pluto's axe inevitably strikes without warning and from nowhere. But while the initial phase of the experience must involve simply coping with the deluge from the external world of events, ultimately the real route to resolution lies in the Plutonic realm of the unconscious and the past. And this route can only be traversed through dreams, revelations and psychotherapy.

The more mature we become, the more we tend to examine our lives and ponder the reasons *why*. Within astrology we can find many of the answers we seek. Whether we choose to meditate on the fate of nations, the cycles that reflect the ebbs and flows of progress and recession, or the vicissitudes of our own lives, we can find an accurate barometer in astrology. As we approach the end of a millennium, the fears of global catastrophe grow in equal proportion to the hopes for world peace, our scientific knowledge and our ability to self-destruct increases in direct ratio to our spiritual understanding and our capacity to transform our consciousness. The outer planets are the flagships in both our individual and collective journey toward the apocalypse – revelation or ruin, death and rebirth, reincarnation and karma.

NOTES

1. The Sun, Moon, Mercury, Venus and Mars.
2. Liz Greene, *Saturn: A new look at an old devil* (Samuel Weiser, 1976)
3. Jeanne Avery, *Astrology and Your Past Lives* (Simon & Schuster, 1987)
4. Saturn spends approximately two and a half years in each sign of the zodiac, thus its placing in a sign alone cannot be the sole justification of a personal theme. In my case, Saturn is conjunct my Sun-ruler, Mars, in Cancer.

5. Transiting Saturn square natal Mars and Saturn.
6. See Chapter 4, pp. 64–5.
7. Guenther Wachsmuth, a collaborator of Rudolph Steiner, who wrote several volumes of work related to spiritual science and modern natural science.
8. Willi Sucher continued the work of Rudolph Steiner in Astrosophy (Star Wisdom). He was the originator of the *Star Journal* (1965–73), which was later taken over by Robert Powell as the *Mercury Star Journal* (1975–81).
9. Liz Greene, from a lecture for the Wrekin Trust in April 1980 published in *The Outer Planets and Their Cycles* by Liz Greene (CRCS, 1983)
10. In *Romancing the Stars* (Aquarian Press, 1988) I suggest that Merlin, the legendary magician and mentor of King Arthur, is an Aquarian – Uranian archetype.
11. The hard aspects in astrology are primarily the conjunction 0°, the square 90°, the opposition 180°, and secondarily, the quincunx 150°, the semi-square 45°, and the sesquiquadrate 135°.
12. Liz Greene, *The Outer Planets and Their Cycles* (CRCS, 1983)
13. In Edward's chart Uranus is the most elevated planet and conjunct the Nonagesimal (the equal house 10th house cusp), thus the revolutionary properties of Uranus became a dominant factor in his life. Also, Saturn is the only other planet above the horizon, and although strongly significant is, in this case, less powerful than Uranus. Had Saturn been conjunct the Nonagesimal, perhaps Edward would have considered his duties and obligations to the monarchy more important than his personal happiness.
14. John Dale, author of *The Prince and the Paranormal* in conversation with Brenda Marsh for *Time Life*.
15. The Imum Coeli, the nadir of the chart and the point directly opposite the Midheaven. In quadrant house systems, the IC marks the beginning of the 4th house cusp and therefore reflects the nature of the family, roots, childhood and one of the parents – usually father.
16. The planet nearest the Midheaven in a chart.
17. The conjunction of Jupiter and Uranus in Charles' 8th harmonic chart reinforces the potential of the powerful natal Jupiter–Uranus opposition. The natal opposition also falls at 29° of the mutables and was triggered in 1988 when Charles came close to death in a skiing accident at Klosters. In Charles' case, his Mars in Sagittarius is linked to this opposition natally, so bringing the reckless, exuberant and also brilliant quality of this combination into the personal sphere.
18. There are three charts commonly in use for Great Britain. The first, and the most often referred to by astrologers is the one erected for the Coronation of William I in 1066 in Westminster at noon:
☉9°♑55′; ☽29°♅08′; ☿16°♑39′ ♀29°♑53′; ♂8°♒28′; ♃7°♍57; ♄16°♍50′ ♅28°♐27′ ♆22°♉12; ☿3°52′; ☊19°♍16′ M.C.8°♑42′; Asc.22°♈17

The Union of England and Scotland: 1 May 1707, London 0 hrs, 0 mins:
☉20°♉29; ☽28°♍10′; ☿11°♉04′; ♀6°♈49′; ♂20°♒01′; ♃21°♌51′; ♄5°♊06′ ♅9°♌24; ♆22°♈06′; ♇23°♌00; ☊0000 M.C.21°♏0000; Asc.16°♑
The Act for the Union of Great Britain and Ireland:
1 January, 1801, Greenwich 0hr. 0 mins:
☉10°♑11′; ☽19°♋29′; ☿17°♐36′; ♀16°♒32′; ♂11°♉47′; ♃1°♌58′; ♄23°♌17 ♅2°♎16′; ♆18°♏43′; ♇5°♓00′; ☊0000 M.C.9°♋0000; Asc.7°♎10

19. Aristotle Onassis – Moon square Pluto
Tina Niarchos – Moon square Pluto. Venus conjunct Pluto
Alexander Onassis – Moon opposition Pluto
Christina Onassis – Moon opposition Pluto. Sun sextile Pluto
Jackie Kennedy – Moon square Pluto
There is some confusion over the exact date of Ari's birth. I took the one recorded in Peter Evans' biography of Onassis, *Ari* (Jonathan Cape, 1986). He states 'the morning of January 20 1900', Smyrna (38°n25: 27°e08). I thought a sunrise birth suited Onassis both in temperament and appearance, thus a GMT time of 5°45′ am yields an Ascendant of 4°08′ and a Midheaven of 24°53′. These axes work will with all the synastry: Christina (11 December 1950, New York, NY 15 hrs.00 EST) – Ascendant–Descendant 25 49 Taurus–Scorpio and MC–IC axis 3°42′ Aquarius–Leo; Tina (19 Mar 1929, no time of birth) – Venus 5°50′ Taurus; Alexander (30April 1948 New York, NY 05,00 am EST) MC–IC axis 6°54′ Aquarius–Leo, Moon 1°52′ Aquarius; Jackie Onassis (28 July 1929, Southampton, NY 14hrs 30 EDT) MC–IC axis 28°55′ Leo–Aquarius, Sun 5°10′ Leo. Ari's Pluto at 14°57 Gemini forms major contacts with his family's charts, most specifically, Jackie whose Mars falls at 14°50 Virgo.
20. See Chapter 2, p. 26.
21. Liz Greene, *The Astrology of Fate* (Mandala–Unwin, 1985)
22. Ibid.
23. C. G. Jung, *Psychology and Alchemy*, Collected Works, Vol. 12 (Routledge & Kegan Paul, 1953)
24. Kenneth Ring, *Heading toward Omega* (Quill, 1985)
25. In *Heading toward Omega* Ring reports that a Gallup Poll conducted in America estimated that approximately 35 per cent of those who have come close to death undergo an NDE.
26. *Heading toward Omega.*
27. The Ascendant–Descendant axis and the MC–IC axis.
28. A finger-of fate, or a yod, is a configuration formed by one planet in quincunx to two others that are in sextile. As the name implies, a theme of fate characterizes this configuration; it is as though the disharmony generated between the one planet in its aspects to the other two can find a resolution through the combined positive 'energy' of the sextile.

6
Past Lives Revisited

The tomb is not a blind alley; it is a thoroughfare. It closes on the twilight. It opens on the dawn.'

Victor Hugo

'Where are you?'

'It's dark . . . very dark. I'm frightened . . .'

'Are you alone? Why are you frightened?'

'I've done nothing wrong . . . they're going to burn me. I don't want to die. I'm frightened.'

'Why are they going to burn you?'

'They say I'm a witch. But I'm not. I've done nothing wrong!'

'Where do you live?'

'In the village.'

'What's the name of the village?'

'Maresfield. It's not nice. Nobody likes me.'

'What's your name?'

'Mary . . . Jowett. I DON'T WANT TO DIE!'

The wracking sobs and the thick country dialect make the impact of these statements chillingly real. And, indeed, it is all too real for Mary Jowett as she lies shivering on the floor of a dark and acrid smelling prison in 16th-century Sussex. However, this is no actor rehearsing her lines, but, middle-aged staff-nurse Jane Kirby reliving a traumatic scene in her past life. And, a far cry from a 16th-century gaol, Mary is comfortably seated in a well-padded arm chair in the drawing room of an English country house; by her side is a tape-recorder, and gently leading her into the recesses of her far memory is psychotherapist, Dr Michael Hopwood.

The technique of hypnotic regression – whereby an individual is enabled to reach an altered state of consciousness in which he can apparently relive a past life – has become an increasingly popular method of exploring reincarnation. This method certainly has its limitations and its critics, but, as I will show later, it also has tremendous therapeutic value. For the moment, however, hypnotic regression must remain on one side.

Since 1417, on the death of great reformer and avatar of Buddha,

Tsong-kha-pa, the choice of each Dalai Lama has depended on reincarnation. When each Dalai Lama dies, a search is mounted for his successor who, as the reincarnation of previous Dalai Lama, embodies Chenrezi, the Buddhist god of grace. The present Dalai Lama, Tenzin Gyatso, was found after an extensive search some four years after the death of the thirteenth Dalai Lama.[1]

Some time before his death in 1933, the thirteenth Dalai Lama had given intimations regarding the manner of his rebirth. After his death, the body sat in state in the Potola in the traditional Buddha posture, looking toward the south. One morning it was noticed that his head was turned to the east. The State Oracle was straightway consulted, and while in his trance the monk oracle threw a white scarf in the direction of the rising sun . . . But for two years nothing more definite was indicated. Then the regent went on a pilgrimage to a famous lake (Chos Khorgyal) to ask for counsel. When the regent, after long prayers, came to the water and looked in its mirror, he had a vision of a three-storied monastery with golden roofs, near which stood a little Chinese peasant house with carved Gables . . . Search groups set out to explore in the year 1937 . . . Following the signs, they journeyed eastward in quest of the Holy Child . . . until they reached the district of Amdo in the Chinese province of Chingnai. In this region there are many monasteries, as the great reformer Tsong Kapa [Tsong-kha-pa] was born there . . . At last after long wanderings they encountered a three-storied monastery with golden roofs . . . they remembered the regent's vision, and then their eyes fell on the cottage with carved gables. Full of excitement, they dressed themselves in the clothes of their servants . . . The servants, dressed in the garments of their masters, were taken to the best room, while the disguised monks went into the kitchen, where it was likely they would find the children of the house. As soon as they entered the house, they felt sure they would find the Holy Child in it, and they waited tensely to see what would happen. And, sure enough, a two-year-old boy came running to meet them and seized the skirts of the lama, who wore around his neck the rosary of the thirteenth Dalai Lama. Unabashed, the child cried, 'Sera Lama, Sera Lama!' It was already a matter for wonder that the infant recognised a lama in the garb of a servant and that he said he came from the Cloister of Sera, which was the case. Then the boy grasped the rosary and tugged at it till the lama gave it to him; thereupon he hung it around his own neck. The noble searchers found it hard not to throw themselves on the ground before the child, as they no longer had any doubt. They had found the Incarnation.[2]

Though their initial meeting with the two-year-old Gyatso appeared to confirm all their hopes, the monks went on to set him many more tests before they felt they had enough proof that he was indeed the reincarnation of Chenrezi; some of these tests involved the identification of objects belonging to the thirteenth Dalai Lama which he was able to successfully recognize. Gyatso also bore certain physical features – strange shaped moles and large ears – considered to be essential marks of an Incarnation of Chenrezi. By the late summer of 1939, some two years after Gyatso's discovery and six years after the death of the thirteenth Dalai Lama, Gyatso and his parents were informed that he was indeed the Tibetan god-king.

The discovery of the present Dalai Lama and the establishing of his 'credentials' is no myth but a matter of historical fact. The Tibetan monks took their task of finding their spiritual leader's successor with the utmost seriousness with no thought of the time or cost involved. Indeed, in order to gain permission to leave China with Gyatso, the searchers had to pay the provincial governor 300,000 Chinese yuan (about $300,000). And while we only have the Tibetan monks' word for it that their investigations were carried out in as objective manner as possible – with no hint of a self-fulfilling prophecy to help draw their conclusions, nor that the parents did not collude with Gyatso to ensure that he became the Dalai Lama – the evidence for reincarnation here seems impressive to say the least.

Of course, the Dalai Lama could be said to be a special case. After all he is a supremely important spiritual leader, and of a faith that has reincarnation as its basic tenet. But he is not the only individual to remember aspects of a past life.

In the 1920s a British newspaper, *The Courier*, asked its readers to send in any of their experiences related to reincarnation. Somewhat to its surprise, the newspaper was inundated with stories from people who had had dreams or waking visions of past lives, or those who simply remembered being someone else. At this time, the academic world had little or no interest in such reincarnation stories. Then in 1979 a professor of English and Humanities at the New School for Social Research in New York, Frederick Lenz, published a book on spontaneous past life memories. For his research he interviewed over a hundred individuals who claimed to have recalled a previous life. Lenz found, like *The Courier*, that the cases tended to group themselves into three categories, those who had strong dreams about a past life, those who had memories of a past life and, most interesting of all, those who had waking visions of a previous life. In this latter category, the individuals would describe the extraordinary phenomena of their environment dissolving and their being transported to some other time and place.

It happened when I was just seventeen. I was at home babysitting for my little sister. My parents had gone out to celebrate their wedding anniversary. I was

> in the kitchen cooking dinner when I heard a loud ringing sound in my head.[4] It got louder and louder until I was very frightened. The sound did not come from outside me, but from within. The room began to shift and fade, and I thought I was going to pass out. The next thing I remember, I was standing on a cliff overlooking the sea. I was watching the waves roll in and break on the rocks far below me. I heard the pounding surf and smelled the salt air. I turned around and began to walk through a field that was behind me. The sun was out and I felt warm and happy. I was returning to my flock of sheep that I had left up at the pasture. As I walked I sang a favourite song until I reached the crest of the hill. I thought about many Greek towns that I would like to one day visit. I sat down near the sheep and, all alone, rocked back and forth singing. The vision ended, and I was back in my kitchen.
>
> I didn't know what to make of what happened to me, and I figured that I had had some kind of vivid daydream. However, several years later when I was on vacation from college, I went to Europe, and one of the countries I visited was Greece. I was very much attracted to some of the small coastal cities. One day while motoring with friends we came to a stretch of road that overlooked the sea. I was filled with a number of conflicting emotions, but one thing was clear: I wanted to get out of the car. I asked my friends to stop for a minute; they pulled over to the side of the road overlooking the sea and looked down. As I did I saw the exact scene I had seen several years before in my vision in the kitchen. I turned around and walked away from the car and my friends. I walked with a purpose, as if I knew the way. I followed a path through a field and began to ascend an embankment. When I reached the top and looked around, I recognised the spot where I had been with the sheep in my vision. It was exactly as I had remembered it. I was filled with memories of places and scenes, and I knew I had returned 'home' again. Although it made no sense, I felt that I had lived there in another time. I returned to my friends in the car and explained my sensation to them. They didn't seem to understand what I was saying, and I finally gave up trying to explain to them.[5]

This transportation to another time and place appears to be a sort of extended *déjà-vu* – where the individual senses (usually very fleetingly) that a current activity or event has happened before. *Déjà-vu* is a common enough experience to have warranted some sort of scientific explanation: reasons that range from the psychological effect of a missed heart beat, to a momentary lapse between the conscious and unconscious recognition of an outer event. Clearly, Lenz's subject was subjected to something far more detailed and profound than the usual *déjà-vu* occurrence, and, of course, there was the added dimension that the experience could be validated by the girl herself when she located the precise area some years later. Lenz himself did not attempt to follow up any of the potentially verifiable past life material provided by his subjects. He took the experiences at face value. Thus, they could only be said to be valid in the psychological sense in that the individuals themselves were deeply affected by their experience and convinced that they had 'relived' a scene from a past life. Although Lenz's work provided no scientific proof of reincarnation it left the field wide open for others to follow.

D. Scott Rogo, American researcher and writer in parapsychology, was one of those who became intrigued by Lenz's work. In 1981 he set about collecting his own sample of reincarnation cases.[6] Like Lenz, he found the experiences grouped themselves into three types, and although there were some distinctly questionable cases, he decided to follow up those of 'twenty highly intelligent and literary people' who gave 'accounts of great clarity'.[7] Rogo was especially fascinated by the waking vision type of past life recall which he considered might well owe its origins to some kind of minor seizure in the temporal lobe. But despite scouring the medical literature for examples of temporal lobe epilepsy, temporal lobe seizures and temporal lobe hallucinations, he could find nothing to match the lucidity and intensity of the experiences described by his own subjects and those of Lenz.

From his study, admittedly of only twenty cases, Rogo was impressed with the way his subjects were completely convinced about reincarnation after their experience, despite the majority having held no such views prior to their past life recall. Also, Rogo was able to corroborate several pieces of information supplied by his subjects from their reincarnation experience. One woman, for instance, had had a recurrent dream since childhood where she was crossing a precarious swaying bridge high above an expanse of water. In her dreams, she was never able to reach the other side of the bridge. Years later, as an adult, she came across an article in *Life* magazine about a bridge over New York's East River that precisely matched the one in her dreams. The bridge, which predated the Brooklyn Bridge, had been of such a treacherous makeshift nature that more than one individual had fallen to his death from it. Rogo's subject believed that she was indeed one of those who had fallen from the bridge, since from the moment when she discovered its existence and recognized it as 'hers' the dream never occurred again. This experience of 'laying the ghost' is one of the most common and important features of past life recalls and, as I shall cover later, has the same therapeutic effect as hypnotic regression.

However, as Rogo readily admits himself, these spontaneous past life recalls although impressive enough to make him 're-evaluate my views on reincarnation . . . are brief and ephemeral phenomena, and a sceptic could dismiss them as hallucinations or delusions . . . [his and

Lenz's work] should only be viewed within the larger context of ongoing research into the reincarnation question.'[8]

Genuine scientific proof of reincarnation is hard to come by, if only because few scientists are prepared to put their name and their university funding behind such apparently spurious research. Fortunately a Canadian, Dr Ian Stevenson, one time chairman of the Department of Psychiatry and Neurology at the University of Virginia and chief psychiatrist of the university hospital was prepared to do just that. In 1960 the American Society for Psychical Research announced a prize in honour of William James for the best essay on parapsychology. Ian Stevenson won it with a lengthy disquisition, 'Evidence For Survival From Claimed Memory Of Former Incarnations'. Stevenson not only drew his material from history, literature and parapsychological works, but from tales of travellers to the East who told of children who could remember previous lives.

Soon after the publication of this essay, Stevenson began his own search for new cases among children who remembered a previous existence. His quest took him to several countries where reincarnation was a widely accepted belief and eventually he began publishing specific case studies from India, Thailand, Turkey, Lebanon and Alaska (the Tlingit Indians).

In a methodical and pragmatic way, Stevenson took each case, investigated it fully and endeavoured to determine whether or not there was any real evidence that the child in question could only have come by the information about another life through actually living that life. In 1966 he published his first book of case studies, *Twenty Cases Suggestive of Reincarnation*. All the examples he chose to include were fascinating and well documented, with detailed lists of each subject's statements – when they were made, to whom and how veracious. The case of Ravi Shankar is typical.

In the early 1950s a two-and-a-half-year-old Indian boy, Ravi Shankar, began asking his parents for toys that he claimed were in a house in which he had lived before. By the time he was six, he was telling his school teacher that in a previous life he had been murdered by two relatives who wished to prevent him from inheriting his father's barber's business. Sporadically Ravi gave intimate details about his former life, naming himself as Munna, the son of Jageshwar, a barber of the Chhipatti District; he described how he had been beheaded by a barber called Jawahar and a washerman called Chaturi; he told of where he had been murdered and that he had lived in the city of Kanauj near Kanpur. Ravi also provided many other details about his life as Munna and he was able to recognize spontaneously relatives and items belonging to his previous life. Most impressive of all, Ravi had a strange birthmark on his neck – a transverse slash some two inches long and between an eighth and a quarter inch thick that resembled the jagged scar of a long knife wound.

As it happened, six months before Ravi was born, on 19 January 1951, a six-year-old boy, Ashok Kumar, commonly known as Munna and the son of Sri Jageshwar Prasad (a barber of the Chhipatti District of Kanauj) had been brutally murdered – his head severed by a razor or a knife. The suspects were two neighbours, a barber (Jawahar) and a washerman (Chaturi). Although the men were both arrested – and Chaturi unofficially confessed to the crime – they were never brought to justice since there were no witnesses.

News of Ravi's memories of a previous life and brutal death travelled the half mile distance from his home in one district of Kanauj to his former father, Jageshwar in Chhipatti; and eventually when Ravi was four years old a meeting was arranged between them. Ravi's present father was reluctant to proceed with the affair and had periodically beaten Ravi to stop him talking about his previous life since he feared his son would want to return to his former parents. Despite the small distance between the two families, they were barely acquainted with each other although news of Munna's murder had reached Ravi's family. Jageshwar was so convinced of Ravi's report about Munna's death that he wanted to renew the legal charges against the alleged murderers. But whether through the time lapse or because the courts would not recognize the testimony of the reborn Munna, this never transpired.

After initially corresponding with an Indian professor about Ravi's case, in 1964 Stevenson visited the families concerned himself. In his book, Stevenson points out some of the discrepancies of the case – most notably that according to some witnesses Ravi had been taken by his father to the home of Jageshwar well before the 'first official' meeting (although this was strongly denied by Jageshwar himself and Ravi's mother and older brother). However, overall, the cases appears to stand out as significant evidence of reincarnation.

In his most recent book, *Children Who Remember Previous Lives*, Stevenson has endeavoured to silence some of his critics by documenting more cases from the Western world, where translation problems are reduced and the information easier to corroborate. Once again his objectivity and attention to detail are much in evidence. The case of Michael Wright is particularly intriguing.

In September 1978 a colleague of Stevenson's at the University of

Virginia was contacted by a distraught Mrs Catherine Wright. As the mother of a three-year-old boy, Michael, she had been disconcerted to say the least when he began to tell her in great detail of an accident in which he had died. 'A friend and I were in a car, and the car went off the road, rolled over and over. The door came open, and I fell out and was killed.' After this revelation, Michael went on to deliver precise names, including his own, Walter Miller, Walter's sister, Carole and the surname and nickname of the other person in the accident, Henry Sullivan. What had disturbed Catherine Wright so greatly was that some eleven years previously, her then boyfriend, Walter Miller had been killed in a car crash. Driving home, somewhat drunk, from a party, with his passenger, Henry Sullivan, Walter had apparently fallen asleep at the wheel and crashed the car. Henry emerged unscathed from the accident, but Walter died instantly from a broken neck.

Although Catherine and Walter had been immensely close in 1968, a year after his death, she had married Frederick Wright. The following year, Catherine had a dream in which Walter informed her that he was not dead and that he would 'come back, and draw pictures for her again', Catherine was affected enough by the dream to conclude that it was an announcement of Walter's impending return to earth.[9] Since Walter's sister, Carole was pregnant at the time, Catherine naturally assumed that the baby would be 'Walter'. But nothing had prepared her for the trauma of discovering that her own son appeared to have become the reincarnation of her previous boyfriend, Walter.

Stevenson makes the point that, although Catherine herself was a firm believer in reincarnation (which could well prejudice the case), in the small town in Texas where she lived such a belief was in no way commonly held. And while Catherine herself might have welcomed proof of reincarnation, she was instead traumatized by the fear that Walter's 'presence' would alienate her much loved husband. He sums up the case in *Children Who Remember Previous Lives*:

> I am far from satisfied with my understanding of the case, but I have thought it worth presenting because it illustrates features found in many American cases of the reincarnation type and in some cases of other countries. Its weaknesses lie mainly in the somewhat overeager attitude of Michael's mother toward her son's remarks and in our inability . . . to verify any of Michael's statements independently with Walter Miller's family or friends.

Stevenson goes on to explain that despite these weaknesses he allowed the counter-arguments supporting the theory of reincarnation greater weight, particularly because the case 'developed in a subculture that I think we can fairly describe as hostile to the idea of reincarnation' and because the Wright family had nothing to gain from the situation.

> . . . one could easily imagine that Mrs Wright thought up the case to torment her husband or that Michael conceived it as a subtle torture for his parents. Maybe they did, but I do not believe it. We should not ascribe a motive for which we have no independent evidence, unless we can point to some gain from its expression. I fail to see that anyone profited from Michael's statements about the life of his mother's boyfriend. And the frantic nature of her first telephone call to us seemed evidence enough that she had no control whatever – at that time – over the psychological forces released in the case.

I have quoted Stevenson at length so that readers can judge for themselves the objective approach he holds to his case material. Others have not been so impressed – including some reputable and highly qualified writers and researchers.

In a conference on reincarnation held by the Wrekin Trust in November 1988 two of the speakers, Scott Rogo and Ian Wilson, voiced serious reservations about the procedures followed and conclusions drawn by Stevenson; both have discussed the flaws in his work in some of their books.[10]

Rogo suggested that one of the main problems with Stevenson's work is that, in most of the case studies, by the time Stevenson had begun his investigations the child's family had already contacted the other family, giving plenty of opportunity for collusion. Also in almost all cases the information is hearsay. Rogo's access to much of Stevenson's unpublished material also led him to believe that Stevenson had had a monumental task sifting the wheat from the chaff of hundreds of conflicting statements and unreliable testimonies, thereby reducing the chances of truly authentic data. Relying on translators and the lack of legal documentation or written records (like accurate dates of birth or significant events) were also a stumbling block to authenticity. Rogo also mentions some anomalous cases of Stevenson's where, for instance, two children each simultaneously claimed to be a reincarnation of the same person, and another instance where the individual who was claimed to be reincarnated was still alive! Perhaps most seriously of all, Rogo reveals that two of Stevenson's ex-research assistants also appear to question the accuracy of his findings. Champ Ranson, a lawyer, used to scrutinizing human evidence, has maintained that every one of Stevenson's cases is flawed because of potential leakage of information to the child. Another research assistant, David Reed Barker, investigated a 'couple of dozen' cases of the reincarnation type in India in collaboration with an Indian psychologist, Dr Sopwink Pasrika, and failed to find *any* cases that were evidential.

Ian Wilson also questions the reliability of Stevenson's investigators. For instance, the late Francis Story, a confirmed Buddhist with no Asian languages to his credit, seemed to have trouble over being consistent with checkable facts – he allowed one Indian child two different dates of birth in two books.[11] Another, Dr Jamuna Prasad, was an ardent Hindu with a special interest in promoting Hindu beliefs in reincarnation. Neither investigator, to Wilson's mind, was likely to have an objective approach to reincarnation.

In both his books concerning reincarnation, *All in the Mind* and *The After Death Experience*, Wilson has raised the pertinent issue of the socio-economic factor. In two-thirds of Stevenson's Indian and Sri Lankan cases the past-life individual was either far wealthier or from a higher social background than the child claimant. Thus, Wilson maintains, the potential of gain from the claimant family cannot be ruled out – after all, a wealthy family would feel obliged to help one of their own if he had fallen on hard times! Wilson also comments that Stevenson has never published any photographs of the birthmarks which number among his most impressive cases. There is also the annoying factor of the inconsistencies over the lapse of time between an individual dying and being reborn: in some cases there is a gap of several years, and in others a matter of mere months. Wilson argues: 'One of the first difficulties for any overall validity of Stevenson's material is the absence among his published cases of any discernible rules that might govern the hypothetical existence of reincarnation.' Amassing research for his book investigating past-life claims and in the process establishing for himself Stevenson's 'impeccable scientific rigour', Wilson travelled to the University of Virginia to interview him. He came away with a 'feeling of unease'[12] and, I suspect, a flea in his ear.

To my mind, Stevenson has responded admirably to his critics in his most recent book.[13] (For a more detailed appraisal of Stevenson's responses, interested readers can turn to pp. 130–131.) Unless we assume that he has lost his mind or his principles and has deliberately fudged his results, I think we can say that he has produced some valuable – if not incontravertible – evidence for reincarnation. However, the main reservations held by Rogo and Wilson on Stevenson's findings and procedures is that there are many more possible explanations than reincarnation for the ability to apparently recall a past life – reasons that I shall be exploring later in this chapter.

Another scientist with an interest in reincarnation was Arthur Guirdham, an English psychiatrist and former senior consultant in psychiatry to the Bath clinical area. In May 1962 a housewife in her early thirties ('Mrs Smith') was referred to Guirdham by a local GP. Mrs Smith was suffering from terrifying recurrent nightmares that had begun when she had almost died from peritonitis in her early teens. Remarkably, the nightmares immediately ceased upon her first visit to Guirdham although she continued to consult him for a considerable time afterwards. Over the course of a four-year period, which involved much correspondence as well as many consultations, Mrs Smith unfolded a fabulous story about a past life as a Cathar in 13th-century France. Guirdham, who had no previous belief in reincarnation, gradually became more and more convinced that this was the only possible explanation for Mrs Smith's memories. The most extraordinary factor about Mrs Smith's memories of her past life, was that they struck more than just a chord with Dr Guirdham himself. As the months went by, it gradually dawned on them both that Guirdham was the reincarnation of her lover, Roger-Isarn de Fanjeaux. Absurd as this might sound, the evidence presented by Guirdham in *The Cathars and Reincarnation* is extremely impressive. When researched by one of the leading authorities on the period, Professor Duvernoy, previously unknown details about the life and times of the Cathars turned out to be true, and, indeed, the fact that Mrs Smith's nightmares were 'laid to rest' through her 'reunion' with Guirdham was, if nothing else, a testament to the psychological validity of the past life. Had Guirdham halted there or, as Ian Wilson pointed out 'even better, accompanied his popular account of the affair with an in-depth psychiatric study of the case . . . [it might have been] possible for his claims to be treated with due seriousness.' However, Guirdham was to publish two further books on the subject which stretched credibility to the limit. In *We Are One Another* and *The Lake And The Castle*, Guirdham describes how, by all manner of strange synchronicities, he met up with several other individuals who had been together with him in previous periods of history, and while the accounts are certainly fascinating and thought-provoking, they cannot be more than suggestive. Not that Guirdham was unscientific in his approach. Colin Wilson maintains that Guirdham has shown him correspondence between himself and various scholars over the 'Smith' material, which in order to avoid confusing his readers, he had felt compelled to leave out of his book.[14] Wilson went on to comment, 'I have no reason to believe he is a Svengali who can persuade his patients to cooperate in his fantasies about previous lives, or that his books are inventions written to gain notoriety. Clearly, he believes every word in them. Moreover, he is far too intelligent to allow his fantasy to run away with him. Ian Wilson points out that if Guirdham had stopped after recounting the "Mrs Smith" case . . . his claims would probably have met with serious attention. He knows as well as anyone that this "group reincarnation" and all the previous lives as Celts and Romans . . . make his story totally unacceptable to most readers. Presumably he would protest, like Sir William Crookes: "I didn't say it was possible – I said it was true."'[15]

If the work of a valued and respected psychiatrist can be treated with scepticism and, like Stevenson's investigative work, come under critical fire, evidence of reincarnation gained through hypnotic regression suffers from even greater bombardment.

In June of 1985 London Weekend Television transmitted a documentary called *Reincarnation* – indeed, the company had such confidence in its audience appeal that it put out the programme between the hours of 11.30pm and 1.00am! The same documentary transmitted in Holland, however, went out at prime time, and was followed up by radio programmes which had the general public jamming the telephone lines. The documentary was riveting. An Australian psychologist and hypnotherapist, Peter Ramster, had selected four women from 1,000 of his subjects to relive scenes from a past life. Then, accompanied by a camera crew, he took them to the other side of the world to visit the location of those past lives. The four women, all second- or third-generation Australians, had never been to their 'past life' locations in Europe; indeed one, Gwen Macdonald, had spent her entire life in New South Wales.

In the first part of the documentary, each woman was filmed being hypnotized. Then, with voice and dialect changes and altered facial expressions, the subjects recounted their experiences in another time and place. Jenny Green's experience was particularly evocative and moving. She was a young Jewish girl at the time of the Nazi holocaust. She had been concealed, somewhat in the style of Anne Frank, behind a false wall in her home. There, in a tiny space filled with her own excrement, half mad from loneliness, starvation and the trauma of her plight, she died a slow and agonizing death. In her last moments, tears streaming down her cheeks, she suddenly 'saw' her father opening his arms to welcome her. It's an experience that affects me every time I summon up the memory.[16]

Gwen Macdonald, on the other hand, was a cheerful peasant living in Somerset, England some four centuries ago. In her West country brogue, she mentioned several words no longer in the English language – most of which an etymologist was later able to authenticate. We watched her being taken to the location she had described and in a hypnotic state, try to get her bearings. After many stops and starts, she found a familiar bend in the river and hurried to locate her home. Her dismay at not finding her cottage (it had been demolished many years ago) was palpable. But with determination, she set off once again to find the cottage of a friend across the field. Fortunately, this cottage was there, but its only residents in 1984 were some prize pigs. Gwen was adamant it was the right cottage, and said that her friend had done a great wrong by stealing one of the flag stones from Glastonbury Abbey and laying it on the floor of his home. Somewhat bemused, the farmer agreed to remove his pigs and clean out the sty. There after two days hard labour, four hundred years' muck had been removed from the floor to reveal a flagstone from Glastonbury Abbey. Gwen, a third-generation Australian, otherwise not interested in or in any way knowledgeable about 17th-century England, had never set foot out of New South Wales.

Peter Ramster's work is some of the most impressive to date. This particular documentary set out to test reincarnation under the most stringent conditions. On the visits to Europe, each woman was accompanied by independent witnesses, all academics, with no connection to reincarnation or the paranormal. To ensure the authenticity of the project, the producers shot 50,000 feet of film (some 23 hours of viewing time); every film sequence was dated and filed for cross referencing; the film crew and the independent observers were thoroughly checked to ensure there was no collusion and the master negative was securely locked away in a Sydney laboratory.

Peter Ramster was not the first hypnotherapist to be exposed to such media interest, but he is the first to have emerged almost unscathed from a blistering attack on his hypnotically derived evidence of past lives. Arnall Bloxam, on the other hand, following in the footsteps of Morey Bernstein and the infamous Bridey Murphy saga[17] did not fare so well.

In December 1976 BBC television transmitted a programme called *The Bloxam Tapes* in which a Cardiff hypnotherapist, Arnall Bloxam, regressed some of his patients to past lives. One of his best subjects, was a 30–year-old housewife, 'Jane Evans'. In front of the cameras, Jane returned to a life in Roman Eboracum (York) where she was the wife of a tutor to the family of a Roman legate, Constantius. The details Jane gave were almost awe-inspiring, especially the matter-of-fact way she dealt with quite complex arrangements pertaining to an historically documented political deal involving the emperors Maximian and Diocletian. Also impressive was the way complicated Latin names tripped off her tongue. It seemed at the time, here was genuine proof of reincarnation. But . . . Some time later a writer-researcher, Melvin Harris, with a propensity for scouring secondhand book shops, came across an historical novel by Louis de Wohl called *The Living Wood*, written in 1947. *The Living Wood* contained scenes described almost verbatim by Jane Evans, plus all the names – and all the mistakes. Livonia had talked about Verulam (St Albans) instead of Verulamium. So did Louis de Wohl. Sadly, all the other past lives included in the programme and subsequently in the book, *More Lives than One?*[18] also proved to be deeply flawed.

If so many learned, highly qualified individuals can be apparently led up the reincarnational garden path, one might question the point of employing such methods as hypnotic regression to investigate reincarnation. But before we look into this we need to establish precisely what people are tuning into if it is not their past lives. Once deliberate fraud is removed as a motive for claims of the reincarnation type, how does this phenomenon occur? Where does the information come from?

One of the most popular theories about the origin of the information is *cryptomnesia*, or as Stevenson puts it, the illusion of memories. Quite simply, the brain is capable of recording everything we have seen, heard or experienced, everything we have ever read or listened to in complete detail from the moment of birth – if not in the womb. Thus in a deep trance access to such memories is made possible. Wilson argues that this is patently the factor at work in Jane Evans's case, and although she may not consciously recall having read *The Living Wood*, nor indeed having had access to any of the other sources of her information for her other lives, at some point in her present life, this she most certainly must have done.[19] I would comment that while Wilson puts up a splendid argument for cryptomnesia in Jane Evans's case and in many others, I do not think it can explain every case. It is very difficult to see how the information about the Glastonbury stone could have been learned in this fashion since the stone's existence had remained hidden from view for almost four hundred years.

Fantasy is another popular explanation for memories of a past life – particularly where children are concerned. Many critics of Stevenson's work have suggested that a child's ability to play act is the fundamental cause of assuming another identity. When a child creates a fantasy figure, he draws from snippets of information he has picked up from others who actually knew or knew of the person concerned. It is even possible that a child using his imagination is able to use psychic powers to gain information about another person's life. This is a highly plausible explanation, but is, to my mind, almost as fantastic as remembering a genuine past life. However, I do believe that fantasy plays an important part in hypnotic regression. From my own work, I have observed that while some individuals dramatically relive experiences from an apparent past life, others appear to enter a state of consciousness where fleeting images are woven into a story line. The story may well include bits of novels or plays and more than just an element of wishful thinking, but within the fabrication lies a precious nugget of truth – a piece of information, a realization that has an important bearing on a present life.

Telepathy, certainly in children who remember being another person, could also explain the ability to recall a past life; in this way, the individual considers the memories of another life are his own when in fact he has tuned into the minds of other's who remember the person in question. This is also a strong possibility. However, if the individual is capable of picking up information telepathically about one person's life, why not others?

Possession is yet another strong possibility, particularly where children take on the very characteristics of a dead person. Possession, of course, is an accepted phenomenon in occult circles – and, indeed the subject of many recent horror films, such as *The Exorcist* – and could well explain how a dead personality could imprint itself on a living one. However, to orthodox psychologists, the concept of possession is almost as unacceptable as reincarnation. Multiple personality, on the other hand, is a well-recognized, if comparatively rare, psychiatric condition. In cases of multiple personality, an individual can exhibit as many as twenty different personalities, or subpersonalities. The personalities will differ to the extent that they will display different handwriting, talk in different dialects and voices, even languages, yet each personality can appear entirely sane and rational. Although most people do not suffer from such dramatic personality disorders, it is possible that the various facets of our own personality could at some level be viewed as subpersonalities but, in 'normal' individuals, the dominant personality ensures that the subpersonalities are held in check so that they can exert only the most minimal influence. It could well be that in hypnotic regression we contact these subpersonalities, even to the extent of creating a suitable historical setting for them.

Inherited memory has also been proffered as an explanation of past life recall. As I discussed earlier,[20] it is possible that memories are genetically transferred from generation to generation. However, in the case of most of Stevenson's children, there is no direct lineal descent from the dead relative to the child. The collective unconscious makes a much more convincing source of past life memories. Individuals could well unwittingly tap the collective pool of information at their disposal and naturally assume it belongs to their own personal past. Of all the possible explanations for past life recall, other than reincarnation, obtaining the information via the collective unconscious seems the most appropriate. Taking into consideration morphogenetic resonance – in which echoes of the past are transmitted across time and influence other developing organisms – we find a mechanism for the process of 'far memory' selection. Individuals by nature of their consciousness are predisposed to respond to certain resonances from the past; put another way, certain memories have a certain affinity with some minds and not others. In deep trance, the individual travelling back in time tunes into these resonances, naturally assuming they belong to his own past.

All these different alternative explanations for past-life recall show, if nothing else, that the mind is capable of some extraordinary feats. Fantasy, hallucination, possession, multiple personality, telepathy, hidden memory and the collective unconscious can in virtually all cases – and certainly the ones I have cited here – account for the apparent memory of a past life. However, it must be said in the face of the large amount of evidence against reincarnation that it does not necessarily prove that reincarnation cannot occur. As the American psychologist and philosopher William James pointed out, 'If you wish to upset the law that all crows are black, you must not seek to show that no crows are, it is enough if you prove the single crow to be white.'[21]

But finding that one white crow appears to be a superhuman task. Not only are the alternative explanations for past-life memory quoted above difficult to refute, but the distinct absence of any common rules about reincarnation also militate against its validity – at least in terms that would satisfy any one other than a firm believer. One of the most forcible arguments against the possibility of reincarnation remains the issue over the length of time allotted between one incarnation and the next. Surely, argues the rationalist, if reincarnation occurs, there must be some regulations over the time it takes. How can one culture claim rebirth occurs immediately, while another state that it takes several hundred years from death to rebirth? (Madame Blavatsky taught that 3,000 years had to pass between successive incarnations.) Likewise, continues the argument, how can one group of individuals believe that one can only reincarnate within the same family, while another consider that rebirth must occur outside the previous family? Then there is the matter of karma. Not all those religions containing reincarnation at their core believe that the actions in one life dictate the terms and conditions of the next. The Shiite Moslems, for instance, teach that a soul must pass through many incarnations in different circumstances, striving at all times for moral and spiritual perfection. But whether an individual succeeds or fails in a particular life bears no influence on the next. Only on the Day of Judgement will all the soul's deeds be examined. Some Buddhists believe that state of the individual's consciousness at death influences his next incarnation and that as soon as an individual dies he is reborn – hence the importance of chanting at the 'bedside' of the dying since it is believed to raise the level of consciousness and so lead to a favourable rebirth. This is one of the main reasons why some Buddhists fear a sudden or violent death since it will almost certainly pitchfork them into a traumatic subsequent life. Individuals from all cultures and creeds seem to fear a violent death, not only at the prospect of pain and suffering, but because it allows no time to make spiritual preparations and reparations. Indeed, some cultures believe that reincarnation only occurs when death has been violent. The high percentage of violent, or sudden, death in Stevenson's cases – 61 per cent, and from across the religious spectrum – would appear to corroborate this. Even in my own small sample approximately 50 per cent of lives ended in traumatic death.[22]

As far as I am concerned, these differences in the mechanics of reincarnation need not interfere with its validity. Not everything in life follows precise guidelines. As the renowned physicist, Stephen Hawking points out: 'With the advent of quantum mechanics, we have come to recognize that events cannot be predicted with complete accuracy but that there is always a degree of uncertainty.'[23] While the human gestation period is given to be nine months, some babies arrive long before their time, while others emerge well after the expected date of delivery. Likewise, from an esoteric standpoint, some souls need longer periods of 'gestation' in a discarnate state than others. Then there is the issue of time itself. All mystics maintain that time as we understand it in term of hours and minutes, days and years, past, present and future has no meaning or parallel in the discarnate state. Indeed, quantum physics goes some way to support this view by establishing that time has no absolute meaning but is conditioned by the situation of whoever lives through it. 'This proof, based on the interaction observed among nuclear particles moving at velocities close to the speed of light . . . allows us to suppose that if two clocks were perfectly synchronised and one left standing while the other moved away at extremely high speed, the time shown on each would be different when the second clock returned to its stationary partner, even though both had been – and still were – ticking along at the same rate.'[24] One of the greatest aims of the mystic is to be able to transcend time and to be at one with the universe. Similarly, as NDEers have all too frequently stated, once consciousness is released from the body a sense of timelessness is experienced so that even if the individual is brought back to life within minutes, he or she has apparently been through a series of events that would take hours, if not days, of earthly time. It is not time itself that changes but our *experience* of time.

Our earthly concept of past, present and future also stands in the way of our understanding how souls appear to multiply, since clearly there are far more people on earth today than there were millions of years ago! This is yet another anomaly frequently raised by the anti-reincarnation lobby. In the eyes of the quantum physicist and the mystic alike, past, present and future are not linear – they exist simultaneously. Thus, in terms of reincarnation, it is entirely possible to experience a first incarnation in 3066 AD (earth time) and the next in 10 BC. If indeed there are a fixed number of souls, there is no reason why they should all incarnate at once, nor take on physical form from the beginning of time (as we understand it) and proceed to reincarnate in a chronological order until the end of time. As Seth, the entity who is channelled through the medium Jane Roberts expresses it:

> Because you [mankind] are obsessed with the idea of past, present and future, you are forced to think of reincarnations as strung out one before the other. Indeed we speak of past lives because you are used to the time sequence concept . . . You have dominant egos, all a part of an inner identity, dominant in various existences. But the separate existences exist simultaneously. Only the egos involved make the time distinction. 145 BC, AD 145, a thousand years in your past and a thousand years in your future – all exist now.[25]

Time and again throughout this book, we have encountered statements to the effect that consciousness is not dependent upon the body for its existence and that the life of the psyche and the soul is immortal. According to most Western and Eastern schools of mystical thought, events from one life to the next and in the discarnate state are imprinted on the soul, or retained in consciousness. And even on a mundane level of existence we know how much the mind can influence experience. This leads to patterns of expectation that are invariably fulfilled and an attunement to certain processes and experiences and not others – whether these expectations and processes are of the nature of heaven or hell or where and when rebirth takes place. In this way it is not too difficult to comprehend how a belief in a particular process of reincarnation can be retained from one life to the next; a factor that not only predisposes an individual soul toward a particular type of rebirth but in turn perpetuates a cultural bias. Thus to the Druses of Lebanon, for instance, reincarnation does occur instantaneously with no time in a discarnate realm, and to the Theravada Buddhists there is an indeterminate amount of time spent in a discarnate realm before rebirth. Both are true. The fact that they are different does not invalidate the whole concept of reincarnation.

Over the past thirty years, a mounting body of evidence has been gathered in support of the belief in reincarnation. Sadly, most of it has been drowned under a deluge of cold water and even the most watertight can be all too easily explained away by the remarkable properties of the mind. My own feelings are that while we must continue to examine the evidence in the harsh light of reason, we must not assume that reincarnation is disproved simply because we have been unable to make the pieces fit established scientific models or been unable to isolate its effect from any other potential source. Science too is continually expanding its frontiers with new knowledge sometimes corroborating previous assertions, sometimes confuting them. As I endeavour to show in the next chapter, through my own research into past life regression, whatever the validity of a past life in terms of hard scientific evidence for reincarnation, there is another, to my mind more valuable, truth to be gleaned from past life memory – and that is the experience of the recall itself and the transformation it inspires. I will leave Hamlet to prepare the way:

> 'There are more things in heaven and earth, Horatio,
> Than are dreamt of in your philosophy.'

NOTES

1. The present Dalai Lama has had to spend his rule in exile. In this way he has indeed fulfilled the ancient prophecy that the fourteenth Dalai Lama would not rule Tibet. However, since the Chinese invasion (1959) forced him out of seclusion in Tibet, his influence on the world's stage has been greater than any of his predecessors.
2. Heinrich Harrer, *Seven Years in Tibet* quoted in *Astrology and Your Past Lives* by Jeanne Avery (Fireside, 1987)
3. Frederick Lenz, *Lifetimes* (Bobbs Merril, 1979)
4. The description of the ringing in the ears prior to the past life recall is a curious anomaly found, incidentally, only in some of Lenz's cases. This

ringing effect is more often described by those who have had out-of-the-body experiences and thus is in no way out of character with a waking vision which shares many of the features of an OBE.

5. Extract from *Lifetimes* taken from *Life after Death* by D. Scott Rogo (Aquarian Press, 1986)
6. D. Scott Rogo, *The Search for Yesterday* (Englewood Cliffs, NJ, Prentice Hall, 1985)
7. D. Scott Rogo, in a Wrekin Trust lecture. 'The Case For Reincarnation', 6 November 1988.
8. D. Scott Rogo, *Life after Death*.
9. Stevenson notes that dreams announcing the return to earth of a loved one are far from uncommon. Indeed, I began this book with the story of Alexandra Samosa (who was not a Stevenson case) whose mother dreamed she would become pregnant with her deceased daughter once more. Stevenson comments in *Children who remember past lives* that announcing dreams 'happen with greater frequency . . . among the Burmese, the Alevis of Turkey, and the tribes of northwestern North America.'
10. D. Scott Rogo, *Psychic Breakthroughs Today* (Aquarian Press, 1987); *Life after Death* (Aquarian Press, 1986); Ian Wilson, *All in the Mind* (Doubleday, 1982); *The After Death Experience* (Sidgwick & Jackson, 1987).
11. In *Rebirth as Doctrine and Experience*, Story quotes an Indian child, Pramod as being born on 15 March 1944. However, in Stevenson's *Twenty Cases Suggestive of Reincarnation* this same child is given a birth date of 11 October 1944. (Source: Ian Wilson, *All in the Mind*)
13. Stevenson answers his critics. *Methods of research* (all quotes taken from *Children who remember past lives*):

> In most cases we do not reach the scene of a case until after the subject and his family have met the family of whom he has been talking . . . Most informants are unaware of the importance of the difference between firsthand testimony and hearsay . . . Consequently, some of our effort goes to telling (and reminding) the informant that he should say only what he has witnessed himself. We never (or almost never) use secondhand testimony . . . Whenever it is feasible, two members of our team take notes during an interview . . . one assistant or colleague acts as the main interpreter (where one is needed); a second assistant makes notes in the language of the informant . . .
> I have to use interpreters for many interviews, and this raises the question of their competence and the possible influence of biases they may have on the information expressed and recorded. Probably some errors in translation have occurred from time to time, as I have noted (when I detected them) in my detailed case reports . . . by recording the questions asked as well as the answers given, I can observe whether the interpreter is asking my questions or pursuing his own line of enquiry.

Stevenson's assessment of his cases (*Children who remember past lives*):

. . . I have no preferred interpretation for all the cases, and I do not think any single one of them offers compelling evidence of reincarnation. Yet I can say that I think reincarnation is, for some cases, the best interpretation.

Stevenson's explanation for the anomaly of more than one child claiming to be the reincarnation of a deceased individual:

. . . human minds may split or duplicate so that one mind can reincarnate in two more bodies: the Eskimo, the Igbo of Nigeria, the Tibetans, the Haida of Alaska and British Columbia and the Gitksan of British Columbia believe this.

Stevenson's reply to the varying differences in time between once incarnation and the next:

Among the cases we have examined, this interval varies from a few hours to twenty years or more, although the median interval (among 616 cases in ten cultures) is fifteen months. In accordance with this wide variation, the members of most cultures believe that no fixed duration exists for the interval between death and rebirth. The Druses and the Jains (of India), however, believe that the interval *is* rigidly fixed for everyone.

Stevenson's comments on the relevance of socio-economic factors:

A substantial number of Indian subjects recall previous lives in socioeconomic conditions distinctly different from their own . . . Among these subjects two-thirds recall better material conditions and only one-third recall worse conditions . . . First, although promotion cases are fewer than demotion ones, they do occur, and in considerable numbers . . . Second, a child obtains no credit for remembering in India a previous life in better circumstances than his own: on the contrary, he will be judged to have done something sinful (in a previous life) that earned the demotion. Third, any comfort from the fantasy of having been rich is more than cancelled in most demotion cases by the trouble the subjects bring to themselves through their boasting, refusal to eat the family's food, complaints about their poverty, and other alienating behaviour. Fourth, attributing such a motive to the subject does not address the question of how some of these children obtained correct information about someone unknown to other members of their families.

In Chapter 5 of *Children who remember past lives*, Stevenson states in regard to *birthmarks in his reincarnation cases* that he has 'photographed several hundred of them'. He later implies that he will publish more material in regard to birthmarks in 'volumes now under preparation.'

14. Colin Wilson, *Afterlife* (Harrap, 1985).
15. Ibid.
16. Although Jenny Green's material was impressively real, when the facts of the case were checked, none of the information tallied. At the address she gave, there was no record of the family having lived there; indeed there was no record of the family having existed at all.

17. The Bridey Murphy saga is one of the most well documented cases of hypnotically derived 'past lives'. An American business man, Morey Bernstein regressed a housewife, Virginia Tighe (now, Ginni Morrow) to a life as an Irish girl in Cork in the 1800s. After some newspaper articles about the regression appeared in 1954, Doubleday published *The Search for Bridey Murphy* in 1956. It became a world bestseller. Virginia not only spoke with an impeccable Irish brogue but produced much correct information about the times – even down to the smallest details. Later research proved her accuracy astounding although no records could be found of her and her family's existence. However, the Chicago *American* – a rival newspaper to the Chicago *Daily News* that had carried a fascinating follow-up to the story – eventually found enough evidence to debunk the whole affair. According to the *American* there were several sources of Virginia's information about Bridey and her times including her own Irish aunt and a real Bridie Murphy Corkell who lived in Chicago, at one time right across the street from Virginia Tighe. The Bridey Murphy case provides yet another source of disagreement between Ian Stevenson and Ian Wilson. In the (British) *Journal of the Society for Psychical Research* (Vol. 55, No. 83, Oct. 1988), Wilson questions Stevenson's inclusion of the Bridey Murphy case in *Children who remember past lives* since it had been 'well exploded'. Stevenson counters (in the same issue) with an extract from a lecture given by Virginia Tighe in 1976 in which she claims that the 'Mrs Corkell' who apparently lived across the street from her in Chicago was a 'put up job'; thus throwing considerable doubt on the whole original newspaper exposé.

    I think the Bridey Murphy case warrants an 'open verdict'.
18. Jeffrey Iverson, *More Lives than One?* (Pan Books, 1977)
19. Ian Wilson, *The After Death Experience*.
20. See Chapter 4, pp. 62–4, and Chapter 5, pp. 101–102.
21. Renée Haynes, *The Society for Psychical Research, 1882–1982: A History* (Macdonald, 1982)
22. My sample included 22 individuals. Full details about the research are contained in Chapter 7.
23. Stephen Hawking, *A Brief History of Time* (Bantam Books, 1988)
24. David Conway, *Secret Wisdom* (Aquarian Press, 1987)
25. Jane Roberts, *The Seth Material* (Bantam Books, 1981)

BIBLIOGRAPHY

Joe Fisher, *The Case for Reincarnation* (Grafton, 1986)

Ian Stevenson, *Twenty Cases Suggestive of Reincarnation* (University Press of Virginia, 1974)

Sylvia Cranston and Carey Williams, *Reincarnation: A New Horizon in Science, Religion and Society* (Julian Press, 1984)

7
Memories, Dreams, Reflections

Rebirth is not a process that we can in any way observe. We can neither measure nor weigh nor photograph it. It is entirely beyond sense perceptions. We have to deal here with a purely psychic reality, which is transmitted to us only indirectly. One speaks of rebirth; one professes rebirth; one is filled with rebirth.

C. J. Jung

When I set out to write this book my intention was not to prove reincarnation, more to persuade others to consider the belief in the light of different systems of knowledge. And one of those systems of knowledge is astrology. As I wrote in Chapter 2, the concept of reincarnation enabled me to make sense out of life's vicissitudes and provided a basis for understanding the mechanism of fate. I reasoned that since a horoscope provides a map of the individual's destiny, his talents and deficiencies, complexes and neuroses, all of which represent the sum total of his accumulated experience and the seeds of future growth, then some astrological themes must, like all patterns, repeat themselves. It was with the intention of discovering whether astrological patterns did indeed repeat themselves that I embarked on a study of hypnotic regression. I hoped that by regressing people to former lives, they might be able to provide the date, time and place of their birth thus enabling me to set up a chart for that life and compare it with the present horoscope. Since I was not a hypnotherapist myself, my first task was to find a qualified practitioner to undertake the regression work for me. As luck, or synchronicity, would have it the ideal person was right on my doorstep. Michael Hopwood and his wife Jean had been friends of mine for some years, and although I knew Michael to be a psychotherapist with a strong spiritual leaning, who had, earlier in his life, been on the psychiatric team at Guy's Hospital, London, I had no idea that he had been exploring hypnotic regression in his psychotherapeutic work. We discussed the project at length and agreed that I should not be present at the sessions in case this made the subjects feel as though they must perform for me.

However, because I was going to write about regression, and since we needed to find the best way to elicit certain information, we both felt that I should undergo a series of hypnotic regressions first. Thus, on 19 November 1987, I placed myself in the hot seat.

Michael began to count slowly backwards from twenty: 'Nineteen, eighteen . . . ten alpha, nine alpha, going deeper and deeper . . . (his voice becoming stronger and more resonant) three alpha, two alpha, one alpha . . . alpha . . . alpha . . . alpha.' I had practised meditation for many years and was thus not surprised to find that I had automatically entered a state of consciousness where I felt still and calm but mentally crystal clear.

To begin with, Michael suggested that I went back to a period in my childhood. I found myself at the age of thirteen on the threshold of adolescence noticing for the first time that my body was showing signs of womanhood. What I had not been prepared for was the vividness of the recall and how I was able to review the experience in such sharp detail; I also gained insight about the conflict I was experiencing at that time between wanting to grow up yet being frightened to leave the safety of childhood behind. Michael then took me back beyond birth 'to a time where it would be useful and creative for you to remember'. My first foray into the distant past found me in Venice – a place I have never visited – in 1740. I had the curious sensation of running lightly over the rugs on polished floors which moved underneath my feet as I ran. I was eighteen, in love and dressed in pink. My name was Angelina.

Despite the flow of information from my first past life, I emerged from the session feeling that I had simply been fantasizing. A week later, we tried again. This time, Michael urged me to let go of my reservations, dismiss the observer-scientist in my mind and let myself flow with the experience.

This time, after a faltering start, where I 'saw' nothing but a huge black void, I let my mind take me into a book I had been reading about Avalon and the sorceress, Morgan La Fay. I felt myself peering into a lake; it was night and the full moon's reflection hovered nervously across the surface of the water. I was using the lake as a scrying glass to peer into the future. From then my life as Sarah unfolded. The period was 1263 AD, I was 25 years of age, and had been born at midnight on 2 March. In this 'past life' I bore five sons, was married to a Duke and was confidante to the King. I had a degree of difficulty remembering who the King was, however – Henry or Harold!

I remained deeply sceptical about this past life, which seemed to contain more fantasy and wishful thinking than truth – at least in the historical, fact-finding sense, although I was surprised and pleased to find subsequently that my birthplace, Carno, did indeed exist, and Henry III was on the throne of England at the time – perhaps his friends called him Harry! But although I was disappointed not to be able to believe in this 'past life' as such, I discovered the experience had enabled me to touch on some areas that I find difficult to deal with in my present life – most notably my fear of rejection and my fear of being wrong. Also there was a moment in the regression where an angel had given me a beautifully bound book with the words 'knowledge is power' written on the frontispiece; he also gave me a blessing which I found exquisitely reassuring. Thus I felt I had gained from the experience, though not in the way I had anticipated, and looked forward to the next session.

The theme that knowledge is power came through in another life as a fifteen-year-old page called, Martinus – once again in Venice, but this time in 1482. In this life I was party to all manner of skulduggery and was eventually smashed to pieces by a stone slab for my troubles. My master, Marcus, was clearly a member of a powerful secret society much concerned with political intrigue. Under hypnosis I talked about sacred geometry, scrolls concealed in tombs, magical ceremonies – even astrology. A fascinating story containing, perhaps just a few seeds of my present life.

Those who know me well were not surprised to learn that I had been a nun in one of my past lives . . . Actually, Sister Ursula was rather jolly (Italian, once again) and a first-class cook. In yet another life I was a rather lonely witch, called, somewhat appropriately, Moira. But perhaps the most impressive of all the lives was that of Anunka.

This regression was the only one where I felt completely within the time and space of that lifetime. I was, somewhat predictably, a priestess, but I really felt the heat of the 'Egyptian' sun and the weight of the gold around my neck and on my head. I spoke with some authority about my life and gave my date of birth as the 'month of the turtle' and 'on the Moon's day'. However, the real impact of this sojourn into the distant past occurred when Michael pressed me to tell him what year I was living in and what gods we worshipped. I became extremely angry with him and impressed upon him that the time period was thousands and thousands of years ago: 'long before what you think of as Ancient Egypt'. I told him I was living at a time when 'men were gods'. I described men as 'giants' and told of how we were able to live on different levels of reality 'moving between worlds'. I informed Michael that I was in a time and place 'on which the *legends* of Atlantis and the Garden of Eden are based.' Asked, by Michael, what happened to this Utopia, I tried to explain that there was an 'energy shift . . . levels (or worlds) moved out of alignment . . . we lost our ability to be as gods.' I was adamant that it wasn't because of some misuse of power (which is generally believed to have caused the downfall of Atlantis) but because of some energy shift.

What intrigued me about this pronouncement, was that it felt absolutely true. At the time I thought that I had genuinely accessed some real knowledge. Nevertheless, I still remain doubtful that it was one of my past lives as such. The point I want to put across, however, is that the validity of the experience need not be measured in terms of whether or not I am the reincarnation of Anunka. In this altered state of consciousness I found something of value and came away enhanced by the experience. And who knows, maybe we did indeed, in a far-distant past, walk with the gods.

One of the greatest problems Michael and I faced with the regression project was inducing subjects to reveal precise data under hypnosis. And because of the astrology involved – effectively the linchpin of the exercise – we needed to elicit the date, time and place of birth of each past life. Hypnotic regression is a process far more suited to the intuitive right brain, not the logical, fact-producing left. I knew from my own experience that a huge shift in consciousness was necessary to evince a definite fact out of a reverie. As it happened, remembering their birth date proved an almost impossible task for several people, let alone the time, but Michael's unusual and rather unorthodox technique of inviting their guardian angel or the higher self to provide the information almost always worked. Another element I was also very keen to explore was the nature of the between-life state. Thus, taking subjects through their death and beyond was another essential milestone to reach.

I had been very impressed with the work of the Canadian-based psychiatrist, Joel Whitton who, together with writer Joe Fisher, had published a book, *Life Between Life*[1] covering some of his research into reincarnation. Whitton, a firm believer in reincarnation, had been researching the area for many years using the technique of hypnotic regression when, in 1974, he was forced to review his understanding of the process of reincarnation. Regressing a patient one day, he accidentally gave her a different instruction from the one he intended. (Since the subject is in an extremely suggestible state in deep trance, exact phraseology is essential.) Instead of asking her to go to another incarnation, he suggested that she went to a previous *life*. To his amazement she began to talk from a discarnate state. Until this time, Whitton had not conceived of a conscious life between death and rebirth. Eventually, based on a deep understanding of ancient texts (notably the *Bardo Thotrol*) and information from his subjects under hypnosis, he began to map the territory of the between-life state. Whitton's subjects describe, sometimes in languages unknown to them in their present life, similar after-death experiences as the NDEers: 'judgement panels' help the discarnate soul to assess its past life and prepare for the new.[2] Thus I was excited by the prospect that Michael and I might achieve similar results.

I was to be disappointed. None of my volunteers talked of a judgement panel, nor were there anything like the vivid descriptions of choosing the next life quoted by Whitton. Nor, indeed, was there any information about sojourns among the planetary spheres. But then here, perhaps, we would be infringing on the ultimate mystery of the life of the soul – an absolute no-go area for any except the exceptionally enlightened. I don't know. However, it must be said that my sample was exceedingly small – only 22 individuals – compared to the thousands of Whitton's subjects. No doubt if I had used more people I might well have covered similar ground as Whitton. It must also be said that while I may have been disappointed at receiving no graphic impressions of the afterlife from anyone on the project, everybody was able to transcend death and enter a timeless state in full consciousness. And while no one had to give an account of themselves to a judgement panel, each did reflect on the meaning of their past life and comprehend the 'stuff' of the next. But before I go into some of these experiences, we need a little more background on the regression project itself.

From the outset I had not intended the study to be a huge research programme. I wanted a small sample just to see if I could discern any connections between the birth charts of past and present lives and find any repeating astrological themes. The regression work was always intended to be just a part of a book covering a huge, largely metaphysical, area. At no time had I thought of amassing any proof as such of reincarnation. And while I personally believe in reincarnation, I remain unconvinced that those past lives revealed under hypnotic regression have a basis in fact. (This, incidentally is not the view shared by most of the subjects in this study.)

Finding volunteers for the programme was not easy. While many people were fascinated and initially enthusiastic about the idea of discovering their past lives, few were actually prepared to confront them. Eventually we found 22 willing souls, of which only five were men. The majority of the volunteers were known to Michael rather than myself; most were psychotherapists and writers (no astrologers), and while the religious background ranged from Catholic to Buddhist, all had been exposed to, for want of a better word, New Age philosophy. The sample was predominantly upper-middle class; all were extremely articulate and the average age was 48 – the youngest being 35 and the eldest 69. In essence we had a group of people well versed in mystical philosophy, individuals who had already spent considerable time working on their own inner development. And although this explains why all but one of the sample found the process of regression rewarding in the sense of self-discovery, it is exceedingly surprising that no one entered another world with 'vast halls of learning equipped with libraries and seminar rooms'. (Such descriptions are almost commonplace in Whitton's work.)

However, even with such a small sample some interesting features emerged. Of all five men, only one recalled a lifetime as a woman, while of the women, twelve out of seventeen experienced previous lives as men – one female remembering four male lives but not one as a woman. Just over a third claimed to have been born close to their birthday in the present life – one was born on exactly the same day, another found he had been born on his father's birthday but not the same year, of course. Two-thirds of the lifetimes recalled were painful experiences, often accompanied by much weeping. Remembering these lives was of enormous therapeutic value, especially those of Chloe and Viola which I discuss at length in Chapter 9. No one was famous, although one person did recall the life of a known soldier at the time of the Battle of Waterloo and another was a French authoress.

All manner of social rank was present, and though people recalled lives in a different country to that of their present life, only one found herself with a radically different skin pigmentation! Indeed, this particular female, 'Sophe' (so blond as to be almost Albino) recalled a life as a tribal African girl; she was used and abused by men and spent the latter part of her short and violent life pretending to be a man. In her present life, Sophe has only been attracted to black men, who have consistently betrayed her and treated her violently. She has been inorgasmic to date, which no doubt accounts for her rather promiscuous life-style. Ironically, Sophe herself found little of value in the regression. The memory, or the creative imagery, which made such sense in light of her emotional and sexual problems, inspired no catharsis. Neither did she express any interest in continuing to try the regression route, nor indeed any kind of therapy, to resolve her current dissatisfaction.

All but five of the sample, felt that they were reliving – as if in the moment – experiences in their past, not merely reporting them. Finally, each person felt that they had been enriched by their regression experiences, indeed, over half saw a positive change in their lives because of them.

One of those who reported a positive change from her regression was 'Susan'. After an initially horrific recall of having her eyes burnt out, Susan described her time in a prison in 15th-century England where she had been gaoled for stealing food. Recently she wrote to me concerning this regression.

> Some time later I realized how ironic it was that I had stolen food, because in this life time I have a constant weight problem. I go through bad phases when I 'binge'. I have never understood why I could not control this area of my life when I have such strong will power and personality. On reflection, it seemed to me that my problem must have stemmed from not having enough to eat in the 1400s. Since the regression, [a year ago] I have been able to control my weight. I have only fluctuated within five or six pounds [of my normal weight] (before it was as much as one and a half stone) . . . and I have had not one 'binge' session.

Another, 'Heather', who relived an experience as a recalcitrant monk, was, in the months that followed the regression, able to release a dormant aspect of her personality: 'It was as if for years the true core of my character had lain dormant. I was existing, not living, under a false pretence of politeness and etiquette, which is absolutely not me at all.'

Eva also found the regressions to her past life as a Viking called Alfric extraordinarily effective.

> Since the regression [nine months before] that feeling of affirmation has remained. I have not wanted to talk to many people about it. When I read the transcript, I was surprised by much of it. And I wept. I found it unbearably moving . . . it could have been a stranger speaking. But the thoughts of the middle-aged Alfric resonated in me – as if somebody had plucked a string that I am only half aware of. I am much clearer about why I work as a psychotherapist. I am more at home with the way I work – I feel that has been endorsed . . . I think a little more clearly than I did.

The past lives revisited ranged from farmers and servants to priests and princes; the periods from thousands of years BC to 1910. One writer and broadcaster went back to southern France in the thirteenth century – a monk who turned against the Cathars to save his own skin, although he knew them to follow the Truth. He was delighted to have returned to this place and time since it had always fascinated him; it also surprised him that he had named places he was entirely unfamiliar with. What I did not attempt to do was suggest that any of the subjects went to a life in the future. As I explained in Chapter 6, our sense of past, present and future is an illusion of time – time is not sequential, except in the psychological sense, but simultaneous. Thus, in theory, there should be no barrier to moving forward to another life. However, I felt that with the already massive amount of research for this book, the scales were weighted too greatly in the direction of hypothesis to warrant any further forays in that direction! Not that I, or rather Michael, would have been the first person to try to *progress* anyone.

Dr Helen Wambach, an American psychologist, undertook a pilot study called 'Mass Dreams of the Future'[3] in which she reported that out of 1,100 subjects, 89 were able to speak of a life between 2100 AD and 2300 AD. Dr Bruce Goldberg, an American hypnotherapist also successfully progressed individuals to a future life, both before and beyond 2500 AD.[4] Apart from the certain comfort to be found in the knowledge that the planet Earth manages to survive beyond the apocalyptic year of 1999, much of the information about the state of the earth in the future provides fascinating food for thought – the subject of another book, perhaps.

Moving through a past life to death and beyond, was a process that everyone on the study underwent. As far as my own sample was concerned, expectations of life after death – in the sense of survival of consciousness – were fulfilled according to the respective belief systems. And although one female – Laura, a psychotherapist – had no belief at all in reincarnation and therefore no concept of a between-life state, she nevertheless successfully managed to recall four lives across the centuries. Interestingly, Laura experienced a vivid recall as the ghost of a ten-year-old boy: Martin had been born in 1600 and was murdered at the age of ten by robbers. After death he began to haunt the castle where he had been brought up. This regression had such a powerfully disturbing effect on Laura that some time after the regression she found a stone, engraved it with Martin's date of birth and death and placed it in consecrated ground. This process of laying the ghost effectively put her distress at rest.

The experience of death and the transition to another state of consciousness was in almost all cases very similar to the events described by NDEers. And like the NDEers, in the main, the regression subjects 'came back' spiritually revivified by their experience. Most returned with a renewed sense of purpose to live life to the full and with the firm belief that love is the most important thing of all. 80 per cent of my sample were convinced that the life they had reviewed was genuinely theirs and the contact with that personality had made sense of particular aspects of their present life and personality. One female, Kathy Eldon, a writer-broadcaster – was impressed enough with her experience to write an article about it.

When Dr Hopwood asked Elizabeth [the past-life personality] whether she believed in heaven, or any kind of life after death, she responded with a scowl, snarling, 'When I die, my bones will rot in hell' . . . [But] as the dead Elizabeth, I felt a sense of total bliss, a release of anxiety and fear and a feeling of floating in a textured space where light and love were fused. I did not wish to leave that sublime existence, and responded slowly to Dr Hopwood when he spoke to me. Instead of rotting bones in hell, I described peace and joy . . . I was a calm, accepting entity for whom love was the only reality.

During hypnotic regression one is completely aware. There is no sense of 'being under' or out of it. I was conscious of street noises, the whirr of the tape recorder, even of the psychiatrist's breathing, and I was also aware of my fascination with the person who fitted so comfortably in my body. Kathy, who continued to think and process information, shared a body with Elizabeth, a 17-century woman who had apparently lived a full life – and died . . .

The traits of Elizabeth . . . live on in me, and now I have the awareness to choose which characteristics I wish consciously to have as part of Kathy. The choice is mine, despite the echoes of the past.[5]

The most profound part of the regression session for most of my sample was the reappraisal of the life past. Heather was a case in point. Before embarking on the project, Heather had hoped that she would return to a life where she had been a dancer; she had held a strong conviction that in a previous lifetime, she had been a ballerina with the Marinsky Theatre in St Petersburg; furthermore, she intuited that her physical disability in her current lifetime stemmed from an accident in her Marinsky life. Contrary to her expectations, Heather returned to a life as a monk called Peter in 19th-century South America. Peter was extremely outspoken and volatile; he managed to alienate many of his fellow priests who, anxious to rid themselves of such a contentious colleague, eventually engineered his death – a particularly grizzly one where after being tortured, his right foot was amputated. Under hypnosis, Michael led her through her traumatic death.

Michael: 'Where are you now? Do you have any sense of other beings of any sort?'
Heather/Peter: 'Not specific ones.'
M: 'What would you call this place where you are now?'
H/P: 'Well, it's not really heaven . . .but it's a lot nicer than earth. I feel

there's higher to go but I'm quite happy where I am . . . I feel I'm being called. There's a sort of tunnel . . . it's as swift as the wind . . . as sharp as an arrow. It's pulling me.'

M: 'What do you feel about being pulled?'

H/P: 'Quite a lot of resistance. I feel as if I've got to restrict this character and squeeze it into some shape . . .'

During this part of the regression, Heather experienced some difficulty in speaking. In order to help her move on, Michael used his, by now, proficient technique of suggesting that she should ask for her guardian angel to intervene. Almost immediately, Heather saw her angel holding up a sword.

H/P: '. . . He's holding a sword and I understand that the sword is unforgiveness. I realize that my unforgiveness consumes me.' [This inability to forgive related to the priests who had not only resented Peter's bravado but committed him to his horrific death.]

M: 'Try asking your guardian angel how you can find the strength to forgive them and yourself.'

Heather experienced enormous difficulty in trying to forgive. As the regression moved on, it became apparent that the next life to come was her present one – and her physical disability is the legacy of her inability to forgive. The regression has had a major transformative effect in Heather's life. Finally, enabled to forgive those who cut short her life as Peter so savagely, she now feels freer and generally happier and her confidence and sense of direction has greatly increased. The facility offered through hypnotic regression of transmuting the legacy of a previous life is the most valuable part of the process of past life regression – something that should become abundantly clear through the case histories discussed later.

Descriptions of lightness and clarity after physical death are common to virtually all the subjects who were taken through a death. Most also contacted a being of light although one individual was faced with the black goddess who informed him that he was not yet ready to pass into the other world. One male felt as though he was being propelled clockwise by a great force, another that she was so full of light and lightness that she could 'dance among the sunbeams'. One female was shown by her 'being of light' two sets of parallel tracks – one she had no further use for and the other that she was now on. 'I'm going along at a much faster rate and I'm being told that I'm on course.' Another described herself in a light and airy place called,

'Palladium'; subsequently a friend told her that she also had visited a place known as Palladium during a near death experience. But out of all the experiences, there is one that truly stands out. This belongs to a doctor, 'Edward' who recalled a life as a small boy, Daniel, living in Dorset in 1789.

Daniel died at the age of nine while playing in a quarry near Bradford Abbas. He passed quickly and easily from his physical body and was immediately greeted by his guide, Machiel: 'He is radiant. He takes my hand as we walk in great peace through a long, dark tunnel – his light radiating the tunnel.' Eventually Daniel emerges from the tunnel and finds himself in a beautiful scene – sea, sun, vivid greenery – and he observes that while he is still 'Daniel', his whole body is 'numinous . . . it's a light form like a thought energy structure rather than a tangible weighty substance.' Filled with exuberance and a sense of great liberty, 'Daniel' plunges into the sea and assumes the shape of a dolphin. As he emerges from the water, back once again in his 'light body', he sees his parents talking to his guide. This throws Daniel, or rather, Edward into utter confusion, for his parents are none other than those of his 20th-century lifetime; both of whom are, indeed, very much alive in 1988.

It is at this point that the psychic edge between Edward as Daniel and Edward as he is now begins to blur. The identification of Daniel as but another aspect of himself, whether from a genuine past life or a construct of the psyche, a subpersonality, perhaps, clearly gives Edward free rein to shift from one part or level of his being to another. Daniel now thinks and speaks as an old soul, not as a nine year-old boy.

Still puzzled about the nature of time 'with some things feeling very strange yet others entirely familiar', Daniel asks Machiel if it might be possible for him to speak to Jesus. Machiel replies that this would be no problem at all since He is not far away.

> We walk across the hill together and there He is, sitting by a stream talking to Carl Gustav Jung. He's very light but difficult to describe facially. He's very welcoming and I say to him, 'I've always wondered at and loved your teachings and your example, but I do have a lot of difficulty with people who designate themselves as Christians as if they're somehow or another different from the rest of the human race.' He says, at once, that he finds anyone assuming false piety or considering themselves one of a faithful élite a pain in the neck too! And we have a big laugh. Then I realise that Jung hasn't been born yet, let alone died, so what is he doing here. I feel I must communicate with them about this . . . and I am given to understand that past, present and future are all one and intermingled. Hence it is quite natural that someone,

who by my earthly sense of linear time hasn't even been born, should be there.

No longer feeling bound by time, Daniel invites 20th-century Edward to join the group. (Edward was later to explain that he was in some way able to see himself talking with Jesus, Jung and Daniel while being simultaneously conscious in 1988.)

It's as if the thought brings him to the group and this seems perfectly all right. Clearly, this is what people refer to as heaven and it's right at hand and it's timeless and it's light and it's loving.

Before Edward returns to earth level, Daniel offers to share with Edward his 'unspoilt view of life, his fresh nature and his openness to experience'. Edward is demonstrably affected by this gesture which bears the hallmarks of a deeply personal revelation.

There was yet another important dimension to Edward's experience under hypnosis. Just before he left 'heaven', Edward was told by Daniel that his one great regret about dying was that he had had to leave his little girl friend, Lucy, behind. It transpired that Daniel had spent as long as possible around Lucy trying to ease her grief, but 'through her lack of openness', she was unable to see or even sense him. This had initially made him very sad. However, Daniel had come to realize that although the external relationship with Lucy had been severed, there was still a spiritual bond that could never be sundered. Daniel had felt compelled to explain this to Edward in order to help him become more in touch with his anima – the feminine, feeling aspect of his psyche.

It's as though Edward hasn't fully recognized what old Jung meant by the anima. He hasn't fully realized the experience – not often anyway, and he doesn't hold on to it if he does. It's intimated rather than fully experienced. I [Daniel] know that the beloved is something that is always available and isn't dependent on a literal, tangible, external person. Edward thinks it intellectually, but he isn't very good at experiencing it with his heart.

At this point Michael brought Edward out of the hypnotic state into ordinary consciousness, suggesting that Edward could clearly remember all that had been said. Some time was then spent reviewing the material and encouraging any other associations or ideas that this experience might have released. Almost immediately, Edward recognized that there was a connection between Lucy and Jung's concept of the anima – the feminine aspect of man's nature. As Machiel had explained, and in the process enabled Edward to experience, there was no real separation between Lucy and Daniel just as there can be no alienation of the anima from the psyche as a whole. This realization also provoked the recall of a dream Edward had had the night before. In the dream, Edward had managed to deeply upset a female member of a small community – and unfortunately the community had taken her side and not his. The woman had been so incensed that she wanted to 'scratch his eyes out'. There seemed no alternative to Edward in the dream but to swim out to sea and drown himself. Before he left, however, he decided to say goodbye to his wife and an old friend he hadn't seen since his days at university. Michael suggested to Edward that the woman in the dream could be representative of his anima and urged him to allow the anima to speak for herself. Edward agreed and in so doing quite literally gave voice to the anima.

I am mostly kept in a different place and I'm not allowed out very often. So I get *very*, *very* angry. I turned up in a dream the other night so outraged with Edward – enough to put his eyes out. Of course, I wouldn't really, but in a manner of speaking I was trying to communicate to him that he didn't need any eyes – he can't see. 'You can't see me, you stupid idiot!' . . . I am a crude, primitive, shadowy creature, but full of absolute beauty if I could be properly released and integrated. But there's a block to him seeing me and maybe there's a block to my trusting him because I'm so angry with him.

Edward, clearly humbled by the force of the anima's vehemence over being so ignored, tried desperately to respond. But while intellectually he could understand why the anima was left in the dark, he felt at a loss to know how to resolve the situation. Ultimately his guide, Machiel came to the rescue.

The barriers between Edward and the anima can only be broken down through the acceptance of suffering. Instead of resisting suffering, or thinking of it as a 'bad' thing, just accept it willingly. Allow the example of Daniel's reconciliation with the inner beloved to act as a beacon for your own union with the anima. Just allow it to be an inspirational, numinous factor – an already-knowing in your being . . . You are already reconciled. It's only the layers of egoic illusion that get in your way. Perhaps you could see what you call suffering is simply a way of allowing the barriers to come down. Just accept. And that is enough for now.

This seemed to bring a natural close to the experience and Edward was brought into 'normal', everyday consciousness. He had total recall of everything that had occurred. He also felt an overriding sense of exhilaration at having touched on so many layers of his psyche and at having been shown in such dynamic terms the conflict between his masculine self (animus) and his anima. What was so elating for him was that he had been able to use a feeling approach to the anima rather than an intellectual one. Perhaps now, the elusive qualities he constantly sought in women that even when found were never sustained, would cease to consume him. Perhaps too, his irritation with those who wear their beliefs on their sleeve would fade and his ability to feel compassion for suffering would be released – all fundamentally the stuff of the anima. While the process of assimilation is undoubtedly a life-long mission, Edward felt that this session had transported him some considerable distance along that path.

Edward's experience is enormously rich in mystical and psychological content and imagery – memories, dreams and reflections, indeed. Taking a mystical stance, Edward's contact with a past life had enabled him to enter heaven, or more probably the astral plane. There, using his mental, emotional and astral bodies he was able to commune with Jesus and Jung. From this stage of being, he was given insight into current problems and allowed a glimpse of what is almost certainly a major karmic issue – to relate to the feeling side of life, to learn compassion for suffering and to recognize that love knows no boundaries, divisions or separations.

From the psychological perspective, Edward had been able to bring into the light some of the content of the unconscious. Creative imagery – both in dreaming and under hypnosis – had enabled him to focus on an inner conflict that was blocking the health and wholeness of the psyche. The symbolism of talking to Jesus and Jung almost speaks for itself. Jung's appearance enabled Edward to surface his thoughts and feelings about the anima and to link it with a recent and powerful dream: in so doing he was able to find a new route to reconciliation with the anima. And who more appropriate to represent Edward's need to identify with love, compassion and suffering, than Christ himself. The anima was not only symbolized by Lucy and the outraged female and reinforced by the presence of Jung, but the settings in the dream and in the regression were a testament to the richness and fertility of nature: water is not only a symbol of the unconscious realm but of the feminine – it was no accident of design that Jesus and Jung should be located by a stream. The sea was an important focus in both the dream and in the hypnotic state. On the one hand, the sea was a welcoming experience where Edward could immerse himself playfully and exuberantly – of course, he needed to assume a different form to do so. On the other hand, the sea represented a source of forgetting:

alienated from his community (ergo his identity) Edward sought to commit suicide, or to give himself up to the sea. Crucially, he felt he had no other choice. In other words, Edward could no longer put off a true meeting with his anima. Although the dream portrayed all Edwards misgivings about confronting the anima, the hypnotic regression showed him that the anima wasn't necessarily going to swallow him up – he could instead find a joyful union. The resolution of this conflict was not only carefully explained by Edward's guide, Machiel, but also symbolized by the confederacy of Christ and Jung: it is through acceptance of suffering (as exemplified by Jesus) that Edward can be reconciled with his anima (the Jungian soul of the feminine).

On whatever level one chooses to interpret Edward's experiences, there is no doubting that hypnotic regression allows for some powerful psychic processes to occur. Thus, while this method may deserve its reputation as a poor source for proving reincarnation, it nevertheless provides a rich tool for growth and awareness. And although it may well be that in some, perhaps many, cases people are recalling a genuine past life, checking historical or geographic data or searching for the present life source of the material is not the only way of validating the experience. The more important truth, at least to my mind, is to be found on the experiential level.

Where hypnotic regression is concerned, despite the convictions of the majority of my volunteers that they did indeed return to a past life, I am much more inclined to believe that in deep trance, heightened consciousness combined with the imagination creates a scenario that enables the individual to relate to some hidden, unresolved feature of the psyche. In the process, he may access a pool of collective information and select a recording – which may be someone else's past – and appropriate it for the purposes of growth and understanding. Yet, as I write this, I am aware there is another equally valid interpretation for what occurs in hypnotic regression: that the higher self, working on behalf of the soul, selects a record from the Akashik library. This record of a past life enlightens and helps the individual to resolve some of the karma of a present life.

Throughout the course of this book, I have endeavoured to show how science, or more specifically modern physics, is 'catching up' with mystical thought. If nothing else, I have tried to show that the division between psychology and the occult is very narrow indeed. In the concluding chapters, using astrology as a language. I shall attempt to weave the many themes of this book together. A truly cosmic quest.

NOTES

1. Joel Whitton and Joe Fisher *Life between Life* (Grafton, 1986)
2. Xenoglossy is a term coined by the Nobel prize-winning French physiologist and parapsychologist, Dr Charles Richet for the ability to speak in a foreign language not consciously known. This is an extremely rare side effect of hypnotic regression and spontaneous past-life memory and has all too often been found to owe its origins to some previous acquaintance with the language in question. Whitton refers to such a case in *Life between Life*.
3. Reference taken from Joe Fisher, *The Case for Reincarnation* (Grafton, 1984)
4. Bruce Goldberg, *Past Lives, Future Lives* (Newcastle Publishing, 1982)
5. From an article for *Signature* magazine, March 1989

BIBLIOGRAPHY

Helen Wambach, *Reliving Past Lives* (Arrow Books, 1979)
Kenneth Ring, *Heading toward Omega* (Quill, 1985)

8
The Astrologer's Case for Reincarnation

Astrology was to the Stoic the study of the manifestation of divine will; modern science is to the materialist the study of the manifestations of undivine accident – but both presuppose the ineluctable operation of cause and effect.

West and Toonder, *The Case for Astrology*

'Reincarnation is to the 1980s what astrology was to the 1960s.' Or so commented Alan Vaughan, the editor of the American magazine, *Reincarnation Report*. And, judging by the rash of astrology books on reincarnation that are presently emerging, it would seem that many astrologers are embracing this zeitgeist with great gusto. Not that reincarnation and karma has been entirely avoided by astrologers until now, for those with their roots firmly in theosophical soil, like Alan Leo and Alice Bailey, for instance, incorporated reincarnation and karma as a central part of their astrological philosophy. Over the past few years – and certainly with the research for this book – I too have come to realize that astrology is spiritually arid without such concepts. However, while I believe implicitly in reincarnation and that the horoscope should in some way reflect such a process, I am not at all comfortable with the concept of reincarnational *laws*. I am sure that there is a divine proportion and harmony to all things in heaven and earth and that the timing of death and rebirth must adhere to some cosmic precept, but I have not yet been persuaded by any work that I have seen that we are close to knowing precisely what these laws may be.

In May 1986 I spent a memorable weekend in Utrecht, Holland, leading a workshop on synastry.[1] At the end of the afternoon session on the Saturday, an astrologer called Monique, who I had known for a year or so, asked me if she could arrange a meeting between myself and another Dutch astrologer before I returned to England. This astrologer, who I am sure would prefer to remain anonymous, wanted urgently to show me the results of some work on reincarnation he had been undertaking. Thus, the following day I arrived at Skipol Airport two hours before my flight in a state of some anticipation. Indeed, the meeting had a touch of a John le Carré novel about it. Before he would open his briefcase, I had to promise the astrologer not to divulge the information he was about to show me to anyone. Nodding my assent, he looked nervously from side to side and produced a thick folder of immaculately drawn charts. 'Here's Elizabeth 1,' he said, showing me her chart. 'And here's Magda's in 1932.' He then proceeded to show me chart after chart from one century to another. Triumphantly, he closed the file. 'You see, I have found the astrological key to reincarnation.' 'Tremendous,' I enthused, 'But what's the method . . . the mathematical laws?' 'Oh, I can't tell you that. It's a secret!'

Nothing I could say would persuade him to let me have copies of his work, despite my protestations that any such discovery should, in the best interests of astrology, be offered up for examination and replication by others. No one, I assured him, would deprive him of his claim to fame. Over the past three years, I have seen nothing in any astrological journal about his theories of reincarnation. Perhaps he's refining things.

Fortunately, other astrologers are more prepared to let the world in on their secrets. Robert Powell's trilogy Hermetic Astrology promises to be one such source of fascinating information. However, at the time of writing, only one volume has been published and, I suspect, the more valuable and practical side of his research will emerge in his subsequent works. At least, I hope so.

Powell is a follower of Rudolph Steiner and has based his astrological 'laws' of reincarnation on Steiner's teachings. Principally, he has followed Steiner's statement that, as the soul prepares to be reborn, 'there remains an endeavour to enter into this constellation [that was present at death], to do justice once again to the forces it received at the moment of death.'[2] Thus, Powell's first 'law', based also on the hermetic principle that the sign of the Moon at conception becomes the Ascendant at birth, concerns the relationship between the Sun and Saturn. '*The angle between the Sun and Saturn at birth is the same as or is the complement of (with respect to 180°) the angle between them at death in the previous incarnation. This is known as the preservation of the angular relationship between the Sun and Saturn.*' His next 'law' becomes the extended first 'law' of reincarnation. Here there is '*an interchange or alignment or mirroring of the zodiacal positions of the Sun and Saturn.*' In other words, the position of Saturn at death can become the position of the Sun at rebirth – or vice versa; or the Sun's position at death repeats itself at rebirth – the same with Saturn. Powell adds that interchange or repetition can occur at the opposite point in the zodiac from the original placing. Powell's second 'law' of reincarnation states, *The sidereal zodiacal position(s) of h-Mercury (heliacal Mercury] and/or h-Venus at birth in one incarnation tend(s) to align with the sidereal zodiacal position(s) of h-Mercury and/or h-Venus at death in the preceding incarnation.*' Then there is the extended second 'law' of reincarnation which involves the juxtaposition of heliacal Mercury or Venus at death with their geocentric counterparts at birth and vice versa. Enlarging upon these basic tenets, Powell goes on to provide many examples of reincarnation where, for instance, Uranus at birth is found at the same position as it was at the previous death, and similarly with other planetary bodies. But before I attempt to comment on or apply any of Powell's ideas, it is worth bearing in mind the approach he adopts to his work on astrology and reincarnation.

> a word of warning must be added here – at the outset – concerning the interpretation of the results of this research. The astrological 'laws' of reincarnation discovered by the author . . . do *not* enable previous incarnations to be calculated. For the mystery of reincarnation is inaccessible to intellectual speculation. No amount of speculative reasoning combined with computational skill can ever penetrate this mystery. It is along other paths – whereby, instead of the brain, the heart becomes an organ of knowledge – that knowledge of reincarnation becomes attainable.

I have to say that I think this sounds like a dreadful 'cop out'. Yes, he's unearthed a formula, but it cannot be put to the test. Heads I win, tails you lose. Indeed, Powell has come under some intense criticism for this attitude to his work, and more than one astrologer has questioned his absolute reliance on Steiner as the fount of all knowledge about reincarnation.[3] While I agree that the mysteries demand a different level of apprehension than the intellect alone can provide – and certainly the Egyptian mystery route was through the heart – order and form exist at every level of manifestation. This is fundamentally what Pythagoras spent his lifetime trying to establish. Ultimately, universal laws must be able to be grasped not just through the intuitive centres but the intellectual ones – albeit not until mankind has evolved to a point where his consciousness can facilitate such understanding. Thus, there are, I am sure, some laws to be found, and Powell's 'laws' could well be signposts toward them. Indeed, through my own work, while I did not so much concentrate on the planetary patterns at birth bearing a resemblance to those at the previous death, I have found that planetary themes tend to echo from incarnation to incarnation. Without meaning to sound patronizing, I do sympathize with Powell's sentiments over his 'laws' not being absolute laws, and thus beyond the reach of present scientific proof. By way of a parallel, any experienced astrologer realizes that the permutations to a single astrological theme are so great that to show any one effect can only occur with one specific astrological factor is almost hopeless. I have always suspected that we twentieth-century astrologers are tackling a jigsaw of cosmic proportions. We have a few of the pieces, perhaps even some of the key ones, but we lack the whole picture and many of the remaining components.

I might also add that while I suspect that Powell's 'laws' point in the right direction of the cosmic design of reincarnation, he does little to help his case by presenting his material in such an oblique and cluttered fashion. It took me hours to establish what these 'laws' actually are since the essential principles involved are hidden in a sea of verbiage – the first 'law' is the only one clearly identified.

Tad Mann – a graduate of Cornell University – is another astrologer to tackle the mechanics of reincarnation. Mann has culled many of his ideas from the late Rodney Collin's work, most notably from his book, *The Theory of Celestial Influence*. But before I expand on Mann's theories, it might be useful to understand Collin's view of reincarnation. For Collin, death did not mark the beginning of a period of time in a discarnate realm prior to rebirth. Death and rebirth, to Collin, were simultaneous; as soon as an individual dies, he is reborn – but with one important departure from the normal conception of instant rebirth. In Collin's view, as soon as a man dies, he is reborn in exactly the same body and proceeds to live the same life again only in a different dimension of time.

> . . . each ending life leaves a residue of effects – upon nature, environment, other men and women – which become the automatic causes of a life to come. The impress left by this body's deeds is the exact mould of the next body's form . . . Being and effects are one. In the moment of death, the pattern of these effects, transformed by this cosmic lightning into a single sign, is struck through time upon the waiting embryo. This is the secret of what happens to man's essence at death. *It causes the same body to be born again, in the same place, of the same parents, at the same time.* Such a possibility cannot belong to ordinary time, that is to man's fourth dimension. It can only belong to his fifth dimension, his recurrence, his eternity.

Collin makes the point that since time 'is round . . . our voyage through it must bring us inexorably to the same years we left behind.'

But Collin adds that the succession of lives should not be viewed in terms of a circle, but perceived as a spiral; in this way, while the pattern of a life remains the same, consciousness changes, so that each 'round' pitches the life onto a new level.

The eternal recurrence is not a new idea, of course, and Collin himself admits that his theories of celestial influence were strongly influenced by Gurdjieff and Ouspensky. Pythagoras taught eternal recurrence and Plato also suggested that an individual lives each life of many hundreds of lives, three times.[4] The Greek Stoic, Eudemus, for instance, believed that eternal recurrence involved a complete return in every detail. As Tadd Mann puts it in *The Divine Plot*, Eudemus 'identified two kinds of recurrence: one is "repetition in time" of the natural order of things such as the seasons, day and night, produced by cycles of the sun, moon, earth and the planets; the second is "repetition in eternity" in which identical things exist in a number of existences.'[5]

Mann has taken these theories about time and reincarnation and, like Collin, has adapted the logarithmic time scale to suit an astrological model – only with a few differences here and there. The concept of this astrological theory is based on the way that time appears to go faster as we grow older.

The reason why time apparently speeds up as we mature is due to the way our metabolic rate decreases with age. The metabolic rate of every living thing determines its perception, or experience of time; for instance, a gnat's entire lifespan may only take 24 hours of clock time, but to the gnat it is experienced as the equivalent of a man's lifetime. To a small child, a day can seem like an eternity, while the same day to an octogenarian appears to flash by. What Mann has done, following in Collin's footsteps, is to express this function of time in astrological terms using the logarithmic time scale – 1, 10, 100, 1000. In this case, 1 represents conception – the first lunar month; 10 represents ten lunar months (or nine calendar months), 100 – 100 lunar months (or seven years) and 1000, 1000 lunar months (or approximately 77 years). The point here is that the lifetime of a human ovum is one lunar month and approximately 1000 lunar months complete the average lifespan of a human being.

But while it may only take ten lunar months from conception to birth, the experience of that length of time to the foetus is the equivalent of some 35 years to an adult! Seen in terms of a logarithmic time-scale made up of equal divisions, it is possible to view a human lifetime comprised of equal biological time periods from conception to birth (1–10), from birth to age seven (10–100) and from seven to 76 (100–1000) (Fig. 16). Man is born after ten lunar months, childhood ceases at seven and maturity (from seven onwards) ends at death – approximately 1000 lunar months from conception.

Fig. 16

Collin named these divisions the octaves of gestation, childhood and maturity. Then, by subdividing each octave, he created nine stages or milestones – at 60 days of gestation, 28 weeks of gestation, birth, 10 months, 2 years, 7 years, 15 years, 35 years and 76 years (Fig. 17).

Fig. 17
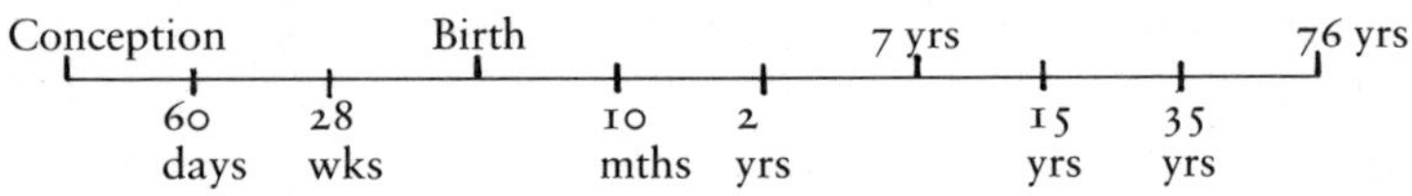

In so doing, he was able to link the cycles of the planets to these nine stages of development. For instance, the first milestone at sixty days, or two lunar cycles, coincides with the foetus as 'a marine creature, possessing gills and fins . . .'.[6] The second milestone at 117 days (28 weeks) coincides with the short cycle of Mercury and the point at which the foetus is capable of breathing. By the 8th milestone at 35 years, coinciding with the cycle of Mars,[7] the individual is at the peak of his powers. (I must add that there is a great deal more to Collin's theories about the part the planets play in the body's development; I am only discussing here what is ultimately relevant to astrological theories of reincarnation.)

I am not entirely convinced that Collin's planetary cycles can be said to precisely coincide with these milestones. However, I remain a great admirer of his work and believe that had he not died so prematurely, he would have emerged as one of the great mystics of the twentieth century.

Tad Mann also appears to have nurtured some doubts over the way the various planetary cycles coincide with the divisions along the logarithmic time scale, since he has not developed this aspect of Collin's theory. Instead, Mann has applied the same logarithmic measure to the horoscopic circle itself. Using the same octaves – gestation, childhood and maturity – he has divided the circle of the houses into three equal parts, beginning and ending at the cusp of the ninth house (Fig. 18).

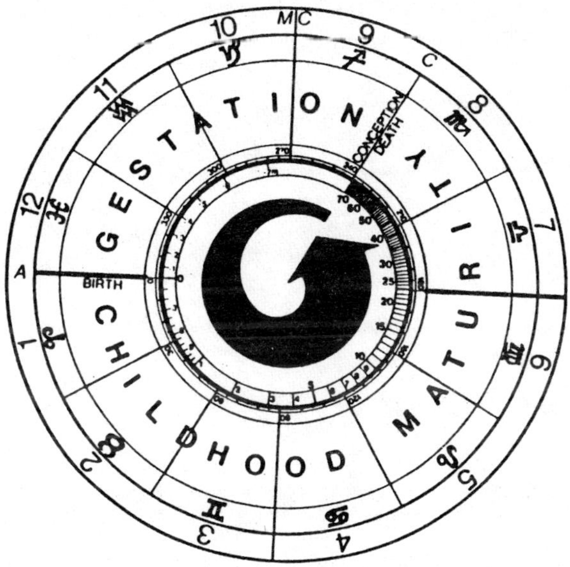

Fig. 18 *Tad Mann's 'Octaves of the individual's life cycle'. Taken from* The Divine Plot *(Allen and Unwin, 1986).*

With this process, Mann has developed his own system of astrology, Life*time Astrology, whereby events in the life – right from gestation to death – can be plotted against the 360 degrees of the zodiac circle.

After what may seem an almost unnecessary digression I will come to the reincarnational point. From relating the logarithmic time scale to the individual life cycle, Mann has applied the same process of measurement to the life cycle of mankind itself – again, using as his base, Collin's thesis. The lifetime of mankind can be viewed in terms of a World Age;[8] as far as Mann is concerned this involves a 50,000-year time span starting at 48,000 BC with the emergence of Cro-magnon man to the end of the twentieth century. In the same way that time appears to go faster as a human being ages, a world age 'speeds up' as it draws toward its end. Seen from an astrological point of view, in the gestation octave of the horoscopic circle, some 45,000 years elapse, while in the octave of maturity there are only some 500 years (Fig. 19).

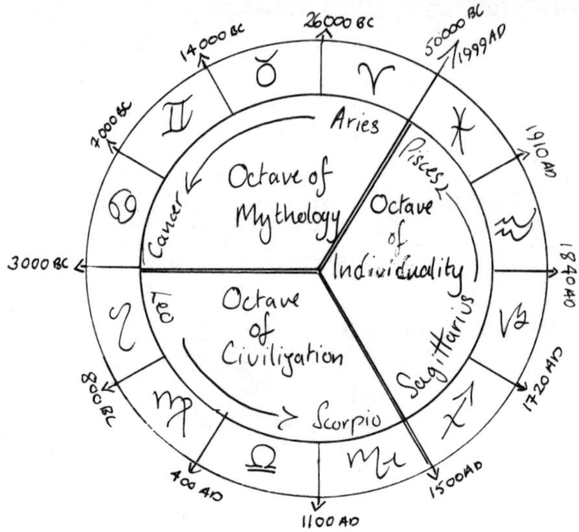

Fig. 19 *Tad Mann's Octaves of mankind's life cycle.*

By creating an astrological model whereby the history of mankind can be traced, Mann has also evolved a way of locating individual past lives. Each degree of the horoscopic circle, beginning from O° Aries and ending 29° 59′ Pisces, can be related to a particular period in history, bearing in mind that due to the phenomenon of time appearing to accelerate, one degree of Aries represents 1000 years, while 29° Pisces becomes the equivalent of only one year. By taking any planet or angle in an individual's birth chart, it is possible to trace the time period in history related to the present expression of that planet or point.

Applying Mann's Astrological Reincarnation Time Scale (ARTS) to my own chart, I find the Sun, according to Mann my 'primary masculine incarnation', relates to around 46118 BC. This means, again according to Mann, that my 'self-awareness and sense of objectivity' is imbued by memories of this incarnation as a primitive, tribal man. On the other hand, my Jupiter which is situated on my Ascendant, correlates to 1021 AD. Mann points out that the Ascendant is of crucial importance since it describes the period in history that my present personality, physical appearance and environmental characteristics originate from. Since Jupiter is also found at the same point, my religious belief system, world view and philosophical stance are also culled from a lifetime in the eleventh century. My moon, incidentally correlates to 1480[9] – precisely the time of Lucretia Borgia! Mann goes on to suggest that aspects between the planets in a birth chart describe the resultant conflict or harmony in terms of attitudes and memories relating to different lifetimes.

> The integration of a birth chart is symbolized by a group of space-time beings in various historical manifestations attempting to discover a higher purpose. Afflicted planets are difficult individuals in their time or indicative of imperfect understanding of a particular life time. Each planet tries to dominate the whole by recreating its natural time and mode of consciousness and behaviour, as sub-personalities can dominate an individual. Present-time reality is a collage of historical beings and their times joining, conflicting or integrating. Everyone is a multi-temporal being, eternally shifting from one identity to another . . . Each individual component is unique and potentially dominant, but the whole is served by integration which experiences all components. The parts must be identified with before we can be liberated from them.[10]

Despite his work meeting with strong criticism from some quarters,[11] I consider Mann's concepts to have much to offer the astrologer in search of reincarnation in the horoscope. Not the absolute truth, perhaps, but more signposts in the general direction.

Although many astrologers have discussed reincarnation in regard to astrology, Collin, Powell and Mann are outstanding in the sense that they have endeavoured to show an astrological mechanism for the process of reincarnation. Within astrological lore there are other suggestions as to what parts of the horoscope provide information about past lives, most notably that the Moon in a present birth chart represents the sign in which the Sun was placed in the previous incarnation and also that the nodal axis[12] and the vertex[13] are thought by many to hold past lives connections.

Ian Stevenson's work provided me with the ideal opportunity to test some of these theories. In his book, *Twenty Cases Suggestive of Reincarnation*, he gives the dates (and occasionally the times) of the death and rebirth of some of his cases – sadly, not all. While I found much of astrological interest in more than one of his case studies, I eventually decided to include Emilia and Paulo as examples. But I must stress that wherever I was able to find the dates and times of death and birth related to Stevenson's cases I subjected them to astrological analysis and found without exception meaningful links between the charts. Why I eventually chose one of Stevenson's Brazilian cases rather than any other is that the theme of suicide gave it an extra edge.

Emilia and Paulo are one of Stevenson's 'Two cases from Brazil' –

curiously, the other Brazilian case (Sinha and Marta) is taken from the same family and demonstrates a family predilection for suicide.

Emilia was born on 4 February 1902, the second child and eldest daughter of F. V. and Ida Lorenz. She had been named after a brother, Emilio who had died in infancy a few years earlier. From a young age, Emilia expressed frustration at being a girl and even informed her brothers and sisters that if there was such a thing as reincarnation, she would come back as a man. She was also convinced she would die single. Emilia was an unhappy girl and attempted suicide on several occasions during her short life; her favourite method was poisoning, from which she died on 12 October 1921. Some time after Emilia's death, her mother began to attend spiritualist seances at which she made contact with Emilia. Emilia told her that she was sorry about having committed suicide and that she wanted to return to her family – this time as a boy. Although she had already borne 12 children, Senora Lorenz became pregnant once more and, on 3 February 1923, she gave birth to a little boy whom she named Paulo.

For the first four or five years of his life, Paulo refused to wear boy's clothes – he would only wear girls' or none at all! He played with dolls, showed considerable natural skill at sewing and enjoyed the company of females. Only when he was given a pair of trousers made out of one of Emilia's skirts did he consent to wearing trousers. Eventually, however, he came to terms with his masculinity to the extent of joining the Brazilian army.

But Paulo's life was not a happy one. He had a history of poor health and retired early from the army through pulmonary TB – respiratory chest infections and bronchitis ran rife in the family, indeed an aunt, Sinha (the other Stevenson case from Brazil) had died of tuberculosis. From 1952 Paulo was employed by the Department of Highways, but apart from an interest in politics, there was little to make his life exceptional or unusual in any way. After retiring from the army, however, Paulo began to become increasingly paranoid. He came to believe that the military government was watching him after a friend of his had fled to Uruguay because of his political affiliations. The paranoid delusions continued until he eventually committed suicide on 5 September 1966. According to his brother, Paulo poured inflammable liquid over himself and set fire to himself at seven o'clock in the morning – he died 10 hours later.

To the more rationalist reader it may seem the height of absurdity to test a possible case of reincarnation – highly speculative in itself – with a tool equally as spurious as astrology. However, astrology is a system that yields, among other things, patterns and degree areas that can be

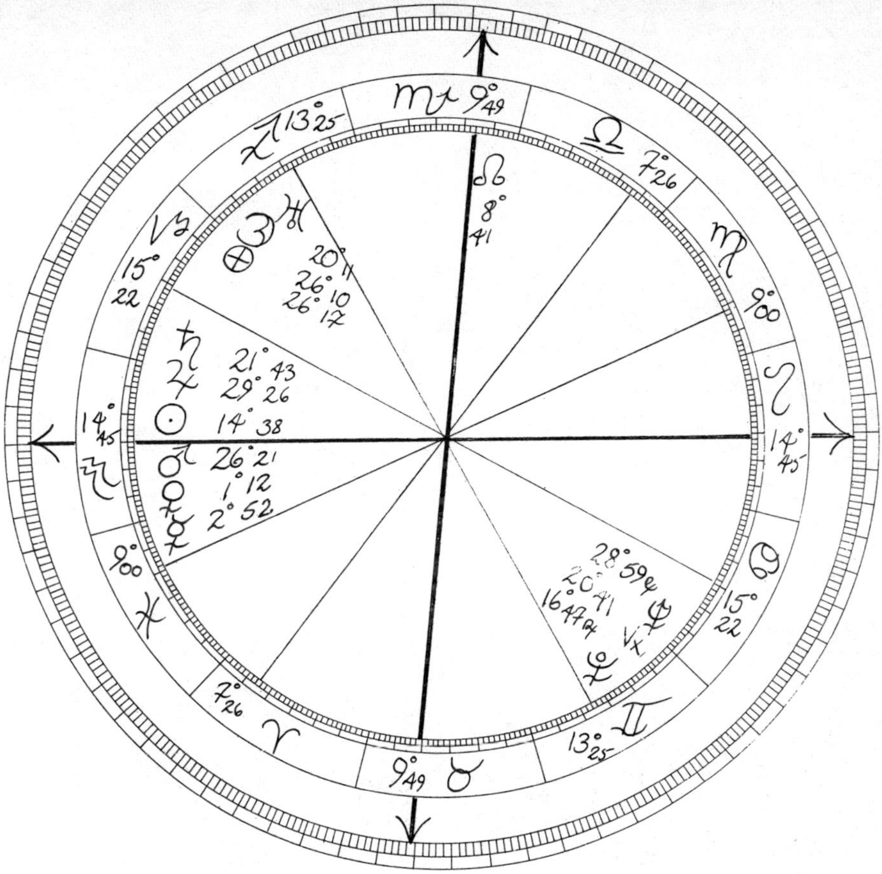

Emilia

4th. February 1902 solar (sunrise) chart: 30°S04: 51°W11

Fig. 20

used to demonstrate certain ties between one individual, or incident, and another or, indeed, one life time and another. While other astrologers have been able to produce some impressive examples of reincarnation through astrology, the case material has been based primarily on conjecture. However, Stevenson's cases have already been thoroughly researched and thus provide a far more substantial base to test any astrological reincarnation theories. Indeed, it is possible to kill two birds with one stone so to speak, for on the one

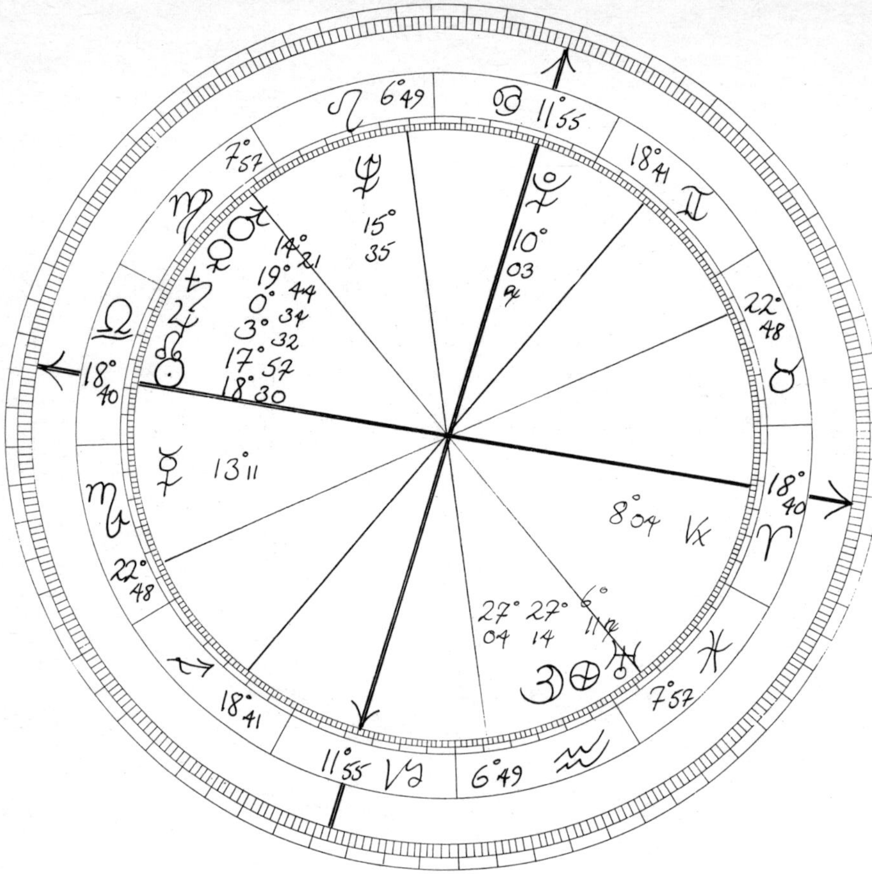

Emilia - death

12th October 1921 : solar (sunrise) chart : 30°s 04 : 51°w 11

Fig. 21

hand we have an unbiased sample with which to test astrological theories of reincarnation and, on the other, astrology can support or throw doubt on Stevenson's conclusions.

As far as Powell's theories are concerned, the charts of Emilia and Paulo do not bear out his first astrological 'law' – the aspect between the Sun and Saturn at Emilia's death is not repeated in Paulo's birth chart. However, Powell's extended 'law' *is* borne out through the charts: the Sun's position at Emilia's death (18° Libra) becomes, give

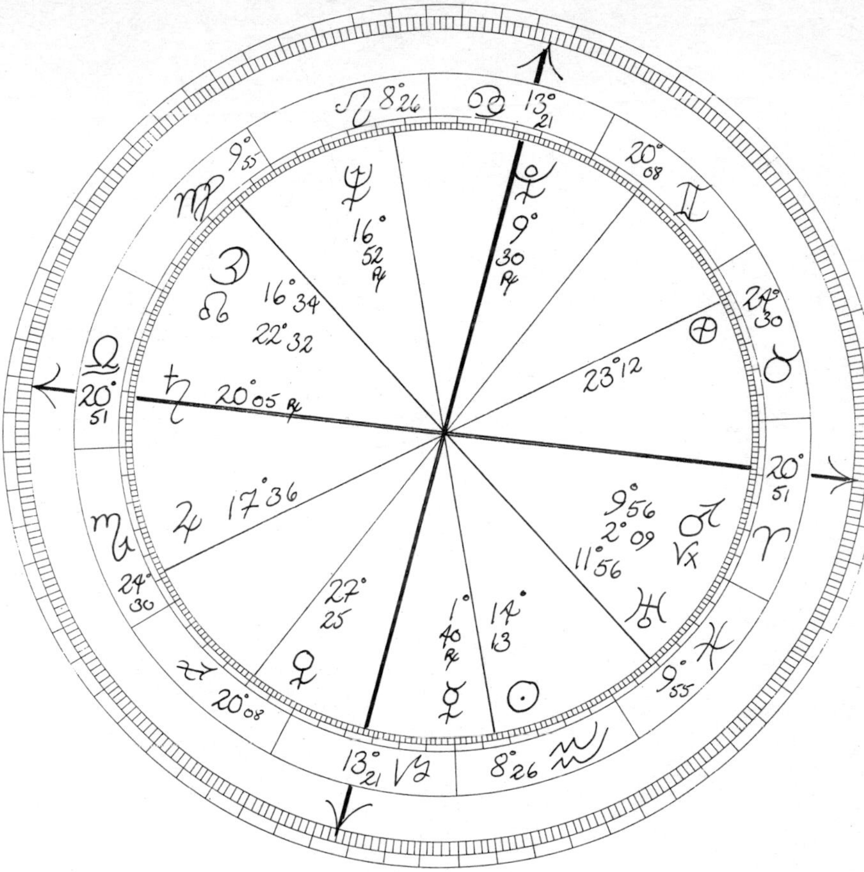

Paulo

3rd February 1923 : 22 hrs. 30′ BZT : 30° s 04 : 51° w 11

Fig. 22

or take a degree or so, Saturn at rebirth in Paulo's chart (20° Libra). And this radical Saturn of Paulo's squares Emilia's natal Saturn (21° Capricorn). Furthermore, by the time Paulo committed suicide Saturn had 'progressed' to 18° Libra – the Sun at Emilia's death. Saturn is assumed, not only by Powell, to play a major role in the process of karma and reincarnation, and the Saturn links between these charts do, I believe, support this belief. Intriguing, if nothing else.

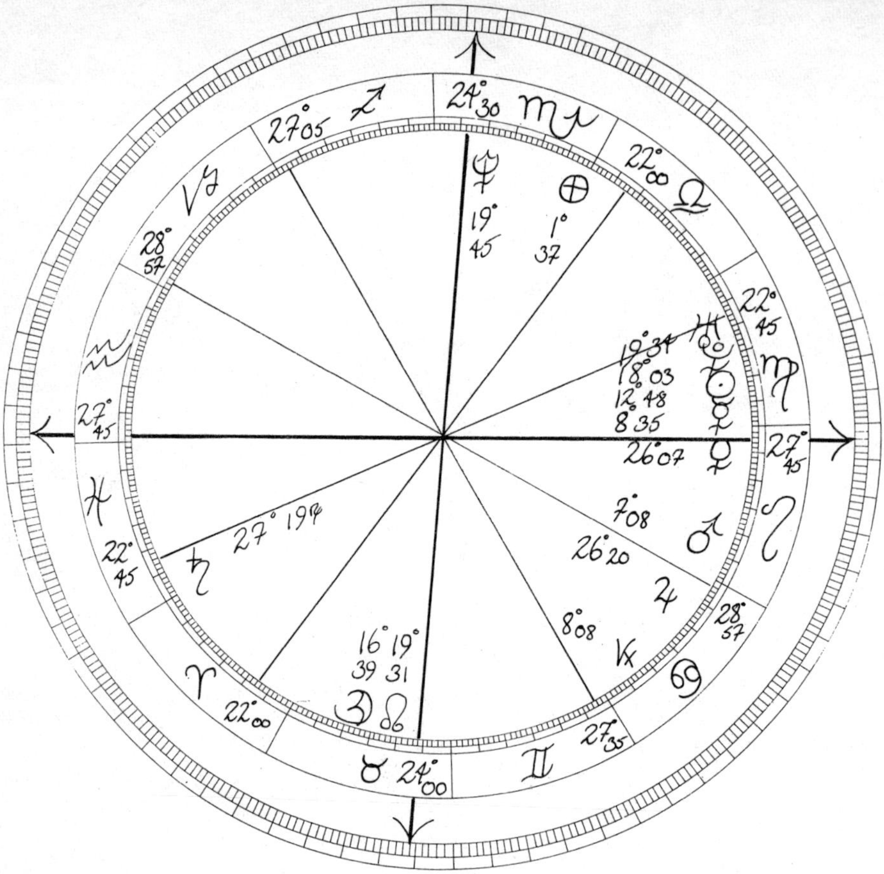

Paulo ~ death

5th September 1966 : 17hrs. 00 B.Z.T: 32°S 00; 52°W 20

Fig. 23 *For a table of the connections and parallels etc. between all the charts, see Appendix to this chapter.*

On the other hand, the charts do not exactly reflect Steiner's teaching, that the soul endeavours to come back into the same constellation as it left at death. Although the outer planets occupy roughly the same position in both charts, this is only because rebirth occurred within 18 months which gave Uranus, Neptune and Pluto little time to move very far. Venus and Mars in mid-Virgo at Emilia's death are echoed by Paulo's Moon in Virgo – at least in the rectified chart – and the Moon–Uranus conjunction at death could be a precursor to Paulo's Moon–Uranus opposition. However, to my mind these astrological similarities assume more importance viewed in connection with the natal charts of Paulo and Emilia rather than those of Emilia's death and 'rebirth' as Paulo. Perhaps with the benefit of precise times of death and birth, Steiner's teachings would be borne out more clearly, but since we have only the planetary positions to work from, we lack vital information about the position of the planets in the diurnal circle and the Ascendant and Midheaven signs. It must also be said that I have neither used the sidereal zodiac nor the heliocentric chart which Powell maintains are the only 'tools' with which to gain spiritual understanding, including such a process as reincarnation from the astrological configurations. Nevertheless, the information gleaned from the planets' positions in the signs is certainly enough to test some of the basic astrological premises of reincarnation – after all, the angular relationships between the planets do not alter from the sidereal to the tropical zodiac.

Unfortunately Tad Mann's theories cannot be put to the test with Emilia and Paulo's charts primarily because the analysis of other past lives (established by linking planetary positions to periods in history) would be redundant to this particular exercise – although I will be referring to his work in connection with other horoscopes in Chapter 9.

Emilia and Paulo's charts fail to give any credence to the 'old wives' tale' that the Moon's position in the current chart represents the Sun's sign in the previous incarnation. Paulo's Moon is very definitely in Virgo and Emilia was a Sun Aquarian. However, Virgo is a 'feminine' sign so the indication of the sex was there at least. But perhaps not all those 'old wives' tales are wrong, for Paulo's nodal axis at 22° Virgo – Pisces could be very significant indeed.

Although we do not know the precise time of Emilia's death, Venus could only have moved a degree during the day of her suicide, thus Venus at around 20° Virgo is close to Paulo's north node. (It is also worth noting that Emilia's natal Uranus is located at 20° Sagittarius – a crucial 90 degrees from the nodal axis.) By progression, Emilia's Moon would also have been near this point in Virgo. What a coincidence that Paulo's natal Moon should be placed in Virgo – possibly in the middle of the sign thus close to both Mars, Venus and the progressed Moon in Emilia's chart at the time of her suicide. What an even stranger coincidence to find that when Paulo also took his own life, Pluto and Uranus by transit were extremely close to this exact degree area in Virgo.

Certainly this clustering in a degree area around the north node would appear to show at the very least that this is an extremely sensitive area for life (and death) events – an area sensitive to echoes of the past intruding on the present.

On balance so far, the astrological case for reincarnation, based on tenets old and new looks fair.

My own feelings about astrology and reincarnation reflect my whole approach to astrology – fluid rather than fixed and absolute. In much the same way as one can establish the composer behind all his many and varied works, one can pin-point an astrological theme despite its many different representations in a birth chart. I am far more comfortable with the concept that an astrological life theme, like a soul name, should be carried through from incarnation to incarnation and this may be demonstrated by planetary relationships, particular degree areas or certain zodiac signs, than I am with by establishing connections between one chart and another with mathematical precision, or by pin-pointing correlations between the configurations at death and those of 'rebirth'. In the way of all things, each life and death is part of a continuing cycle – each death and rebirth but a resonance of an essential theme – one unfolding to the next retaining its connections with its original source. Thus, in the case of Paulo and Emilia, I am far more struck by the way Moon and Uranus are coupled together in both natal charts, that the luminaries are opposed by Neptune and there is a shared Aquarian–Sagittarian theme than that the charts dovetail precisely with one another. I must admit, of course, that it is a bonus that in this case (and, indeed in those included in the next chapter) there are some extremely close connections between the charts concerned.

I have already briefly referred to some of the similarities between Emilia's and Paulo's natal charts. One of the other striking connections is that because Paulo was born within a day of Emilia's birthday, the Suns' positions are extremely close – not merely in Aquarius but around 14° Aquarius. Of course, family members often share the same birthday but in this case Emilia informed her mother that she would be reborn into the family as a boy, thus arriving almost to the day of her birthday appears to be a confirmation of this prediction – after all, it would be almost impossible for her parents to contrive a birth at exactly this point in the year.

We know from Stevenson that Emilia was extremely frustrated with being a woman. She despised the constraints that existed on women at the time and wanted, above all, to have the freedom to travel. Stevenson also mentions that she had a great gift for needlework. Emilia's natal chart with its progressive, libertarian Aquarian emphasis and its thirst for adventure and wide horizons (depicted by the Moon–Uranus conjunction in Sagittarius and the Mars, Mercury, Venus stellium in Aquarius–Pisces) is in keeping with Stevenson's description of her character. That she was unhappy with her sexual identity is also suitably expressed by the Moon–Uranus conjunction in opposition to Neptune. Now I realize that this is a speculative sunrise chart, but even if she was born right at the end of 4 February, making the conjunction between the Moon and Uranus so weak as to be almost obsolete, the opposition to Neptune would still have remained throughout the 24 hours. This latter contact between the Moon and Neptune is often coincident with women who are confused about their femininity, if not downright disappointed about it. That Paulo has a Moon–Uranus opposition (effective throughout the birth date) and that on the day of Emilia's suicide there was a Moon–Uranus conjunction suggests to me that she may well have a natal conjunction between these two planets and that this may very well be a soul theme, or at least an issue requiring expression repeatedly. Emilia's sewing skills emerge through the conjunction of Mercury and Venus in Pisces trining Neptune – again, a configuration that is sustained throughout the 24 hours.

Paulo's Moon–Uranus opposition may well be a throw-over from Emilia and, with its erratic emotional overtones, certainly supplies a reason as to why he avoided entanglements with women. Emilia maintained that she wanted to die single and Paulo remained unmarried at his death at the age of 43. In Paulo's case it was not the Moon, the seat of femininity that was opposed by nebulous Neptune, but the Sun – his masculine identity. Thus in both cases the same ambivalence about sexuality is expressed. Indeed, one of the most striking parallels between these two charts is that while Paulo has a clear 'T'-square configuration involving the *Sun*, Neptune and Jupiter, Emilia also has a three-way relationship between the *Moon*, Neptune and Jupiter (Moon sextile Jupiter; Jupiter quincunx Neptune). Like Emilia, Paulo displayed a Mars–Neptune trine which is, without the benefit of the Ascendant to go on, the only area of the chart to reveal his similar great talent for sewing. Paulo, as another Aquarian soul with a Sagittarian Venus, a Mars in Aries and a Sun–Jupiter square, was able to fulfil all Emilia's frustrated desire to travel but, as Stevenson comments, he appeared to seek freedom at the expense of loneliness.

Apart from the Sun–Neptune opposition and the Mars–Neptune trine, there is little to account for Paulo's effeminate ways. (Stevenson makes the point that when he met Paulo aged 39, he was noticeably effeminate.) However, because of the importance of Venus around the time of Paulo's suicide, I began to speculate that Paulo may well have had Libra rising (making Venus the ruler of the chart) or Venus rising in Sagittarius. Both these configurations would bring a degree of gentleness and courtesy into the picture – at its extreme, a certain effeminacy – but I feel the Libran Ascendant has the edge. One of my reasons for favouring the Libran Ascendant is that the Sun was in Libra at the time of Emilia's suicide, thus it might be appropriate to find the same sign rising in the next incarnation; but perhaps, more importantly, the progressions and transits to Venus at the time of Paulo's suicide are more in keeping with the significant role of a ruling planet rather than a rising one.

Before I cover these progressions and transits, it might be worth examining the natal charts of Paulo and Emilia to see where the suicidal tendencies emerge. As far as Emilia is concerned, self-destruction is not a theme at the top of the list – but, here again, knowledge of the Ascendant and Midheaven might make all the difference. Mars is in the same sign as the Sun, but a little too far away to reflect any of the self-destructive and aggressive qualities of such a conjunction. Venus and Mercury in Pisces infer a tendency toward melancholia and despair, and the Moon–Uranus–Neptune configuration indicates a basic emotional instability. Paulo, on the other hand, has a very tight Mars–Pluto square (and from fiery Aries to Cancer) – so his galloping paranoia and fiery suicide are entirely in keeping with such an aspect.

Yet another route to establishing suicidal tendencies in a chart opens up through the work of one of astrology's most respected sons, Charles Carter. In his *Encyclopaedia of Psychological Astrology*,[14] Carter names Uranus as the 'principle afflictor' in cases of suicide and cites Jupiter's presence in Saturn signs or in aspect to Saturn as another indication of suicidal tendencies. He also states that 'The commonest zodiacal areas are about 15th of the cardinals (often tenanted also in the nativities of murdered people irrespective of suicide), about 25° of the fixed, a notably violent area in many respects, and about 26° of the mutables.'

Emilia and Paulo meet Carter's guidelines in more than one regard. Emilia not only has Jupiter in Capricorn (Saturn's sign) but conjunct Saturn; furthermore, at the time of her suicide, Jupiter was once again conjunct Saturn in Libra – the sign of Saturn's exaltation. Emilia also has Mars at 26° of fixed Aquarius and possibly her Moon at 26° of mutable Sagittarius. For his part, Paulo has Venus at 26° (or 27°) of mutable Sagittarius and at the time of his suicide (7 am) Venus was at 25° of fixed Leo.

The most significant progression at the time of Emilia's suicide was the Moon's square to natal Uranus – which was situated at the sensitive 20th degree of the mutables – and the progressed Sun was separating from a conjunction to natal Venus and Mercury. Transiting Neptune was separating from an opposition to her natal Sun and transiting Saturn was squaring natal Neptune – both highly indicative of a period of depression and confusion. Another extremely significant feature of Emilia's suicide was that the Sun was situated on the eclipse point – a factor revealed by its conjunction to the nodal axis. By great coincidence, Paulo also committed suicide with a luminary – in this case the Moon – at the nodal point. While for Emilia, this occurred in the Venus-ruled sign of Libra, for Paulo it was the other Venus-ruled sign of Taurus. Even if the fact of the two suicides occurring at the eclipse points has no bearing on the reincarnation issue, it reinforces the astrological belief that eclipses bode fateful events.

Venus again looms into significance with Paulo's suicide. On 5 September, transiting Saturn was at 27° mutable Pisces squaring natal Venus, while transiting Jupiter in Cancer was a quincunx away from natal Venus. At the moment of death, Venus (at 26° of Leo) was setting, trining its radical position. By progression Venus had reached a conjunction of the Sun while the progressed Sun was square natal Venus. I think these factors would persuade most astrologers that Venus must play a singularly important role in Paulo's horoscope.[15] Of course, there were other significant astrological features of Paulo's suicide. At seven in the morning when he set himself on fire, Pluto and Uranus were on the Ascendant and the MC–IC axis precisely squared Paulo's nodal axis. By the time of his death, the Moon was in close conjunction to the north node opposing an elevated Neptune suggestive, if nothing else, of a peaceful passing away.

I realize I have introduced a great deal more into the astrology of Emilia and Paulo's case than the reincarnation issue perhaps demanded. However, the charts provided such an irresistible opportunity to look at a whole range of astrological features, it seemed a pity to waste it. However, to conclude, I feel on balance that the astrology could well reinforce the possibility that Paulo was indeed the reincarnation of Emilia – there are a few too many connections and parallels between the charts, degree areas repeated, even some astrological tenets about reincarnation fulfilled, to justify mere coincidence. Yet I cannot overlook the fact that since Emilia and Paulo were brother and sister, the connecting and repeating astrological themes may be present simply because they are family themes. However, Stevenson also provided the birth dates of some other members of the Lorenz family and after setting up their solar charts I failed to find anything like as many 'coincidences'.[16]

The search for astrological laws of reincarnation is clearly a continuing one and the astrological case for reincarnation hardly 'sewn up'. However, I believe there is more than just a hint of promise that something beyond the laws of chance is revealing itself in the repeating degree areas and mirror images – whether of death and rebirth or life after life. Although with Paulo's case I suspect that the family link may mask the astrological reincarnation theory, I have come across cases where hereditary links are not present to confuse the issue – two of which I discuss in the next chapter. It may be that Powell, with his Steinerian background, is on the right track – even if he is adamant that his 'laws' should not be used to test reincarnation; it may also be that Mann has cracked the astrological reincarnation code. For my part, I prefer to consider that resonances are carried through from life after life, chart to chart, and that these resonances can be perceived in the astrology albeit with subtle variations in the harmony which allow for change and growth from one life to the next – whatever the sequence in chronological time. Yes, cosmic laws must play a precise part in the process and timing of reincarnation, but we need a far more powerful 'telescope' with which to view the totality of the picture.

NOTES

1. Synastry is the name given to the astrology of relationships. It is derived from two Greek words, *syn* (meaning bring together) and *astron* (star).
2. Rudolph Steiner, *Life Between Death and Rebirth* (Anthroposophical Press Inc. New York, 1968)
3. In a letter published in *Correlation*, the *British Journal of Research into Astrology*, Vol. 8, no. 1, June 1988, Richard Nolle comments, 'Proof [that certain people are the reincarnation of others] comes easy for Robert Powell. He simply accepts the authority of Rudolph Steiner . . . If Steiner claims that he was the reincarnation of St Thomas Aquinas (and he did make such a claim), that's all it takes to convince Powell.
   . . . All things considered, it seems fair to state that *Hermetic Astrology* presents a doubtful case for Robert Powell's theory of the astrological 'laws' of reincarnation. This won't deter Powell in the least, for he considers his Hermetic' approach to be above and beyond criticism. ('The results of karma research,' Powell maintains, '. . . ought not to be treated in the same way as scientific facts.')

   Richard Moxon adopts a similar critical stance in his comments on Professor Rudnickis' review of *Hermetic Astrology*. I refer those interested to *Correlation*, vol. 7, no. 2, December 1987.

4. A. T. Mann, *The Divine Plot* (Allen & Unwin, 1986)
5. Ibid.
6. Rodney Collin, *Theory of Celestial Influence* (Robinson & Watkins, 1973).
7. Table taken from *Theory of Celestial Influence*:

PLANET		*CONJUNCTION*	
		Earth, Planet, Sun	*Earth, Planet, Sun, Zodiac*
(Moon		29½ days)	
Mercury	117	days (4 lunar cycles)	× 25 = 8 years
Venus	585	,, (20 ,, ,,)	× 5 = 8 ,,
Mars	780	,,	× 7 = 15 ,,
Asteroids[25]	468	,,	× 7 = 9 ,,
Jupiter	398	,,	× 11 = 12 ,,
Saturn	378	,,	29 = 30 ,,
Uranus	369	,,	83 = 84 ,,
Neptune	367	,,	163 = 164 ,,

8. The concept of world ages is common to many cultures and religions. In Hindu tradition cosmic time is divided into sections of hundreds of thousands of years known as Yugas; the Hopi Indians also believe in massive cycles of time that constitute the four worlds – almost identical in qualities to the Yugas. Astrology also takes into account huge epochs called Zodiacal Ages spanning some 25,952 years; these ages are derived from the phenomena of the Precession of the Equinoxes. Mann bases his belief in the 50,000 year duration of a world age on 'the consensus among anthropologists that humans became conscious about 50,000 years ago at the time human pigmentation occurred. Richard Leakey states that homo sapiens is 50,000 years old . . . The Jewish Jubilee Cycle is 50,000 years and added importance was given to the year AD 1000 as the beginning of the last thousand-year Jubilee Year . . . The astronomical-astrological mechanism of the precession of equinoxes also corresponds to the duration of about 50,000 years as two equinoctial cycles – a night and day of creation similar to the night and day of Brahma.' (*The Divine Plot*)
9. Although, as I discuss in Chapter 9, Mann's ARTS did not appear to 'strike home' with either of the past-life case histories discussed in this book, my life as Martinus (Chapter 7, p. 135), a character involved with magical practices and political intrigue in Italy, was indeed born in 1482 – a time period precisely earmarked by my Moon in Scorpio.
10. *The Divine Plot*
11. A particularly harsh review of *The Divine Plot* was penned by Nicholas Kollerstrom in *The Astrological Quarterly* of the Astrological Lodge of London, vol. 60, no. 4, Winter 1986.
12. The north and south node of the Moon are the points at which the Moon

in its orbit intersects with the ecliptic. The interpretation of these points in astrology is by no means uniform or clearcut, but most astrologers agree that they are sensitive areas for transits and progressions and in synastry. The association of the Moon's nodes with fate and karma stems from the fact that the nodal axis is the point where eclipses occur – astrologers of antiquity believed that eclipses portended events of great magnitude. In Hindu astrology, the nodes are supremely important and given the names of Rahu (Dragon's Head – the north node) and Kethu (Dragon's Tail – the south node).

13. 'Astrologically the Vertex is a term originated by the modern astrologer Johndro, arising from a theory (perhaps based on a suggestion made by Collin) that the existence of a magnetic field within and around our earth postulates that there must be two "Ascendants" (or more properly, two Ascendant Descendant axes), one being magnetic the other electrial' (Fred Gettings, *Dictionary of Astrology* Routledge & Kegan Paul, 1985). In my work with synastry, the vertex appears to figure strongly when two individuals experience a sense of *force-majeure* in the relationship. I have also noticed that transits or progressions to the vertex, rather like the nodal axis, coincide with periods of great and unexpected change.
14. Charles Carter, *An Encyclopaedia of Psychological Astrology* (Theosophical Publishing House, 1972)
15. There is a consensus of opinion among astrologers that Venus often assumes a significant role at death. However, I feel in Paulo's case, there are so many progressions and transits involving this planet that it warrants a powerful role in the natal horoscope.
16. Out of all the Lorenz family members Stevenson mentions in *Twenty Cases Suggestive of Reincarnation*, he includes the birth dates of only Marta and Waldomiro. Marta 14 August 1918, Waldomiro 10 May 1913. Neither of these dates produces as many of the same features as those shared by Emilia and Paulo, although, interestingly, both the Suns fall in the mid-fixed signs, like Emilia's and Paulo's.

The connections between the charts of Emilia and Paulo:

EMILIA'S NATAL CHART (SUNRISE)	PAULO'S NATAL CHART (SPECULATIVE)
☉ 14°♒	☉ 14°♒
♄ 21°♑ (in own sign)	♄ 20°♎ (in sign of exaltation)
☽☍♆	☉☍♆
♃	♃
☽♆	☉♆
♂△♆	♂△♆
☽☌♅	☽☍♅
☽☌♅ in 3rd decanate ♐	♀ (chart ruler) in 3rd decanate ♐

EMILIA'S DEATH CHART (SUNRISE)

Transiting ☉ (@ 18°♎) ☌ eclipse point

(N.B. Paulo's ♄ rad. 20°♎)

Transiting ♀ @ 20°♍

Progressed ☽ @ 21½°♍

(N.B. Paulo's ☊ rad. 22°♍

Transiting ♆□☉ rad. (@1½° of orb)

Transiting ☽☍♆ (the day prior to suicide)

P ☉☌♀ rad. (2° of separation)

PAULO'S DEATH CHART

Transiting ☽ (@ 17°♉) ☌ eclipse point

Transiting ♅☌♇ @ 19°♍

(At 7 am when he set fire to himself

Asc: @ 18°♍; M.C. @ 22°♊

Transiting ♆□☉ rad. (@ 5° of orb)

Transiting ☽☍♆ (6 hours later)

P ♀☌☉ rad. (exact)

P ☉□♀ rad.

T ♄□♀ rad.

T ♀☌ desc. □ M.C.

BIBLIOGRAPHY

John Anthony West and Jan Gerhard Toonder, *The Case for Astrology* (Penguin, 1973)

9
Transformations

> Ask and it shall be given you; seek, and ye shall find; knock, and it shall be opened unto you.
>
> Matthew 7:7

Over the 18-month period that Michael was regressing everybody on the project, I in turn listened to the tapes of the sessions – most of them riveting – and set up all the charts concerned. It was extremely satisfying for me to note the many astrological coincidences between the charts of a past life and those of the current life and just how well the past life horoscope could be interpreted according to the history provided. Details of personal characteristics and descriptions of childhood tallied uncannily with past-life charts – one individual who claimed he was a soldier with a fiery temper had Mars rising in Scorpio, another who spent her life in a nunnery had a crowded 12th house. On several occasions, when the past-life personality would give an age when a major event in the life occurred, it could be seen reflected in the progressions and transits at the time. In one of my own past lives as Sarah, the year in which my husband died, progressed Venus had reached the conjunction of Neptune in Sarah's 7th house of relationships, while transiting Saturn also opposed radical Neptune; in the month I maintained that he had died (October) the progressed Moon was squaring natal Saturn in the 8th house – all most apposite for the death of a spouse. Sometimes, of course, there were anomalies. One man described a life as a Syrian monk, Hashim, who worked with the healing power of plants. He was a fanatic and talked repeatedly about the conflict he experienced between Christianity and Sufism. Although the past-life horoscope bore some features of the life and personality described, Hashim seemed far more of a reflection of the current life chart. In this horoscope, situated in the solitary and mystical 12th house, there is a stellium of planets including the Sun in Taurus (a sign synonymous with the fruits of the earth), a Sun–Pluto square and a Moon opposition Saturn–Neptune – again involving the 12th house. However, perhaps it was no mere coincidence that this individual felt that he was indulging in a marvellous fantasy during the regression rather than reliving a past life.

At the end of the day, there were any number of fascinating case histories that I could have included here, but I had to limit myself to two. I have done my best not to clutter the text with a constant liturgy of astrological degrees and aspects and have therefore included only the most relevant horoscopic details – astrological devotees will be able to peruse all the data connected with these case histories in the appendix to this chapter (pp. 202–3). Also I have deliberately refrained from adopting an objective stance to these case histories, fearing that I would interrupt the flow of information. In turn I would urge readers to suspend disbelief for the course of this chapter and allow themselves to be simply borne along by the narrative.

Viola's regression was one of the first I dealt with. I sat in my study at the top of the house one sunny morning in early September 1988 listening to the tape of the session. At first her voice was very faint and she seemed to be trying, with Michael's help, to get her bearings. Then suddenly she began to cough – great choking coughs and rasping breaths. 'My God . . . my God . . . I'm burning!' she shrieked! A *frisson* rippled along my body like an electric charge. I had never heard anything so horrifically real. Michael gently moved her forward in time, but it took some minutes before she could be calmed. Eventually, she was able to say who she was and tell her story.

Anne was born on 2 July 1760 at twenty minutes past eleven at night in Goan, Scotland. She was illegitimate and her mother had died when she was two years old. Her Aunt Ellen took care of her after her mother's death, but she was cruel and eventually Anne ran away. In her teens she lived in the wild with a young man called Jim, but her youthful happiness was cut short when she was abducted by soldiers and forced to cook and care for them. The bulk of the regression, however, centred on Anne's trial. She was accused of being a witch and ultimately sentenced to be burnt at the stake. The peak moment of the regression occurred when she recognized the judge who had condemned her to death – he was none other than her mother, Grace, in her current lifetime.

As a child, Viola had had all the privileges that a middle-class background in Rhodesia (now Zimbabwe) could provide; what she did not have was love and attention – at least from her mother. Her father, on the other hand, did give her affection, although as a staunch Christian Scientist he tended to withdraw frequently into his inner spiritual sanctum. Viola described her mother as a 'rather distant creature'; a socialite who was 'out to lunch' in more ways than one. As a child, Viola cannot remember being kissed by her mother; indeed, her only recollection of any kind of demonstrative affection was when her mother once placed her hand on her forehead when she had a temperature. No doubt as a reaction to her rather distant family life, Viola became a wild and unruly child, and was often beaten for her bad behaviour. Her great escape proved to be the world of drama and, at the age of eighteen, she left Rhodesia to study acting in England. She had a successful career as an actress and married a renowned scenic designer. Tragically, her husband died when she was only 29, and she did not remarry until she was 37. Fate was to strike another blow for her a year later when her second husband was killed in a car crash – a matter of weeks after she lost their child in pregnancy. Viola, now no longer an actress, initially taught drama, then after completing a clinical psychotherapy course felt the pull of a more spiritual path. She studied yoga – which she subsequently taught – primal therapy and bio-energetics. She now works as a psychotherapist, incorporating art and drama as a dynamic aid to therapy, and is concerned to expand her spiritual horizons.

With such a rich and varied background in metaphysics and psychotherapy, Viola had been able to work through many of her psychological 'blind spots'; however, the one difficulty that would not go away, and the one problem that no amount of therapy seemed able to resolve, was her relationship with her mother, Grace. A normally calm and intelligent woman, Viola had been known to go to extraordinary lengths to avoid her mother. Apart from living some 10,000 miles away in the first place, when Grace visited, Viola spent much of her time trying to avoid close contact – on one occasion actually retiring to the inner recesses of her bedroom cupboard. Viola did not need to be a psychotherapist to recognize that this kind of behaviour was odd.

It was with the intention of trying, yet again, to get to the bottom of her mother-problem that Viola decided to join the regression project. And indeed, the realization that the judge who sent her to an horrific death in 1808 was her mother in this current lifetime turned out to be the breakthrough Viola had sought for so long.

Under hypnosis, Michael took Viola beyond her death as Anne and suggested that she contact her spiritual guide for some help in resolving the trauma of this lifetime. Her guide told her,

> What you, Anne, need to do now is forgive your judge. He was acting in good faith, protecting the society in which he lived from what he thought was the evil he saw in you. It is for you to forgive him. He was doing his job. He believed what he was doing was right. And he did not do it out of any personal revenge or hatred.

Viola somewhat reluctantly agreed to forgive the judge, rationalizing, 'if I did what was right for me in my lifetime, then I can accept that what he was doing was also right.' After the regression, Viola felt refreshed and certainly fascinated about all that had been revealed, but she experienced no sense of any great burden being lifted off her shoulders. Three weeks later, Viola went back to see Michael in the hopes that another regression might enable her to cope with her mother's imminent visit. During this 'regression', no attempt was made to return to her life as Anne, nor indeed any other. The aim of the session was to take Viola into an altered state of consciousness where further insight and potential resolution might occur. With this in mind, Michael suggested to Viola that she assume the role of Buddha and allow him to speak on the nature of the problem.

We are all part of one another. There is no separation and nothing to reconcile. You and your mother are both part of each other. Forgiveness presupposes that there has been a wrong done; the only wrong is to oneself. So it follows that we must forgive ourselves . . . Approach your situation with an open heart. Love and let go the resentment.

Once again, at the end of the session, Viola was disappointed that she felt no sense of great release; she considered, therefore, that there had been no cathexis. However, she was mistaken. To her great amazement, some days later when Grace arrived, Viola found her usual distress had disappeared. As she told me some time later in our astrology session, 'Yes, I found her irritating but all the strong emotions had gone; all the fear had gone. Before, even when I just talked about her, my heart would be leaping up and down, I'd be twitching and my head would start going round and round. That just stopped. It was like the charge had gone out of the relationship.' On her mother's return Viola found no need to constantly write to her as she had done in the past. 'I feel it's finished business. My whole life has changed. This great constant shadow has totally vanished.'

Viola's chart is redolent with a parental problem – especially a maternal one. The Moon, symbolizing (among many themes) mother, emotions and childhood, is rising to the Ascendant and squaring Neptune on the MC–IC axis – planets on the angles assume far greater significance. Venus, the ruler of the chart, is placed in the compassionate, victim-saviour sign of Pisces and is drawn into a mutable 'T'-square with Mars and Saturn. (I appreciate that Venus is 10 degrees more than the requisite 90 from Saturn, but because Mars, which is square to Venus, *is* opposing Saturn, Venus in turn becomes linked to this difficult planet.) Neptune's conjunction to the IC which I

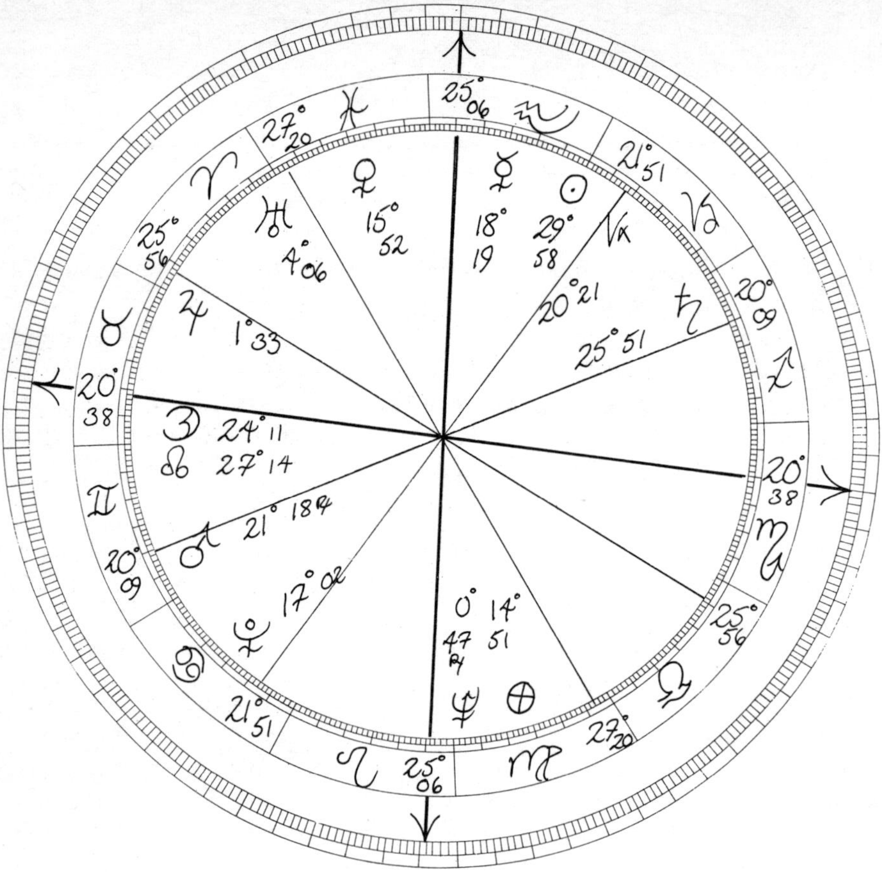

Viola

January 20th 1929 : 14 hrs 00 LT : 26°S15 ; 28°E00

Fig. 24

have discussed earlier in this book[1] rarely suggests that family life is plain sailing. That Neptune is directly linked to the Moon by hard aspect suggests mother is an indistinct figure – in fact, all the qualities in Grace that Viola describes. But my consultation with Viola was to reveal something even more powerful about this angular Moon – Neptune aspect and Venus's position in Pisces in the 10th house[2] – a veritable family ghost, or shadow, as it were.

During World War I, Grace's father had been sent to South Africa

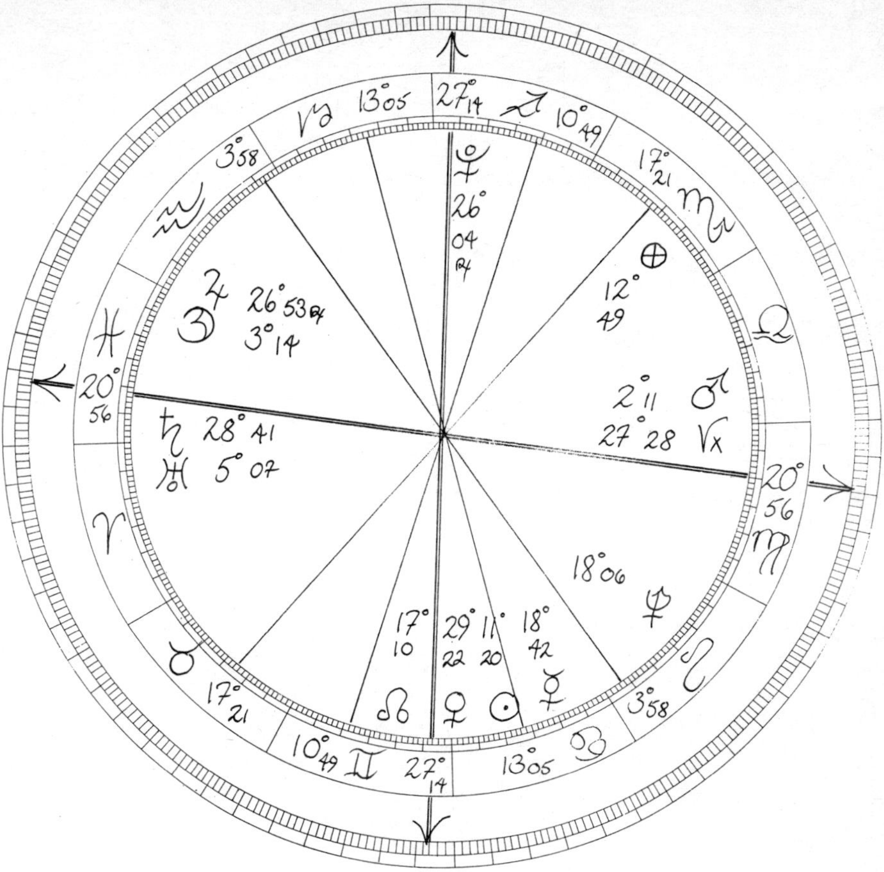

Anne

July 2nd 1760 : 23hrs. 20 L.T. : 55°N50 ; 4°W 26

Fig. 25

while she, her mother, three sisters and a brother remained in England. Grace's mother missed her husband greatly and, unable to wait any longer, she decided to take herself and the children out to join him. They went by sea and, in mid-Atlantic, the boat was torpedoed and sunk. Grace and her brother were the only members of the family to survive and after 36 hours in a dinghy, they were miraculously rescued. It was an event that must have haunted Viola's mother all her life and she has never been able to speak about the incident. (Grace,

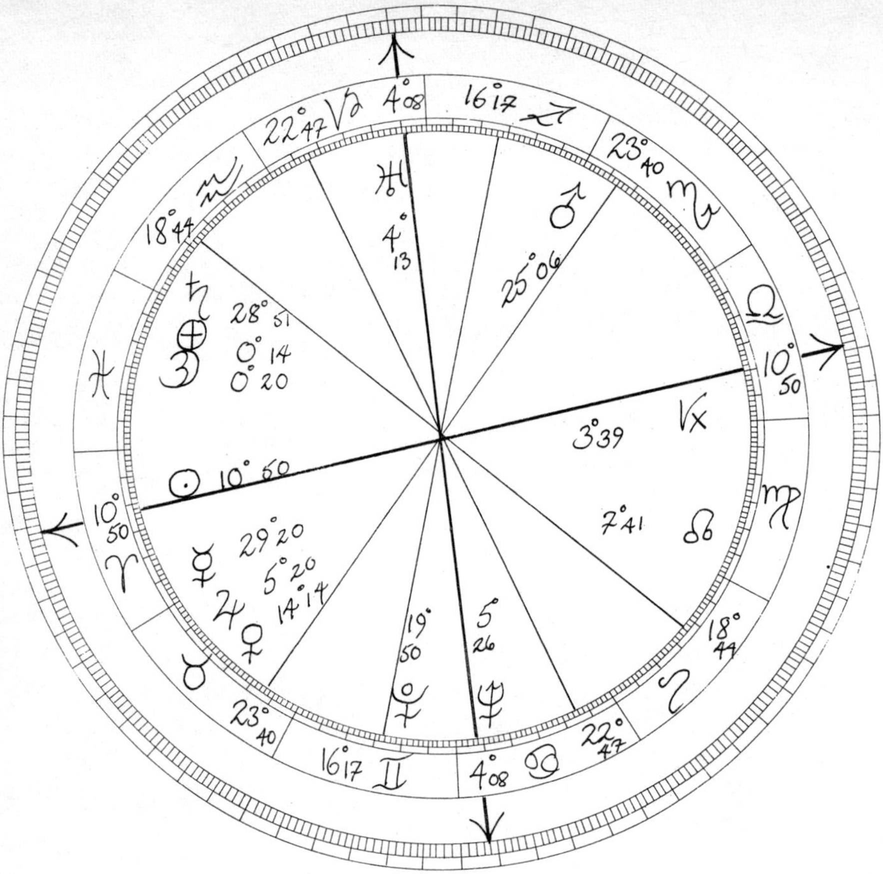

Grace

April 1st 1905 : Solar (sunrise) chart : 51°N30 ; 0°W10

Fig. 26

incidentally has a cardinal 'T'-square involving Sun, Neptune and Uranus in her horoscope.) Clearly, this trauma is implicated in Viola's mother's inability to express love; she must have experienced considerable guilt over her survival while her mother and sisters had died; in the process she detached herself permanently from her emotions. However, it does not explain why Viola bore the brunt of this emotional withdrawal, for Grace seemed able to express her love and affection openly for Viola's brother.

At the risk of labouring the point, such themes as the sea and drowning, on the one hand, and guilt, sacrifice and suffering, on the other, are entirely Neptunian. Thus Neptune's position in the family seat of Viola's horoscope can be interpreted not only as the insubstantial emotional life of the family and its effect on Viola, but as a symbol of the ancestral cross the family bears. Viola's family tragedy is imprinted in her horoscope, and in the way of the collective nature of these outer planets, it is as if she became the focus for this family ghost and because of it came within a whisker of fulfilling the role of the sacrificial lamb.

How fascinating then to find that there is a strong Neptunian theme not only linking Viola and her mother, but uniting Anne's and Viola's chart. Anne has Pisces rising with Neptune, the ruler of the chart, squaring Viola's Ascendant and opposing Viola's Mercury; Anne's Moon in Pisces is also in opposition to Viola's Neptune. The Neptunian theme in Anne's chart is certainly a reflection of her sense of being in the grip of fate and a victim of circumstance – a powerful resonance to span across two lifetimes. Also significant is the placing of Anne's Jupiter at 26° 52′ Aquarius which is Viola's Midheaven and Grace's Saturn; this degree area also squares the all-important nodal axis and Grace's Mars.[3] But perhaps most fascinating of all, Anne's Grand Cross in mutable signs contacts Viola's Saturn thereby triggering Viola's mutable 'T'-square. In both cases Venus and Mars are the personal planets locked in conflict with Saturn – and in poor Anne's chart, Pluto as well.

These mutable configurations resound to a theme of rejection, frustration and emotional hardship. In Anne's case, the involvement of Pluto and its placing on the Midheaven suggest that this conflict may indeed involve authority and that, as her life so vividly portrayed, she was tied to the stake of an inescapable destiny. In Viola's case, apart from the sense of emotional rejection that she suffered as a child and a general lack of appreciation for her gifts – very typical of a Venus –Saturn square – with Saturn in the eighth, she has found herself widowed twice. (It is also worth commenting that Viola's marriages were unhappy, not because the content of the relationships were sexually or emotionally unfulfilling or the partner cruel and indifferent, but because both her husbands through dying rejected her and provided her with much ensuing pain and hardship.) To find a mutable Grand Cross in a claimed past-life chart and a mutable 'T'-square in the current lifetime involving the same planets and similar degree areas is stretching the laws of coincidence a little too far to my mind.

Given that Grace was also a key figure in Anne's life, I wondered if there might be some links between their two charts, particularly any contacts to Anne's Grand Cross. But with the lack of a time of birth for

Grace, the all-important four angles of the chart are missing and therefore some potentially crucial astrological contacts. The most significant link to the Grand Cross is formed by Grace's Pluto – again, like Anne's, in Gemini – although it is a little too far away to be truly significant. However, Pluto is not an insignificant planet to play a key role in this situation given its awesome power and its association with death and rebirth and, while it may not precisely contact Anne's Grand Cross, it forms a close square aspect to Anne's Ascendant from a 10th house, authoritarian position. (Grace's Pluto, of course, forms a close conjunction to Viola's Mars and is thus attached to her sensitive mutable 'T'-square.) I think the Plutonic link between Grace's and Anne's chart carries more than just a flavour of the part Grace played in condemning her to a slow and painful death for witchcraft. And perhaps because this Pluto is in turn touching Viola's sensitive 'T'-square, the echo of a past life can be seen as the underlying reason for the fear and anxiety Viola experienced over her mother.

One other extraordinary set of coincidences, this time between Anne's and Viola's charts emerged in the progressions. I decided to progress Anne's chart forward to Viola's birth – some 169 years. I will leave these progressions to speak for themselves.

Anne's progressed (p.) Sun 27° 38′ Sagittarius – conjunct Anne's radical (r) Pluto and triggering Grand Cross and conjunct (by 1) Viola's r. Saturn and 'T'-square.
Anne's p. Moon in Taurus in the area of Viola's Jupiter, Ascendant, Moon and north node.[4]
Anne's p. Mercury 26° 03′ Sagittarius conjunct Anne's r. Pluto and triggering her Grand cross and Viola's Saturn etc.
Anne's p. Venus 28° 49′ Capricorn is conjunct Viola's r. Sun.
Anne's p. Mars 27° 56′ Capricorn is also conjunct Viola's r. Sun.

It also occurred to me that Tad Mann's reincarnation timescale (ARTS) could be deployed to find out if Grace and Viola were connected in the eighteenth century. Of course, I was hoping that Pluto, Saturn, or indeed any of the participating planets in the mutable configurations would be implicated. I would not say that the connections were overwhelming so much as interesting, and sadly, none of the main planetary characters are involved. Grace's Uranus' at 4 Capricorn, which ricochets around all three charts at 4 to 5 of the cardinals, yields a period of around 1740 which would indeed coincide with Anne's and the judge's lifetime. Uranus viewed as the higher self, rather than the principle of revolution, would endow this synchronicity with more significance. So perhaps here the ARTS can be seen to reflect the past life – just. However, all-important Pluto, which conjuncts Viola's Mars, is around 21° Gemini and synchronizes with 8500 BC, and so fails to register with the relevant time period, as does every other planet in the crucial mutable configurations.

I do not think this cross-reference with Tadd Mann's ARTS either confirms or denies his hypothesis nor Viola's past life. Mann shows evidence in support of his theories in his book, *The Divine Plot* and I urge readers to peruse his results before drawing any firm conclusions from my own findings. But I might add that in Chloe's case, which I will discuss shortly, once again the ARTS failed to resonate with the time periods involved in any of the lifetimes.

In Viola's case, the connections between all the charts concerned and the degree areas involved persuade me that at the very least something more than just coincidence is at work. But whether the astrology, good as it is, can really be said to add substance to the belief that Anne was a genuine past life, is open to opinion. The ability of the psyche to construct a history and synchronistically find suitable birth data to reflect the fantasy life is to many minds far more plausible than the ability to remember a past life. From the astrological point of view, incorporating the chart of the past life with Anne's traumatic existence etched in its symbolism, brought new insight to Viola's current life horoscope. The planetary symbols and configurations in Viola's chart not only reflected her present life traumas and problems but also those of her past life. In this way, as an astrologer, I was able to benefit from a much broader perspective and deeper understanding of the symbolism. Viola's problem with her mother – mirrored in the Moon – Neptune square and the 'T'-square – might merely have been interpreted as Grace's inability to show love and affection to Viola and its subsequent damage to their relationship; with the knowledge that there was a deep mutual hatred and mistrust stemming from a distant past suddenly the reasons for Grace's distance and Viola's fear became absolutely clear. But, leaving aside the astrology, what cannot be denied and what is of paramount importance is the response these memories and realizations evoked in Viola's present life. After thirty years of persistently trying to resolve her fear of and difficulty with her mother, it was only through recalling a life as Anne, together with the wisdom gained through the dialogues and the act of forgiveness that such a cathexis could occur. To Viola, her past life was absolutely real and the transformation a testament to that reality.

*

Chloe is a vivacious, glamorous and highly intelligent female. At sixteen she left the United States, travelling via Europe to South Africa where she studied English literature at university. She married an English lawyer, Stephen, in 1968 and by 1974 had produced two children – a girl and a boy. Eventually, frustrated by the shackles of domesticity, she joined a national newspaper as a journalist and by the early 1980s had worked her way into a lucrative, successful and high-powered career in television. In 1986 she met and fell in love with an Italian writer and, during the course of their affair, left her husband and moved to London to be with her lover. Over the past three years, she has launched a second successful career in film and television in both England and the United States.

At the time I first met Chloe, in the summer of 1988, she was in a state of some anxiety and confusion alternating between periods of great depression and manic elation. The primary reason for her state of being was the state of the relationship between herself and her lover, Andreas.

Andreas had been introduced to Chloe by a close friend at a lunch party. Within three days they were in bed and passionately in love. 'We both knew something extraordinary had happened to us. We knew there was no going back. This was no brief affair, but something much, much greater. It seemed to have a grip over us and we both felt as if we had been taken over by some immense cosmic event.' After much to-ing and fro-ing between her husband and her lover, Chloe eventually left Stephen 'permanently' and moved in with Andreas – a move which involved leaving Johannesburg for London. However, wracked by guilt over leaving Stephen and the children, in May of 1988 she went back to South Africa; a decision that proved somewhat short-sighted for some two months later she returned to England to be with Andreas again. Not surprisingly, Andreas refused to take her back.

Thus Chloe was in the centre of this emotional furore when we met. She had been referred to my colleague, Michael, who considered her an ideal candidate for the astrology-regression project. And he was right.

Chloe proved to be a perfect 'deep trance' subject. At each of the regression sessions, she slipped almost effortlessly into another time and space: her tone of voice, facial expressions and dialect changed dramatically and the information she gave was full of interest and relevance. By the end of October 1988, I too began to work with her, using the astrology to shed light on the many faceted aspects of her personality and her complex relationships, thereby encouraging the gradual and painful process of transformation.

Margaret Stewart, her first incarnation, was a whore – an illiterate, foul-mouthed whore. She hated men, hated sex and hated what men had done to her. Men had only hurt and controlled her. Her mother – who was also a whore – had died when Margaret was seven. With no one to care for her, Margaret had been forced into prostitution at the tender age of 12.

This regression involved Chloe in a great deal of distress. She wept copiously throughout and had to be hastily moved forward in time by Michael when Margaret found herself in an advanced state of labour. The experience of Margaret had a profound effect on Chloe – the knowledge of this person 'inside' herself and the grief and pain she had touched on allowed her to relate in a compassionate way to her own suffering.

It was in the process of taking Margaret beyond death that Chloe contacted her spiritual guide. In dialogue with him, she gained some illumination over the reason for such a tragic life.

> Margaret is a part of Chloe which she has sought to deny . . . Bringing Margaret out of the shadows will help Chloe to understand why it is that she felt this way about the men in her life. If she can acknowledge that the pain she feels in this existence [as Chloe] stems from something on another plane in another time, she can reconcile within her that she has no further need to nurture these feelings. She no longer needs to feel a sense of unworthiness; she no longer needs to feel abused, raped and tortured – either physically, mentally, verbally or emotionally by men. She can leave that behind . . .
>
> To forgive, to let go through forgiveness will enable Chloe to move on free – free, at last. It will be difficult for her because there is no conscious memory of that which she must forgive. Such forgiveness must be done as an act of faith.

Some weeks later, in a further regression, Silas made himself known to Chloe. This little boy living near Chelmsford, England, spoke in a high childish voice about missing his father who had 'gone off a very long time ago'. Silas described his life from the age of seven, when his father had left, to his peaceful death at 83. He had married a girl called Nell, fathered four children – one who died – and throughout his long and uneventful life he had farmed the land his father had left. Silas had many of the characteristics of a Victorian patriarch; his attitude to his wife, for instance, was that she was the mother of his children and not an object of lust. He hankered after 'ladies of the night' but ploughed all his sexual energies into the land. He seemed dull, boring and narrow-minded. However, once through the 'gates of death' and into the 'realms of light', the reason for this prosaic life became clear to Chloe. She perceived that Silas had a measure of control over his existence and that through losing his father he had endeavoured to rise above his fate and make something of his life. Her guide had this to say.

Chloe has had everything in life, but does not really know it. She is moving away from female receptiveness . . . taking hold of her existence in a more masculine way. This is a fate she has created. Moving from Margaret, who was a victim of fate, to Silas who rode his fate and surmounted his obstacles . . .

Coming to terms with yourself on so many levels can be confusing at first. Accepting that the many levels are possible is the first step in recognizing the ongoing nature of the soul. The fact that you are here today is no coincidence. What you choose to do with this information will reflect in the coming role you have as a disseminator of what you call higher knowledge. Your life is unfolding in ways that you never thought it would.

Jane complained of a pain in her head. 'I'm in a vice-like clamp . . . and the pain won't stop.' Thus, in yet another life, Chloe was to experience a sense of pain and hopelessness. Jane had been born in Baton Rouge, Louisiana in 1904. She was retarded and put into an institution for the mentally ill after killing a man. Since Jane was so intellectually impaired and verbally inarticulate, Chloe's guide had to come to the rescue repeatedly. It transpired that Jane's mother had died when she (Jane) was six and that this had affected her so greatly that she never grew up. She was a child inside a 28-year-old woman's body. A genetic neurological disorder was the source of her crippling headaches. Apparently she had become 'the crazy woman in town who people visit' and had killed the man who was supposedly her guardian because he was sexually abusing her. Chloe's guide revealed,

In your character, Jane, lies another victim, another person used and abused, another person without control of her life and destiny. In your character, Jane, lies an entity without direction, ambition or aim. Imprisoned within her mind and imprisoned within an institution. Within your character, Jane are the threads of Margaret.

You ask, 'what then is the value of such an aimless existence?' . . . You, Chloe are in a present lifetime where you have much to do and much to create; you are actively 'growing'. Jane and Margaret were also lives of growth – though you cannot understand it; they were lives of *passive* growth.

Chloe's guide also revealed to her that the man Jane had killed in her lifetime was Andreas – Chloe's present-day lover.

While in the discarnate state, Jane–Chloe stated that her next incarnation was to be the present life. She inferred that the decision to reincarnate was 'not a decision made by one entity alone but agreed upon by more than one . . . I am aware of a decision-making process based on the needs of the soul. I am aware of a focus of light which is directed into the womb [of the mother] which is the light of the soul, the spirit.' Chloe also described being inside the womb, yet as soon as she emerged from the birth canal – and this is a process she goes through – she could not communicate verbally at all. (As she was later to recollect, 'in the womb I could communicate well – I seemed to have all the appropriate machinery – but as a baby, while I could understand what Michael was asking me, I just couldn't find the mechanism to speak.')

This regression as Jane took place after Chloe and I had started our astrological sessions. And it was some of the information and experiences culled from this past life that brought several of the features in her birth chart into sharper focus – particularly the role Andreas had played in her Jane lifetime. The regressions had a major effect on Chloe's life, not only in the realizations and resolutions they engendered but in Chloe's newfound skills as a medium. It was as though the regressions had opened a vault in the psyche and allowed her dormant psychic skills to emerge. She visited several highly regarded sensitives who concurred that she had mediumistic potential and, in the process, gave her even more information about her past lives – crucially, a life in thirteenth-century Italy, where her husband, upon discovering her *in flagrante delicto*, had murdered her lover on the spot. The husband was Stephen (her present-life husband), the lover Andreas.

Chloe's chart is the stuff of an analyst's dreams. There, in the deeply mysterious 8th house – the area of death and rebirth, the forbidden, the taboo, sex and the subconscious – are a Venus–Pluto conjunction and a Mercury–Saturn conjunction. Of course, there are many 'lighter' aspects in the natal chart – an expansive Sun–Jupiter trine (clearly operative in her successful career), Venus trine the Ascendant (reflecting her abundant charms and her ability to win hearts and flowers wherever she sets foot) and a compassionate, sensitive and artistic Moon–Neptune trine which is one of the sources of her natural mediumistic skills, her spiritual leanings and her loving, imaginative, empathetic qualities. But, back to the 'nitty gritty'.

Saturn in the 8th house is a problem. Yes, it is through Saturn's infamous learning attributes (and karmic lessons) that growth can

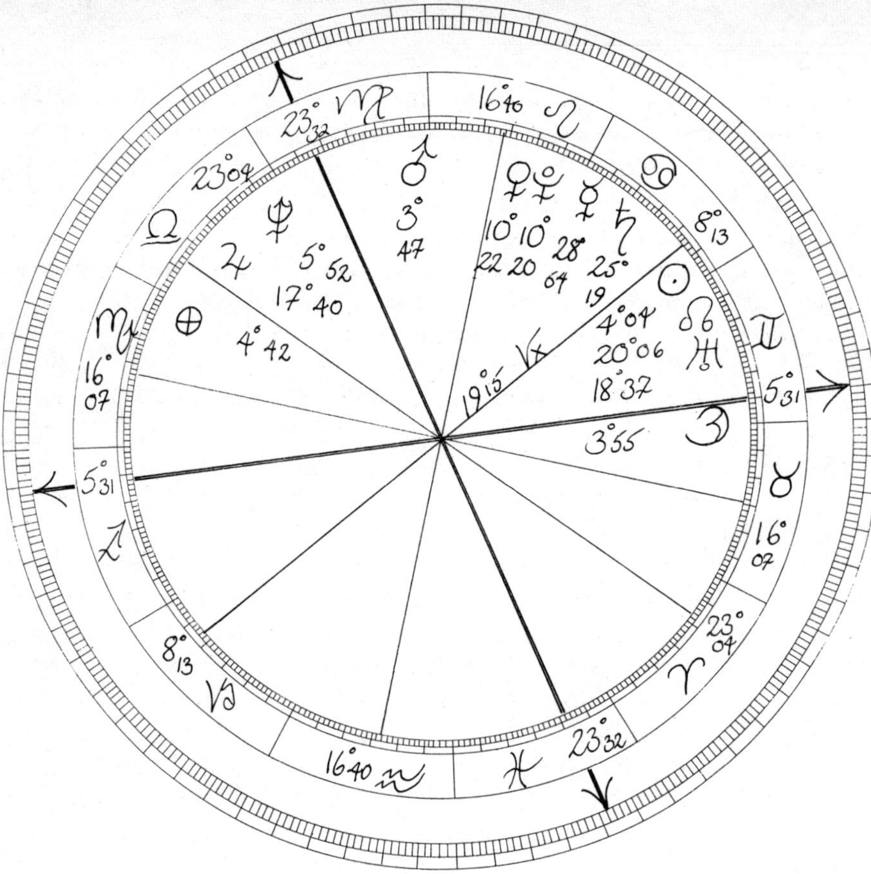

Chloe

June 26th 1946 : 17hrs 25 C.S.T. : 41° N59 ; 91° W40

Fig. 27

occur, but Saturn in the 8th is not a happy lot. Sexual frustration, a poor return for emotional investments, emotional hardship, loneliness and pain are all too often the legacy of an 8th house Saturn. That Saturn is conjunct Mercury suggests communications, particularly the intimate variety, are fraught with obstacles – if not seriously blocked at times – but also that the intellect is structured and efficient.[5] The presence of this conjunction in the 8th house indicates a tendency to analyse this area of life and, where sex is concerned, much talking and

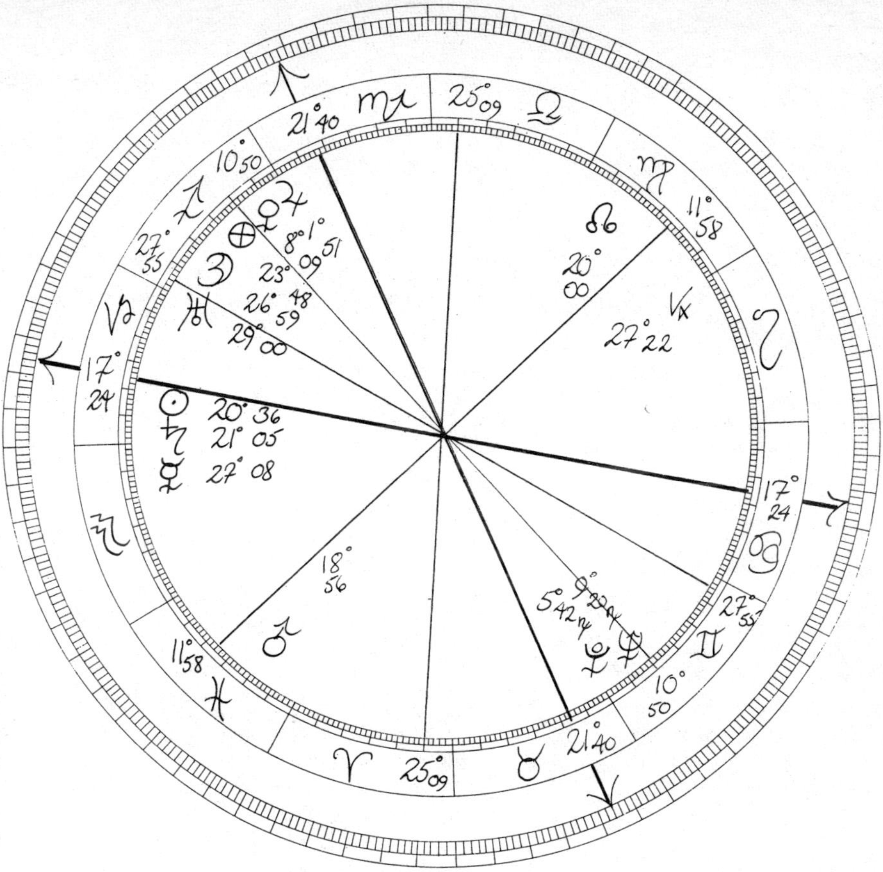

Margaret Stewart

January 2nd* 1402: 8hrs:00 am g.m.t. 50°N50:0°W46

* Gregorian calendar

Fig. 28

perhaps not enough doing! Venus–Pluto tell another story, however.

Venus alone in the 8th house, and in the fiery and passionate sign of Leo, would indicate a love for all 8th house events; its conjunction to powerful and transformative Pluto – indeed, the ruler of this house –

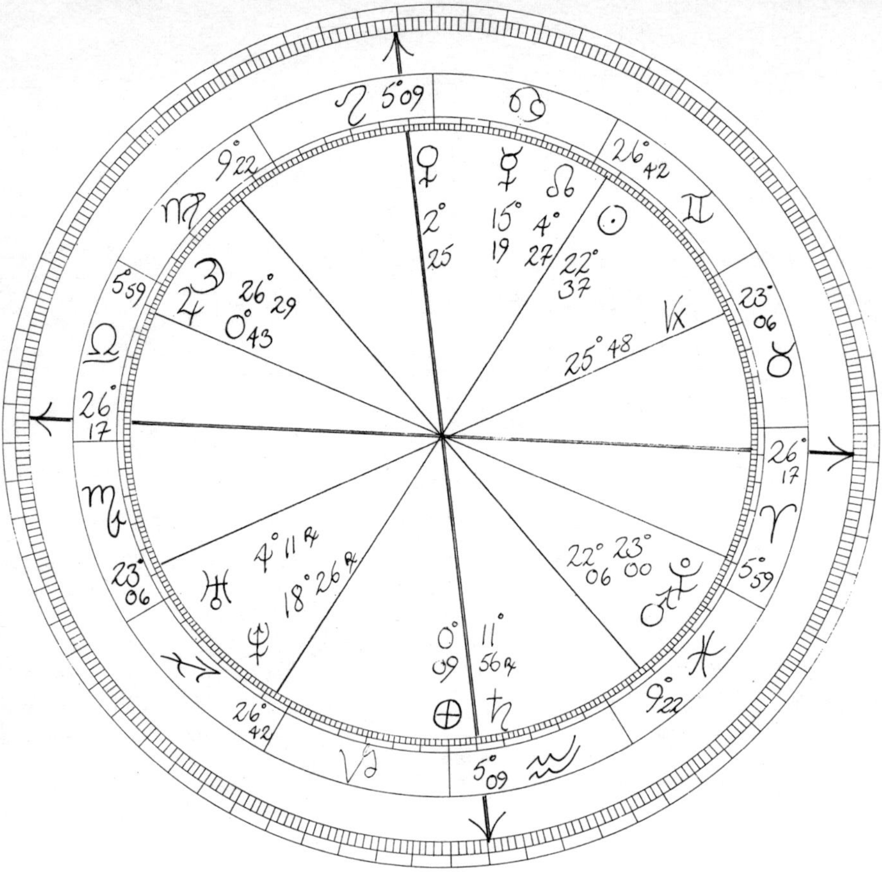

Silas

June 14th 1815: 15hrs 0 GMT: 51°N44; 0°E28

Fig. 29

puts the Venus expression onto another level entirely. Passion, sexual magnetism, sexual fascination and the highest expression of sexual love, kundalini, are all inherent in this conjunction. But the other side of the coin manifests as sexual abuse, fear of sex and sex for money – even, perhaps, death linked to sex.

What on earth, one might ask, did this have to do with effervescent, beautiful Chloe sitting in Hampstead one mellow Autumn afternoon?

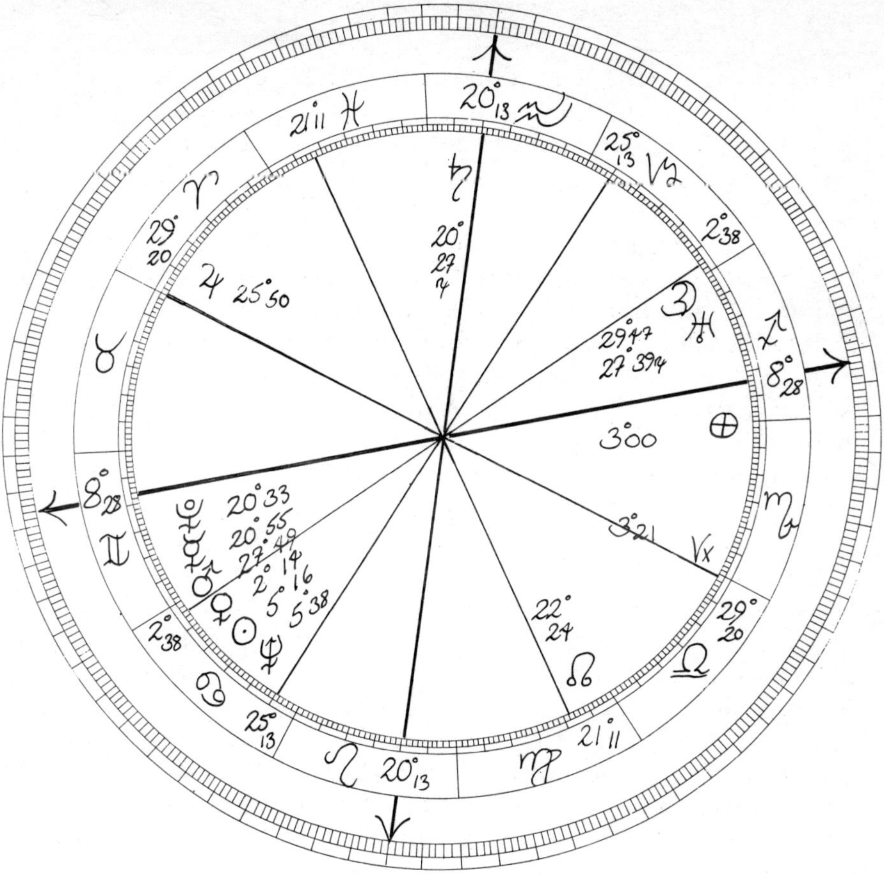

Jane

June 27th 1904: 3hrs: 15 a.m. C.S.T.: 30°N 27; 91°W 11

Fig. 30

Sex, for Chloe, had been the source of almost all the heartache in her life. She had been loved and adored by her husband, Stephen – and she in turn had loved and cared for him and their children – but she had been utterly unsatisfied by him. She had felt 'in an emotional void – empty, imprisoned in a shell of a marriage'. They had no arguments. They got on well. But they could not reach each other where it counted. Chloe also had a deeper problem. She was inorgasmic and her desire to be sexually fulfilled had driven her from lover to lover. On the surface of her life, the promiscuity was not a problem, especially as Stephen chose to ignore her affairs, but deep inside Chloe despised herself. Then suddenly, at the age of forty, it seemed as though her problems were at an end. Into her life walked Andreas. And at last she was able to reach orgasm. The relationship with Andreas was the supreme turning point of her life; it was as though she had been released from a prison sentence. She stripped off the past and plunged financially and emotionally naked into the new.

Astrologically, Chloe's description of an emotionally vapid marriage and a sexual lack that drove her to promiscuity is the personification of her 8th house cluster. We could in fact leave matters there; after all, we have located the source of her troubles and, without any therapy or astrological insight whatsoever, fate sorted things out nicely: Chloe fell in love, became orgasmic and started a new life in another country – all wonderfully Plutonic. But there's a little more to it than that. And while one of Chloe's problems was resolved, she had opened a Pandora's box of new ones.

Chloe had never sought any kind of psychological help in life. She had worked hard, become successful and lived an enviable life. Sexually she was a little at sea, but she could live with that – just. And it never occurred to her to question the reasons why she was unable to become sexually fulfilled. And while it may seem as if Andreas was simply a Latin lover with fantastic sexual prowess, their relationship was almost a year old when Chloe achieved her first orgasm – on the day she left Stephen and moved in with Andreas. Indeed, it was in recognizing the connection between these two events that prompted the realization that her inability to be able to let go sexually might have had something to do with a deep fear and mistrust of men. She was only able to move in with Andreas when she trusted him totally; and with this total trust, she was able to achieve release sexually.

The regression work enabled Chloe to see why she had this deep mistrust and fear of men. As Margaret, she had learned to hate men because they hurt her and degraded her. She hated sex. Jane too was badly treated by men and committed murder because she was sexually abused. Even Silas held some rigid attitudes about sex and was notably inhibited. For Chloe these lives were absolutely real, and understanding that she no longer had to hang onto these feelings of being 'dirty' and unworthy helped the healing process to continue – despite having to cope with Andreas's refusal to take her back.

The regression work also helped Chloe with present-life traumas that had been buried in the unconscious. Taken back through her

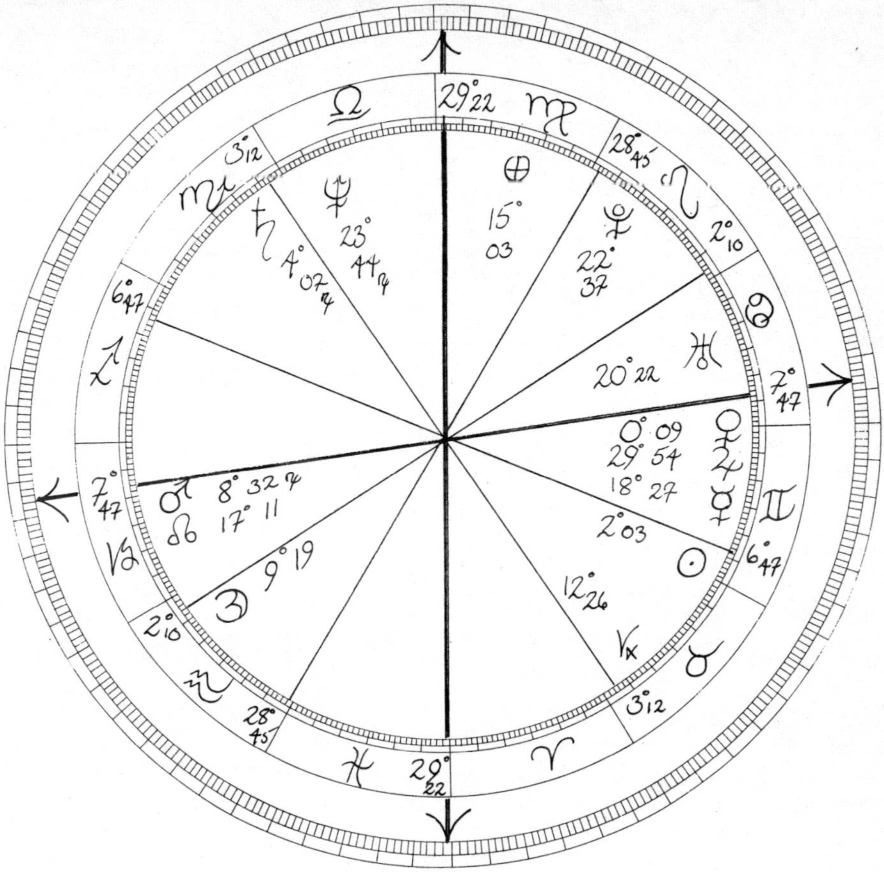

Andreas

May 23rd 1954 : 20hrs. 00 LT : 20°S09; 28°E36

Fig. 31

present life to an age that held significance for her, Chloe immediately found herself at the bedside of her mother. She was only five years old and distraught at seeing her mother so ill. Chloe's mother had suffered a nervous breakdown and although no one had told Chloe what was wrong with her and why she was in this condition, she had picked up the strongest signals that it was her sister who had 'hurt' her mother. Little Chloe's world was upside down, not only was her mother ill, but her fifteen-year-old sister, Diane, had been sent far away and for a very

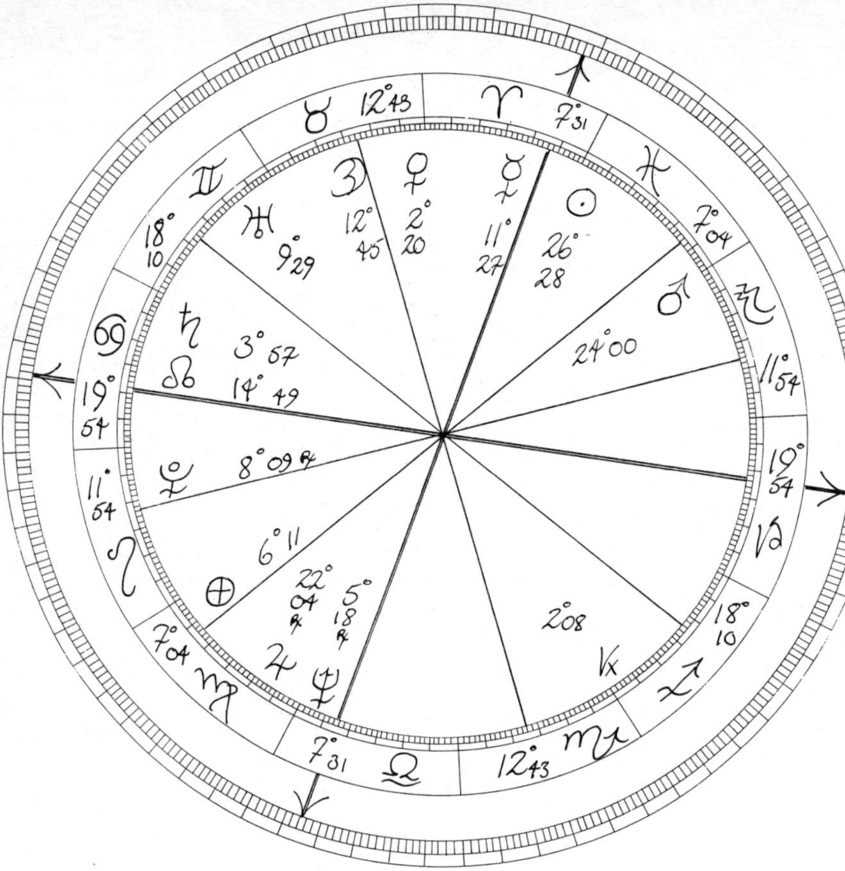

Stephen

March 17th 1945 : 12hrs 30 LT. : 32°N04; 34°E46

Fig. 32

long time. When Chloe was older she came to understand that Diane had disgraced her staunchly Methodist family by becoming pregnant, thereby necessitating immediate 'excommunication' to the other side of America. Never once was Diane's demise openly discussed in the family, thus it clung to the collective psyche like an everpresent shadow – unspoken and unacknowledged. Although she was too young to understand all that had happened, the events registered loud and clear on Chloe's subconscious and, as she grew into a young woman, the unconscious association of sex with betrayal, disgrace and abandonment inhibited her own sexual response.

In the early months of her return to England, Chloe not only wanted some reassurance that she and Andreas would get back together, but needed greater insight into the relationship – a task tailor-made for astrology. One of her first concerns was to find out if their shared feeling of a destined union could in any way be borne out.

Pluto, as I have mentioned before, is the planet most associated with that sense of *force majeure*. Thus, even before I set up Andreas' chart I suspected that Chloe's Venus–Pluto conjunction would form a major contact with his chart. And it did. Andreas' Moon, the symbol of the feminine and indicative of his emotional attunement, is placed at 9° Aquarius – exactly opposite Chloe's Venus and Pluto. Furthermore, his Saturn at 4° Scorpio intersects this opposition forming a 'T'-square in the fixed signs. There is a sense of the inescapable about this configuration, especially as Saturn, either in his role of teacher or harbinger of karma, is involved.

One of the great myths existing in astrology is that if there are strong Saturn aspects between a couple's charts, especially involving Venus or Mars, sexual attraction is minimal – and the relationship doomed. In my experience as an astrologer specializing in relationships, I find almost the reverse. Time after time, I am presented with Saturn –Venus, Saturn–Mars couples whose sexual interaction is intense, and while they may indeed ultimately encounter darker and more difficult areas in their relationship – which may indeed cause them to separate – the physical side of the relationship invariably wields a strong hold over them both. Certainly, in Andreas' and Chloe's case, their sexual relationship was supremely passionate and mutually rewarding, right up to the bittersweet end.

The Moon–Venus–Pluto–Saturn contact in the synastry was an echo from Andreas' own chart, for although his Pluto is a little too far from his Moon to form an exact aspect, I would suggest that the 'flavour' of the opposition is there – and, not insignificantly spanning the 8th and 2nd houses. But whether or not the Moon–Pluto opposition can be held to blame for all Andreas' emotional unrest – which I will explain shortly – Saturn's square to the Moon, more than compensates for any trouble of the emotional variety.

Andreas's childhood was also painful. His mother, a nurse and an immensely nurturing and caring individual, had seven children including Andreas. His father was a drunk and, in his alcoholic rages, he frequently battered his wife and his children. Andreas hated and feared his father, but saw his mother as a 'saint'. As in Chloe's situation, an unspoken problem hung over the entire family; but in Andreas' case it was not concerned with sex, but alcohol and violence.

On balance, astrologically, it would appear that Andreas had more of a mother problem than a father problem. The Moon is a primary indicator of mother, and it is the Moon that suffers from the planetary onslaught rather than the Sun or Mars (both masculine symbols). The Moon–Saturn–Pluto trio may indeed reflect the pain and hardship his mother experienced at her husband's hand and that consequently Andreas' lunar experience of childhood was marred. But why, when he clearly experienced his mother as a Neptunian saint and received only emotional nourishment and abiding loyalty from her, did he then assume that women could not be trusted? Was it a case of the anima speaking louder than words? Andreas, reflecting the difficulty and inhibition of his Moon–Saturn square, has nurtured a deep mistrust of women throughout his life: he decided to be sterilized at the age of 21 – on the one hand because he did not want to bring any children into the world, perhaps in case he proved to be as inadequate a parent as his father – and probably unconsciously because he wished to avoid a commitment like marriage. After all, most women would be deterred from forming a permanent union with a man who was unable to father a child. As far as I can see, one of the possible explanations for his mistrust of women – an explanation that would account for his anima problem – is that in the past, the distant past, he has been fatally wounded by a woman. This certainly begins to look a likely proposition when we discover that Chloe not only in a past life as Jane murdered him, but in another life was the cause of his death. Before we leave Andreas's chart, it is worth noting that Neptune colours the family experience: on the one hand Neptune rules the fourth house and on the other, it is situated in the 10th. From the 10th house perspective, Neptune represents his saintly mother; from the fourth, his alcoholic father.

While the powerful cross-connections between Andreas's Moon and Saturn and Chloe's Venus and Pluto showed that fate could well have played a major role in bringing Chloe and Andreas together, it is equally clear that they were both drawn to each other through their mutual disabilities. Both of them came from disfunctional families where they felt abandoned; both were mistrustful of the opposite sex. Consequently they clung together in their mutual vulnerability – united by their common insecurity and need to absolve their family inheritance of pain and guilt. (Ironically, once again we find Neptune associated with the fourth house and symbolizing, once more, a family shadow.)

One crucial factor I have left out until now is that at the time of their meeting, Pluto, by transit, was close to the square of Andreas's Moon and Chloe's Venus–Pluto. It was as though the time had come for Pluto to bring into consciousness much of the repressed material in their psyches and so bring about a massive transformation. It may also be that the hands on the cosmic clock had reached a point where destinies were set to link and some unfinished business attended to. For the first time in Chloe's life, Pluto formed a major hard aspect to its natal position and to Venus; in the process, Chloe went through a period not only where her sexual and emotional life was transformed but a time when she was able to unlock some secrets from the past.

One of the most fascinating themes to emerge in Chloe's past lives was her loss of a parent around the age of seven. In our work together, I asked Chloe if this was a reflection of her current life? Had her parents divorced when she was six or seven, or had one of them died? (At the time I did not know of her mother's nervous breakdown.) Chloe then divulged the family history and told me that her mother's illness when she (Chloe) was five made her feel as if she had been abandoned – a feeling she had re-experienced with seering intensity in the regression of her current lifetime. Was that sense of abandonment an echo from a previous life, or a childhood trauma that found a source of resolution through creative imagery? Were we seeing a pattern that resonated through life after life or a construct of the psyche? Was mentally retarded Jane a reflection of her mentally ill mother, and was Margaret's life as a prostitute (the result of her mother's death) an elaborate way of associating Chloe's promiscuity with her own mother's abandonment of her?

Chloe's past life remembrances could be said to be valid from either perspective since their justification lies in the transformative effect they had on Chloe's life. However, the extraordinary astrological coincidences between the charts of Chloe's past lives and her present horoscope tempt one to believe that these lives might well be genuine.

Chloe seemed to relate most strongly to the life of Margaret. Remembering this life allowed Chloe to make sense of her fascination with prostitutes. She had written about them, been involved in documentaries about them and wherever she went in the world she would make a point of visiting their haunts. She was fascinated with their lives, fascinated about their needs, their attitudes and their ways. Realizing that she had once been a whore herself at last made a sense of this obsession.

Astrologically, Margaret has much in common with Chloe. At eight in the morning of 12 January, 1402, Capricorn was rising with an exact Sun–Saturn conjunction on the Ascendant – how symbolic of a life haunted by rejection, hardship and struggle. What is so supremely significant about Margaret's chart, however, is that Venus was in hard aspect (opposition) to Pluto – and Pluto is on the precise degree of Chloe's current life Ascendant-descendant axis and squaring natal Mars and Moon. Chloe's powerful Venus–Pluto conjunction is echoed by every one of her past life characters' charts. And it is not the only theme or degree area to repeat again and again. But for the moment, I would like to take Margaret's chart a little further.

With Mars in Pisces, Margaret became one of life's victims and with an exact opposition from Venus to Neptune, suffering through love was her unwanted lot. With her Piscean Mars in opposition to the north node in Virgo in the 8th, was it any surprise that she found her destiny in prostitution? Her Moon, in hard-working Capricorn, is tucked away in the 12th house of institutions, and although it is trined by Pluto and Neptune, she found no spiritual comfort through these contacts. She suffered and died believing there was no God. Forgiveness for her suffering – a superbly Neptunian theme – was an issue taken up by Chloe's guide in reference to her life as Margaret. The Neptunian content of Margaret's chart clearly resonates in Chloe's horoscope with its elevated Neptune in tight square to the Sun and in trine to her Moon. And although Margaret was unable to find a spiritual route through which to express her Neptunian potential, Chloe, with her gentle Moon–Neptune trine and elevated Neptune has fulfilled the promise instead.

Silas – Sun in the 8th house, Mars conjunct Pluto and Venus opposition Saturn (picking up the same degree area in the fixed signs of Chloe's Venus and Pluto) – was a farmer with fixed attitudes to life. And quite right too, with the Venus–Saturn opposition straddling his MC–IC axis. Silas also had a mutable cross to bear, with the Sun in opposition to Neptune squaring a Moon–Jupiter conjunction opposite Mars and Pluto. To use a colloquial expression, Silas's and Margaret's charts were a case of 'same meat different gravy'. With Saturn in his fourth house, it is no surprise that Silas was deserted by his father and found his life from childhood onwards sheer hard labour. Chloe's guide informed her that Silas' life was crucial because he 'rode his fate, and surmounted his obstacles'. Considering the mutable cross, and the presence of Mars in Pisces (which I have already suggested indicates a tendency for victimization) it would indeed appear that Silas found the inner resources to triumph over his fate.

Poor, much-abused Jane was born with an exact Mercury–Pluto

conjunction rising. Her Ascendant, also in Gemini, is close to the degree of Chloe's Ascendant-descendant axis, and, like Silas and Margaret, she has a powerful angular Saturn. Jane, with her birthday the day after Chloe, has her Sun within a degree of Chloe's, and she has an almost exact Sun–Neptune conjunction. As with all four charts, Neptune is also a key figure, forming hard aspects to the Sun in three cases and, by way of compensation, a hard angle to Venus in the other. Jane's Mercury–Pluto conjunction is entirely descriptive of her mental difficulties – Mercury, the principle of communication, is crippled by the repressive nature of Pluto. Mars too is close to this pair, and, because Mars is conjunct Venus, Venus is also drawn into the stellium. Thus Jane has an extremely 'heavy' configuration between these four planets, which certainly reflects her impaired sexual and intellectual functions. Reflecting with her guide upon the reasons for this lifetime, Chloe was helped to understand that in her nature lay 'this entity without direction, ambition or aim'. With five planets and the Ascendant in mutable signs and the Sun conjunct Neptune, Jane's life was indeed the epitome of confusion and lack of direction. Yet with Saturn on the Midheaven there is the implication that there was much to learn from the life – even though its purpose had to be revealed some seventy years later in another lifetime.

There are just so many links and repetitions between all these charts that to discuss them all would take another book. Thus, I have listed all the connections and repeating themes in the appendix to this chapter. I would like to draw attention here, however, to one or two key features of the astrology. In three of the charts (Chloe's, Margaret's and Jane's), the nodal axis is around 20° of the mutables and in two cases within two degrees of the same sign – Virgo. In the fourth chart (Silas's) the North node at 4° Cancer is the degree of Chloe's Sun in two lives and square Neptune in the same two. In the preceding chapter, through the astrology of one of Stevenson's cases, the node was also seen to feature prominently. This makes me inclined to believe that the nodal axis is crucial in some way to the process of reincarnation. Also significant to the astrology of Chloe is that in three of her lives (Margaret's, Silas' and her own) Mars is in Pisces or Virgo and in the fourth chart. Mars is in another mutable sign in conjunction to Neptune. The feeling of unworthiness and of suffering is quintessential to Neptune and it would seem that in this lifetime Chloe has been able to evolve to the point where she can appreciate the higher levels of this planet. The Neptune theme is carried over strongly from lifetime to lifetime – as is the Pluto theme – which suggests not only that the attributes of these two planets must be experienced time and again one way or another but that perhaps these planets could be said to be predominant 'soul notes'. Returning to some of the earlier discussions in this book about the part the chakras play in the formation of the body and the way the harmony of the spheres resonates within us from conception, it may well be that for the purposes of Chloe's soul, the key resonances required to bring the soul into physical life involve these two outer planets in some hard aspect to the personal ones.

As is clearly and repeatedly demonstrated in Margaret's, Silas's, Jane's and Chloe's charts, Neptune and Pluto are resonances that cannot be ignored. In Chloe's chart, the pattern of her life over the past three years has been highly influenced by these two planets. As transiting Neptune squared natal Neptune and opposed the Sun and, as transiting Pluto approached the exact square to natal Venus and Pluto, Andreas came into her life; through the powerful nature of their relationship, she walked away from her marriage and her children. Sacrifice and abandonment through Neptune this time around involved her in the role of protagonist – not the victim. Yet she subsequently suffered great anguish and guilt over this apparently wanton act of abandonment and returned to the family. When she left them once more, it was with the family's blessing; her daughter (aged 14) encouraged her to follow her newfound path.

Venus–Pluto evoked a different quality altogether. Here Chloe experienced the compulsive nature of this planet; both she and Andreas felt they were powerless in the face of such a strong sexual attraction and consuming love for each other. Stephen, on the other hand, undergoing a similar Pluto transit to his natal Moon–Venus square to Pluto, was on the receiving end of the Plutonic love affair – he experienced only severe fallout. He had no control over the situation. His world was in ashes.

As Chloe's guide told her, through her remembrance of Silas she should perceive that she had to ride her fate and gain some measure of control of her life. While Chloe could do nothing about Andreas's refusal to take her back, there was still much she – and he – could learn from their relationship. It took nine months, between the November of 1988 and August of 1989, for the process of resolution to occur.

Throughout their love affair, unlike her relationship with Stephen, there had been as many passionate arguments as there had been passionate nights and, consequently, despite Andreas's determination not to continue living together, there was still a great deal of life left in their love. Andreas was clear that he was still deeply in love with her, but he simply could not take the risk of committing himself once more only to have Chloe leave him again. For her part, Chloe assured him that she would never leave him and that she loved him absolutely. Throughout the nine months as they continued to meet, sometimes in anguish, sometimes in joy, they gradually came to an acceptance of each other's needs and attitudes. For both of them trust had been a crucial issue. Neither had ever truly trusted another individual before they fell in love with each other; the trauma then of encountering a betrayal of that trust – Chloe in leaving Andreas and returning to Stephen, and Andreas in terminating the relationship – was potentially highly damaging. Chloe's memories of her past lives with Andreas enabled her to see that it was imperative that they resolved the issues between them with love and retained their newfound ability to trust, otherwise they would be torn apart in life after life until they eventually understood. It was a lesson they had to learn through each other. By the August of 1989 they realized they had done so. They made love for a final time and said good-bye. 'It was a perfect passing away for both of them, and at the same time the most intolerable accession into being.'[6]

Throughout these same nine months Chloe had also to make her peace with Stephen. It took much heartache and much honesty, especially on Stephen's part, to accept any blame for the breakdown of the marriage and to face the fact that despite the end of the love affair, Chloe was not coming back to him. For Chloe, the realization that she had been Stephen's wife in the thirteenth century and that he had murdered Andreas enabled her to see why she found with Stephen an emotionally arid marriage. As her thirteenth-century husband he had been cold and heartless. He had treated her with contempt and never let her forget her infidelity. 'This loveless marriage where I lost my beloved and the lives where I lost a parent have enabled me to resolve my fear of abandonment and betrayal. I feel truly free and totally transformed.' Almost to the day that Chloe and Andreas made their peace, Stephen and Chloe parted with love. Synchronistically, each had chosen to fly to a different part of the world. And while Chloe felt that a karmic lesson had been well and truly learned, one can only speculate that Andreas and Stephen felt that they had reached the end of a long and painful, but ultimately enriching, chapter of their lives.

Transformation, the ultimate Plutonic event, has been the core of Chloe's experiences. At the time of her first regression, transiting Pluto was exactly squaring her Venus–Pluto conjunction; it was in this regression as Margaret that she experienced the pains of labour and recounted her life as a prostitute. Some weeks later on, in her third regression, Chloe experienced life in the womb and emerging through the birth canal. In all her regressions she experienced death. In this way, Chloe dramatically worked through an entirely Plutonic process – death and rebirth – on an entirely new level and was transformed by it. Through the regressions she was able to relate to the underlying reasons for her complex sexuality and able to comprehend the ties that bound her to both Stephen and Andreas. Through the astrology, she was able to see that she had brought a symbolic process vividly to life. She also came to see that Pluto was instrumental in leading her to another stage in life and so unfolding another part of her destiny. Through Andreas, she had left behind a country, a career and a marriage. Having made the transition, new doors were opening at almost every turn of the way. She stands to become one of the most sought after individuals in her field – fame and fortune are within her grasp. But, perhaps most important of all, the kindling of her latent psychic abilities appear already to be leading her towards the role of a disseminator of higher knowledge – just as her guide had informed her. Without the regression process, it is doubtful transformation on so many levels could have occurred. But then, perhaps this is all part of fate's grand design.

Chloe's case may be a particularly fascinating one. I chose it, of course, because it allowed me to discuss a wealth of different themes. But all the individuals on my sample who provided me with enough material to set up charts presented similar planetary themes and degree areas from one life to another. It was this factor that persuaded me perhaps these past lives are not mere figments of the imagination. I am not overwhelmed by proof but am impressed by the great coincidences! Of course, in the way of synchronicity, it could be that in an altered state of consciousness not only does one tune into an appropriate life, but an appropriate date, time and place. Certainly, I believe this process of remembering a past life, or constructing a damn good fantasy, is a marvellous tool for therapy. I also believe it opens up a whole new arena for astrology and puts it onto a different level.

All good practising astrologers recognize that the planets convey a hierarchy of meaning; each planet is a symbol for many different expressions of a central theme. When we interpret a chart for an individual, only some of the effects of a particular planet tend to emerge in that person's life – a factor which cannot be explained by that planet's relationship to other planets or its position in the horoscope. Taking the step of combining astrology with psychology (particularly Jungian psychology) which was undertaken earlier this century by Alan Leo, enabled the astrologer to widen and deepen his understanding of the horoscope. To my mind, the next step – at least on the interpretive level – must be in incorporating past life material (primarily via the hypnotherapeutic route) to reveal an even greater and deeper understanding of the planetary patterns and symbols. The karmic reasons for a situation need not be quite so speculative any more and need not rely on the astrologer or the clairvoyant to give the information to a client, it can be perceived directly by the individual, thus allowing the realizations to be personally meaningful; with the use of past life charts we can trace the distant origins of an issue and through the therapeutic process make way for resolution and catharsis. As we have seen through Chloe's example, the Venus–Pluto conjunction had been lived out in every way from sexual abuse, the death of a lover, lack of orgasm to kundalini. These things are contained within the psyche, whether as some kind of genetic memory, or experiences culled from the collective unconscious, or the soul's memory of its own personal past. An astrologer can now find a route to understanding and interpreting a horoscope on a far richer level. He can also incorporate the concept of fate without fearing that it denies individual free will. With an overview of life after life one can perceive how something engendered in one life takes seed and flowers in another. Thus one's particular lot in a lifetime is not the result of a blind uncontrollable force but a process meted out by the soul itself. Fate as such is contained in every feature of the horoscope; past and future experience lodged in every characteristic of the birth chart, just as our fate and our past and future experience is secreted within the psyche. We now have a mechanism with which to tap that information and stimulate, even accelerate, the process of growth and awareness. I can only conclude with an echo from Chapter 2: we are our fate; we create our destiny.

*Major themes and degree areas in Chloe's present and 'past life' charts**

	Chloe	Margaret	Jane	Silas
Planetary themes common to all charts reflected in aspect patterns.	♀☌♇ (orb: 0.0)	♀☍♇ (3.6)	(♀☌♇) ☿☌♇ (0.4) ♂☌♇ (7.3)	☉□♇ (0.4) ☽☍♇ (3.5) ♂☌♇ (0.9)
	☉□♆ (1.1) ♀✱♆ (4.5)	♀☍♆ (0.0)	☉☌♆ (0.4) ♀☌♆ (3.4)	☉☍♆ (4.2) ♀⚼♆ (1.0) ♂□♆ (3.7)
	☽△♆ (2.0)	☽⚻♆ (2.3)	☽☍♆ (5.9)	
		♄☌Asc.	♄☌MC.	♄☌IC.
Significant degree areas 4°–5° of the cardinals	☉ 4°♋ 44 ♇ 5°♎ 52		☉ 5°♋ 16 ♇ 5°♋ 39	☊ 4°♋ 27
2°–5° of the mutables	☽ 3°♊ 54 ♂ 3°♍ 47 Asc. 5°♐ 31	♃ 2°♐ 01 ♇ 5°♊ 41	⊕ 2°♐ 29	
20°–23° of the mutables	☊ 20°♊ 06 MC. 23°♍ 32	☊ 20°♍ 27 ♂ 19°♓ 41	♇ 20°♊ 33 ☿ 20°♊ 55 ☊ 22°♍ 24	♂ 22°♓ 06 ☉ 22°♊ 37 ♇ 23°♓ 01
Other significant features between all charts All charts have Uranus in mutable signs: in Jane and Margaret's charts within 1½ degrees of each other.	♅ 18°♊ 37	♅ 29°♐ 03	♅ 27°♐ 39	♅ 14°♐ 11
All charts have Mars in mutable signs.	♂ 3°♍ 47	♂ 19°♓ 41	♂ 27°♊ 49	♂ 22°♓ 06

On 3 occasions the north node is around 20° of the mutable signs and on the other its position, 4°♋27, is the Sun in 2 lifetimes.

On 2 occasions, the Ascendant is between 5°&8° of the mutable signs.

On 2 occasions the Sun is found to within a degree.

Chloe	Margaret	Jane	Silas.
☊ 20°♊06	☊ 20°♍27	☊ 22°♍24	
Asc: 5°♐31		Asc. 8°♊28	
☉ 4°♋43		☉ 5°♋16	

*There are many other less significant connections and similarities between the charts and also many major contacts in the synastry between Chloe, Andreas and Stephen. However, I will leave it to the enthusiastic astrologer to discover these for himself!

NOTES

1. See Chapter 5, pp. 93 and 94.
2. The 10th house of the horoscope is traditionally associated with life direction, ambition and aims, but the cusp of the 10th house (MC) and its opposite point (IC) is known as the parental axis. While the 4th house is more usually associated with father, the 10th house invariably describes mother.
3. Repeating degree areas in the charts of past and present lives, and, indeed, the charts of members of the same family is a phenomenon that I found occurring time and again with the research material for this book. In Viola's case, the linking of Jupiter, Saturn and the Midheaven between all the charts concerned binds together the themes of justice (Anne's Jupiter) immutable law (Grace's Saturn) and aims in life (Viola's MC).
4. It is curious that in all three of the major cases discussed here, Paulo (in Chapter 8), Viola and Chloe, the progressed Moon in the chart of the previous incarnation features strongly (by sign) in the horoscope of the subsequent life.
5. Hard aspects, like the conjunction between Mercury and Saturn seem to have an either-or effect; either the intellect is brilliant or considerably hampered – if only by poor education.
6. D. H. Lawrence, *Women in Love*.

Death and transformation are man's unchosen and unchangeable fate. All that he can choose and change is consciousness. But to change this is to change all.

Rodney Collin, *The Theory of Celestial Influence*

Epilogue

I do not want to conclude by restating the themes discussed in the book in the way of a lawyer summing up his case. I would like to leave the reader with a feeling that, no matter how he may disagree with some of the ideas I have put forward, he may be inspired to think about the world he knows in a different way. Raymond Moody in *Reflections on Life after Life* handed over the stage to Plato to conclude his book. And so will I. The text is taken from Plato's *Republic* and involves a dialogue between the philosopher Socrates and another man, Glaucon.

Picture men dwelling in a sort of subterranean cavern with a long entrance open to the light on its entire width. Conceive them as having their legs and necks fettered from childhood, so that they remain on the same spot, able to look forward only, and prevented by the fetters from turning their heads. Picture further the light from a fire burning higher up and at a distance behind them, and between the fire and the prisoners and above them a road along which a low wall has been built, as the exhibitors of puppet shows have partitions before the men themselves, above which they show the puppets.

All that I see, he said.

See also, then, men carrying past the wall implements of all kinds that rise above the wall, and human images and shapes of animals as well, wrought in stone and wood and every material, some of these bearers presumably speaking and others silent.

A strange image you speak of, he said, and strange prisoners.

Like to us, I said. For, to begin with, tell me do you think that these men would have seen anything of themselves or of one another except the shadows cast from the fire on the wall of the cave that fronted them?

How could they, he said, if they were compelled to hold their heads unmoved through life?

And again, would not the same be true of the objects carried past them?

Surely.

If then they were able to talk to one another, do you not think that they would suppose that in naming the things that they saw they were naming the passing objects.

Necessarily.

And if their prison had an echo from the wall opposite them, when one of the passers-by uttered a sound, do you think that they would suppose anything else than the passing shadow to be the speaker?

By Zeus, I do not, said he.

Then in every way such prisoners would deem reality to be nothing else than the shadows of the artificial objects.

Quite inevitably, he said.

Consider, then, what would be the manner of the release and healing from these bonds and this folly if in the course of nature something of this sort should happen to them. When one was freed from his fetters and compelled to stand up suddenly and turn his head around and walk and to lift up his eyes to the light, and in doing all this felt pain and, because of the dazzle and glitter of the light, was unable to discern the objects whose shadows he formerly saw, what do you suppose would be his answer if someone told him that what he had seen before was all a cheat and an illusion, but that now, being nearer to reality and turned toward more real things, he saw more truly? And if also one should point out to him each of the passing objects and constrain him by questions to say what it is, do you not think that he would be at a loss and that he would regard what he formerly saw as more real than the things now pointed out to him?

Far more real, he said.

And if he were compelled to look at the light itself, would not that pain his eyes, and would he not turn away and flee to those things which he is able to discern and regard them as in very deed more clear and exact than the objects pointed out?

It is so, he said.

And if, said I, someone should drag him thence by force up the ascent which is rough and steep, and not let him go before he had drawn him out into the light of the sun, do you not think that he would find it painful to be so haled along, and would chafe at it, and when he came out into the light, that his eyes would be filled with its beams so that he would not be able to see even one of the things that we call real?

Why, no, not immediately, he said.

Then there would be need of habituation, I take it, to enable him to see the things higher up. And at first he would most easily discern the shadows and, after that, the likenesses or reflections in water of men and other things, and later, the things themselves, and from these he would go on to contemplate the appearances in the heavens and heaven itself, more easily by night looking at the light of the stars and the moon, than by day the sun and the sun's light.

Of course.

And so, finally, I suppose, he would be able to look upon the sun itself and see its true nature, not by reflections in water or phantasms of it in an alien setting, but in and by itself in its own place.

Necessarily, he said.

And at this point he would infer and conclude that this it is that provides the seasons and the courses of the year and presides over all things in the visible region, and is in some sort the cause of all these things that they had seen.

Obviously, he said, that would be the next step. Well then, if he recalled to mind his first habituation and what passed for wisdom there, and his fellow bondsmen, do you not think that he would count himself happy in the change and pity them?

He would indeed.

And if there had been honours and commendations among them which they bestowed on one another and prizes for the man who is quickest to make out the shadows as they pass and best able to remember their customary precedences, sequences, and co-existences, and so most successful in guessing at what was to come, do you think he would be very keen about such rewards, and that he would envy and emulate those who were honoured by these prisoners and lorded it among them, or that he would feel with Homer and greatly prefer while living on earth to be a serf of another, a landless man, and endure anything rather than opine with them and live that life?

Yes, he said, I think that he would choose to endure anything rather than such a life.

And consider this also, said I. If such a one should go down again and take his old place would he not get his eyes full of darkness, thus suddenly coming out of the sunlight?

He would indeed.

Now if he should be required to contend with these perpetual prisoners in 'evaluating' these shadows while his vision was still dim and before his eyes were accustomed to the dark – and this time required for habituation would not be very short – would he not provoke laughter, and would it not be said of him that he had returned from his journey aloft with his eyes ruined and that it was not worth while even to attempt the ascent? And if it were possible to lay hands on and to kill the man who tried to release them and lead them up, would they not kill him?

They certainly would, he said.

Plato, *The Republic*, Vol. VII, trans. Paul Shorey (Cambridge, Mass: Harvard University Press, 1935)

Index

Page numbers in *italics* refer to diagrams and illustrations